Favorite Flies

Favorite Flies

A COMPREHENSIVE GUIDE TO TYING AND FISHING THE BEST FLIES AVAILABLE

David Klausmeyer

Skyhorse Publishing

Skyhorse Publishing books may be purchased in bulk at special discounts for sales promotion, corporate gifts, fund-raising, or educational purposes. Special editions can also be created to specifications. For details, contact the Special Sales Department, Skyhorse Publishing, 307 West 36th Street, 11th Floor, New York, NY 10018 or info@skyhorsepublishing.com.

Skyhorse® and Skyhorse Publishing® are registered trademarks of Skyhorse Publishing, Inc.®, a Delaware corporation.

Visit our website at www.skyhorsepublishing.com.

10 9 8 7 6 5 4 3 2 1

Library of Congress Cataloging-in-Publication Data is available on file.

Cover design by Daniel Brount
Cover photo credit: David Klausmeyer

Print ISBN: 978-1-5107-4303-8
Ebook ISBN: 978-1-5107-4304-5

Printed in China

Contents

NYMPHS AND WET FLIES

SALTWATER FLIES

Chapter Nine: Match the Hatch Saltwater Style: Flies That Imitate Common Baitfish   459

Acknowledgments

101 FAVORITE DRY FLIES CONTAINS A FISTFUL OF PATTERNS you can use to catch trout wherever they swim. I have included a few of my own flies, but have also relied on the help of many friends in compiling this small collection. They are all expert anglers and fly designers, and when they recommend a pattern, we should all listen.

But I am writing in the present tense, which is not entirely accurate: two of the contributors—Fran Betters and Warren Duncan—are no longer with us. Their influence on fly fishing and tying, however, will remain timeless.

My heartfelt thanks to the following gentlemen (and ladies) for helping with this project:

Tom Baltz
Al and Gretchen Beatty
Fran Betters
Gary Borger
Bill Black
David Brandt
Dennis Charney
Warren Duncan
Jay "Fishy" Fullum
Keith Fulsher
Aaron Jasper

Claes Johansson
Craig Mathews
Dennis Potter
Jesse Riding
Al Ritt
Mike Romanowski
Ted Rogowski
Ed Shenk
Mike Valla
Ken Walrath
Sharon E. Wright

Saltwater

A great many anglers have played key roles in my development as a fly fisherman and tier. Without them, my life and fishing would be poorer. The following folks—in no particular order—have offered important contributions to this book, and I offer them my thanks. Tie or buy their flies, and you will catch fish.

Dick Brown	Mike Hogue
Al Ritt	Barry and Cathy Beck
Drew Chicone	John Kumiski.
Bob Veverka	Henry Cowen
Aaron Adams	Lenny Moffo
Tim Borski	Chris Newsome
Alan Caolo	Peter Smith
Lefty Kreh	Jonny King
Patrick Dorsey	Steve Farrar
Tom McQuade	Thomas Kintz
Bob Clouser	Page Rogers
Dan Blanton	Kate and Bill Howe
Bob Popovics	David Skok
Lou Tabory	Keith Fulsher
Craig Mathews	Bob Hines
Matt Ramsey	Chuck Furimsky
Kirk Dietrich	Art Sheck
Brad Buzzi	Richard Murphy
Stu Apte	Lex Hochner
Joe Blados	Greg Miheve
Jack Gartside	

Introduction

IN ORDER FOR YOU TO UNDERSTAND HOW I WROTE THESE books, I have to tell you a little about myself and how I came to the craft of fly tying.

I was raised in Oklahoma at a time when hardly anyone fly fished. Every Wednesday evening, around suppertime, a local television station broadcast a thirty-minute show dedicated to hunting and fishing—mostly deer, turkey, bass, and crappie. With respect to the fishing, almost everything revolved around using purple plastic worms or small spinner blades. I had a tackle box full of those baits, and they did catch fish.

One evening, this show featured a gentleman who caught trophy black bass using a fly rod and his very own flies. I was aware of fly fishing—I saw photographs of fly anglers in Field & Stream and the other popular outdoor magazines—but this was the first time I heard anyone explain the nuances of the sport. I was very young and only a fledgling angler, but everything he said made perfect sense to me.

A local department store with a large hunting and fishing department sponsored that television show, and at the end of the evening's broadcast, the host said that their guest would be at the store the following weekend to tie flies and talk about fly fishing. I asked my parents to take me to meet this man, and they agreed.

I faintly remember watching this fellow tie flies. He explained how a heap of deer hair, lashed to a hook and trimmed just so, could imitate a mouse or other tiny critter that might scurry along the edge of a stream or lake, fall in, and get gobbled by a fish. He described how to cast a fly, and most importantly, how to retrieve it to encourage a bass to attack. Once again, what he said made sense. At the end of the day, my parents purchased a fly-tying kit for me, and I took the first small step in my fly-tying career.

In addition to being a devoted angler, I have always been a voracious reader. About the time I discovered fly fishing, I also lived close to a public library. I would peddle my bicycle to the library and spends hours thumbing through the small section of books devoted to hunting, fishing, and even taxidermy. I checked out each of those books over and over again. One of those volumes became important to my growing love of fly fishing.

Streamers & Bucktails: The Big Fish Flies, written by Col. Joseph D. Bates, is a classic piece of fly fishing literature. In this great book, which first appeared in 1950, Bates tells the stories of hundreds of flies and the men—and even a couple of women—who created them. From the title, you might think this is a book about how to tie flies, but it actually contains very little tying. *Streamers & Bucktails* is primarily a book of history, exploring the world of fly fishing through the patterns used to catch fish.

It was impossible to read *Streamers & Bucktails* and not dream about rivers filled with landlocked salmon, ponds full of rising trout, or tropical flats visited by leaping tarpon. In addition to the wonderful stories, Streamers & Bucktails contains hundreds of fly patterns with notes about color and material substitutions. But rather than writing a mechanical fly-tying manual, Bates brought the sport alive through his stories about flies.

I have written hundreds of articles and several books about how to tie flies, but for my own reading, I return to Streamers & Bucktails and other books like it. I fell in love with Bates's book long before I became a proficient tier, and I still return to it for inspiration. Whether I'm looking for a good fish-catching fly to tie, want to learn more about the history of our sport, or simply want to be entertained, this type of literature fills an important place on my bookshelf.

In the *101 Favorite Flies* series of books, I tell the stories of some of the very best dry flies, wet flies, nymphs, and saltwater patterns. Many of the flies are obvious choices, but many others have never appeared in print. I selected many of the patterns from my own fly boxes, but guides and other exceptional anglers offered their own favorite flies; one of my personal goals when writing a book is to explore new aspects of our sport, and I am always eager to learn what other flyfishermen use to catch fish. My thanks to all the anglers who opened their fly boxes and shared their best patterns.

This collection of more than three hundred patterns spans more than two hundred years of fly fishing. I am especially proud to include flies tied by some of the most famous anglers and pattern designers in the history of our sport: Fran Betters, George Grant, Al and Gretchen Beatty, Ed Shenk, Oliver Edwards, Warren Duncan, and many more. And, to the best of my knowledge, this is the first time a Royal Wulff—actually tied by Lee Wulff—appears in print.

If you tie flies, you will discover many tips that will improve your time at the vise. If you fish with flies, you will learn many tricks that will help you catch more fish. I think this book contains something for everyone who enjoys our great sport.

Good tying, and good fishing!

DRY FLIES

Deciphering the Challenge of the Rising Trout

SUCCESSFULLY CASTING A DRY FLY TO A FEEDING TROUT IS the pinnacle of the fly angler's art. The first steps are identifying what the fish is eating, selecting the correct forgery, and choosing the proper position in the river from which to cast. Even the angle of the light and potential shadows that might alarm your quarry must be considered.

You fall into rhythm with the rising trout and the flowing water. You cast the fly just ahead of the fish, and just a moment before it should return to the surface to snatch another winged morsel. You tend the line both before and after it drops to the water. The bits of feather and fur, tied to a piece of bent wire, bob with the speed of the current. You wait and watch.

If you've considered the problem correctly and handled your tackle properly, a slick wet nose will poke through the surface to suck in your fly. You may now consider yourself a good angler. A very accomplished fly fisher can do this repeatedly, intuitively going through the steps that lead to tugs on the end of his line.

It's said that nymphs catch more trout and streamers fool bigger fish, but nothing beats the joy of seeing that wet nose intercept your fly from the top of the water.

This book is about dry flies. Not all dry flies, but *favorite* dry flies—101 flies, to be exact. I have selected some of my favorite patterns, and a group of angling friends chose some of theirs. What follows is a collection of floating flies that will catch trout anywhere.

Each entry contains a clear—and hopefully artful—photograph of the fly, a precise materials recipe, and a small story describing the pattern. Sometimes I tell the history of the fly or offer a few tying or fishing tips. Other times I discuss what the pattern imitates and give a brief lesson in streamside entomology. The material is as varied as the flies themselves.

There's no way a small book can contain *every* favorite fly; in fact, I am including a few patterns that have never appeared in print. But, each fly has been chosen and tied by an experienced angler, the kind of fisherman who can intuitively decipher the challenge of the rising trout.

David Klausmeyer

CHAPTER ONE

Matching the Hatch: Mayflies, Caddisflies, and Stoneflies

Slow-water,
Blue-winged Olive

Hook: Standard dry-fly hook, sizes 20 to 16.
Thread: Olive 8/0.
Tail: Dark pardo Coq de Leon.
Body: Stripped peacock quill, dyed olive.
Thorax: Olive Superfine dubbing.
Wing post: White Hi-Vis polypropylene yarn.
Hackle: Grizzly.

THE SLOW-WATER, BLUE-WINGED OLIVE IS EXTREMELY
productive in slow-water scenarios where the trout are ultra selective. The
body is very slender, and when combined with a light-wire hook, this pattern is extremely buoyant.

The parachute-style hackle on the Slow-water, Blue-winged Olive
makes the fly float on the surface with the body resting in the film like a
real emerger. This pattern creates a realistic-looking silhouette on the water,
which is necessary when fishing for very discerning trout in slower moving
sections of a stream.

Feel free to swap other colors of yarn for the wing post. Hot pink and
orange are easy to track on the water—even in failing light, and the fish do
not seem to notice these bright colors.

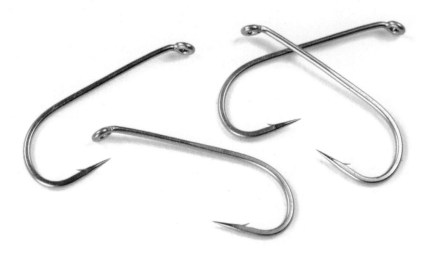

Hovering Green Drake Emerger

Hook: Partridge Klinkhamer hook, size 10.
Thread: Brown 6/0.
Tail: Dingy olive marabou tips.
Abdomen: Dingy olive marabou.
Rib: Extra-fine copper wire or clear monofilament.
Thorax: Peacock herl.
Wing bud: Cul de canard.
Hackle: Grizzly, dyed tan, or Cree.
Indicator: Closed-cell foam.

AS AN AUTHOR, IT'S FUN TO SHARE SOME OF YOUR OWN patterns, and this is one of mine—well, sort of. I made several changes to the classic Quigley Cripple, so many, in fact, that most fly designers would claim it as an entirely new pattern. When I look at the Hovering Green Drake Emerger, however, I still see the basic form of Bob Quigley's famous fly, so I think of it as more of a second or third cousin. It's different, but there is no denying the family resemblance.

The tail and feathery abdomen, which hang down in the surface film, do an admirable job of imitating a beefy green drake or *Hexagenia* mayfly nymph. Counter-wrap the rib over the abdomen to protect the marabou fibers. The cul de canard wing bud, full-hackle collar, and foam indicator keep the head of the fly above the water like a real emerger.

Tying the Hovering Green Drake Emerger

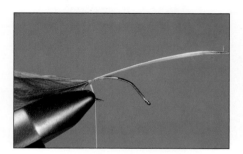

1. Wrap a layer of thread on the end of the hook shank. Strip the fibers from the base of a marabou feather. Tie the bare stem to the hook using two or three loose thread wraps.

2. Pull the marabou to form the tail of the fly. Tighten the thread to lock the marabou to the top of the hook. Tie on a piece of extra-fine copper wire.

3. Twist the marabou into a tight rope. Wrap the twisted feather up the hook to create the abdomen of the fly. Tie off and cut the surplus marabou. Counter-wrap the wire (in the opposite direction of the marabou) to make the rib. Tie off and cut the remaining piece of wire.

4. Tie on a small piece of cul de canard for the wing bud. Strip the excess fibers from the base of a hackle. Tie the feather to the hook.

5. Tie on three or four strands of peacock herl. Wrap the herl on the hook to make the thorax. Tie off and clip the surplus herl. Tie a piece of closed-cell foam to the top of the fly.

6. Wrap the hackle collar. Tie off and cut the remaining hackle tip. Tie off and snip the thread.

Carol's Caddis

Hook: Regular dry-fly hook, sizes 20 to 12.

Thread: Size 6/0, color to match the body.

Body: Any dry-fly dubbing, color to match the caddisflies on your local waters.

Underwing: Light gray mallard-flank fibers, slightly longer than the hook shank.

Wing: Natural snowshoe hare foot fur.

JAY "FISHY" FULLUM DESIGNED CAROL'S CADDIS TO HONOR his favorite angling companion, his wife. (Carol Fullum was once a production fly tier, so Fishy's flies have to be spot-on to get her approval.)

In describing the origins of this pattern, Fishy said, "I was replenishing my inventory of caddisflies when Carol took a minute to see what was coming off my vise. She retrieved her vest and checked out her supply of caddisflies. Carol said she had an idea for a simple, durable pattern that she could see on the water. While she hasn't tied flies in many years, she definitely knows what she wants in her patterns."

They have used Carol's Caddis to catch trout in a dozen states. The materials always stay the same, but they change colors and sizes to match the local caddisflies. They recommend sprinkling a little powdered flotant on the fly before fishing.

Dark Visible Dun

Hook: Regular dry-fly hook, sizes 16 to 12.
Thread: Black 8/0.
Tail: Deer body hair.
Body: Stripped peacock quill.
Wing: White calf tail.

FLY-TIER KEITH FULSHER IS ONE OF THE LEGENDS OF FLY fishing of the last half of the twentieth century. His Thunder Creek series of streamers, designed to imitate dace, minnows, and other forms of common baitfish, was his answer to the dry-fly purists' mantra of "match the hatch." While well known for his unique family of streamers, Keith is always eager to fish dry flies when the trout start rising, and I was so pleased to receive a package containing two of his original surface patterns.

Keith wrote about the Dark Visible Dun for the June/July 1962 edition of *The Sportsman*, which was the publication of the Southern New York Fish & Game Association. (Keith included a copy of that article in the package.)

In Keith's cover letter, he said, "Most of my dry-fly fishing was with standard patterns, but sometimes I changed them a bit. For instance, on the Royal Wulff, I always put on a white tail instead of the brown. The Dark Visible Dun has been a good fly and has served me well."

Yarn Wing Dun—Dark Hendrickson

Hook: 2X-long dry-fly hook, size 16 or 14.
Thread: Brown 8/0.
Tail: Dark dun hackle fibers.
Abdomen: Brown dry-fly dubbing.
Thorax: Dark brown dry-fly dubbing.
Hackle: Brown.
Wing and head: Dark gray polypropylene yarn.

BEFORE MAKING THE YARN WING DUN, TIER GARY BORGER bends the first one-third of the hook up about twenty degrees. This makes the fly land on the water thorax first. The bend also anchors the thorax in the surface film and allows the fly to rest on the water like a real insect.

When tying the tail of the Yarn Wing Dun, first wrap a tiny ball of dubbing at the end of the hook shank. Next, tie on the tail. The hackle fibers will splay around the ball of dubbing and improve the fly's appearance and flotation.

Check out the great-looking wing and head; Gary makes these using polypropylene yarn. It's easy to imagine tying the wing, but you must do something to prevent it from collapsing onto the fly when fishing. Gary places a small drop of cement on the base of the wing to stiffen the fibers.

This pattern begs for variations. Swap hook sizes and colors of materials to tie imitations of almost any medium to large mayfly dun.

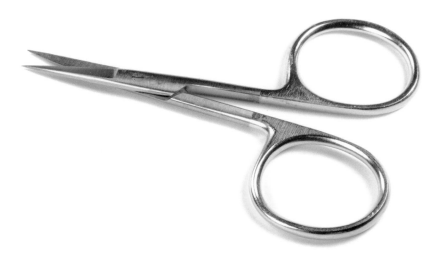

Opal & Elk Caddisfly

Hook: Tiemco TMC100, size 12 or 10.
Thread: Fifty-denier, gel-spun thread.
Body: Opal Mirage tinsel.
Rib: Fine gold wire.
Wing: Natural, dark cow elk hair.
Hackle: Dun.

THIS IS DENNIS POTTER'S TAKE ON AL TROTH'S GREAT DRY fly, the Elk-hair Caddis. According to Dennis, the opal tinsel used for the body makes this the best all-round, hackled-caddisfly imitation he has ever used. In fact, he carries no caddis imitations tied with dubbed bodies; they all have opal tinsel bodies. Dennis is so enthusiastic about this pattern that I think it's worth tying and fishing.

Be sure to use a slightly undersized hackle when tying the Elk-hair Caddis, Potter's Opal & Elk Caddis, and similar patterns; the fibers should be equal to or only slightly longer than the width of the hook gap.

Also, Dennis Potter has joined the growing group of tiers using gel-spun thread for making dry flies. They can apply a lot of pressure to the thread and tie durable patterns without adding a lot of bulk.

Crowd Surfer Stone

Hook: Regular dry-fly hook, size 8.
Thread: Orange 6/0.
Abdomen: Foam, ribbed with tying thread.
Tails: Brown goose or turkey biots.
Underwing: Tyvek.
Wing: Elk hair and white polypropylene yarn.
Thorax: Bands of orange yarn or dubbing.
Legs: Rubber legs.

THE CROWD SURFER STONE, A PATTERN SOLD BY RAINY'S, is a creation of expert fly-tier Clint Goodman.

The Crowd Surfer Stone is a brilliant, high-floating imitation of the western salmonfly. The foam abdomen makes the pattern almost unsink-able, and the rubber legs give it a great splayed appearance on the surface of the water.

The salmonfly hatch is one of the most anticipated events of the western fishing season. After living in the water for three years, the large nymphs emerge to turn into winged adults; look for the empty cases of the nymphs along the edges of the river. The adults return to the river to mate and lay eggs, and the trout eagerly feed on this smorgasbord of giant insects.

In addition to matching the salmonfly, swap colors and tie the Crowd Surfer Stone to imitate almost any large, adult stonefly.

March Brown Emerger

Hook: Partridge 15BN Klinkhamer, size 14.
Thread: Orange 6/0.
Tail: Three golden, pheasant-tail fibers.
Abdomen: Tannish yellow dry-fly dubbing.
Rib: Stripped center quill from a duck, primary or secondary feather.
Wing: Light dun Hi-Vis yarn.
Thorax: Tannish yellow dry-fly dubbing.
Hackle: Cree or reddish brown and grizzly mixed.

THE STRIPPED MALLARD-QUILL RIB GIVES THIS PARACHUTE
March Brown a very realistic appearance. Stripping a mallard quill is easy.
Hold a duck pointer or secondary feather with the good side facing up.
Nick the center quill near the tip of the feather with a razor blade, creating
a small tab. Next, grasp this projecting piece of quill with hackle pliers and
pull straight down toward the base of the feather, unzipping the quill. If
done properly, you'll get a beautifully segmented quill.

The quill has a tendency to curl as it is stripped, so soak the stripped quill
in a bowl of water, and it will straighten nicely. Spend an evening preparing
stripped quills for a future tying session. Allow the soaked quills to dry and
then store in a plastic sandwich bag.

Blue Dun Snowshoe

Hook: Regular dry-fly hook, sizes 16 to 12.
Thread: Gray 8/0.
Tail: Dun snowshoe rabbit foot fur.
Body: Tying thread.
Wing: Dun snowshoe hare foot fur.
Hackle: Medium dun.

"BLUE DUN" IS A VERY OLD FLY-TYING TERM. THE DISCUS-
sion of exact shades of color always encourages friendly debate among tiers.
With respect to blue dun, think of medium gray with a slightly bluish cast.
Flip through the pages of old fly-tying books, and you'll find many other
descriptions associated with dun: light dun, medium dun, dark dun, honey
dun, and more.

Snowshoe hare fur is a fascinating material. You'll find the cured feet in
fly shops in natural cream and a variety of dyed colors. The fur from the
bottom of the foot is corkscrewed and holds air bubbles. These bubbles
help the Blue Dun Snowshoe and similar patterns float on the surface of
the water. This simple pattern is great for novice tiers looking for an easy-
to-tie dry fly.

Mahogany Quill Spinner

Hook: Tiemco TMC100, size 12.
Thread: Black 6/0.
Tail: Brown, spade-hackle fibers.
Wings: Light medium dun hen hackles.
Abdomen: Brown neck-hackle, stripped quill.
Thorax: Dark brown dry-fly dubbing.

MAHOGANY MAYFLIES (*ISONYCHIA BICOLOR*) ARE SOME OF the most important insects to fly fishers. *Isonychia* duns molt into spinners within a couple days of hatching, and when they return to mate and lay their eggs, they provide much more concentrated action than during emergence.

Isonychia bicolor mate in swarms twenty to thirty feet in the air. The females usually drop their eggs from high above the water and then fall spent on the surface; this is when they become available to the trout.

Sharon E. Wright's Mahogany Quill Spinner is a fine mayfly imitation. She artfully uses hen-hackle tips to imitate the splayed wings of the natural insect. The stripped-quill abdomen matches the slender profile of a real, adult mayfly.

Heckel's Tape Wing Caddis

Hook: 2X-long dry-fly hook, sizes 20 to 14.
Thread: Size 8/0, color to match the body of the fly.
Body: Hare's mask or rabbit dubbing.
Body hackle: Rooster dry-fly hackle.
Wing: Hen-saddle hackle on tape.
Front hackle: Rooster dry-fly hackle.

FLY-TIER BILL HECKEL CREATED THIS UNIQUE PATTERN, and it is sold commercially by the Spirit River Company.

Three things come to mind when regarding this fly.

First, select materials in colors to match the real caddisflies on your local water; black, brown, and tan are the most common. Also, tie this fly in several sizes to match any caddisflies you encounter.

Second, just like when tying an Elk-hair Caddis, the fibers of the body hackle should equal or be slightly shorter than the width of the hook gap.

And third, Heckel places a hen feather on a piece of 3M Scotch Hand Packaging Tape and then clips the wing to shape. Next, he ties the base tip of the trimmed wing to the top of the fly. A roll of tape is inexpensive, and there is enough material to create the wings for dozens of flies. The tape helps the feather hold its shape and creates a durable wing.

Egg-laying Rusty Spinner

Hook: Regular dry-fly hook, sizes 18 to 12.
Thread: Dark brown 6/0.
Tails: Light dun microfibbets.
Egg sac: Yellow embroidery floss.
Abdomen: Turkey biot, dyed rusty brown.
Wing: White McFlylon or polypropylene yarn.
Thorax: Mahogany brown beaver dubbing.

THIS IS OBVIOUSLY A SPINNER IMITATION, BUT WHAT IS A "rusty" mayfly?

This term usually applies to the Baetidae family of mayflies. It is one of the most prolific varieties in North American trout streams. Baetidae often have three generations per year and hatch in impressive numbers.

The genus *Baetis* and its species are often misidentified. Many anglers call them *Baetis*, especially if they're olive in coloration. In reality, the prominent *Baetis* is only one of several very similar and abundant genera in the family Baetidae. Many other anglers call them Blue-winged Olives, but this name is unwittingly applied to dozens of species across several families of mayflies.

Okay, enough of the bug Latin. Suffice it to say that this pattern comes in handy when matching a large number of small mayfly spinners. These spinners, which gather in large numbers over the water, often lead to impressive feeding action from the trout. At times such as these, a spinner imitation will definitely improve your catch rate.

Life & Death Callibaetis

Hook: Daiichi 1100, sizes 18 to 14.
Thread: Tan 8/0.
Tail: Mayfly tails, black barred white.
Abdomen: Gray, stripped quill.
Wings: White organza.
Wing post: Orange Hi-Vis or polypropylene yarn.
Thorax: Adams gray Superfine dubbing.
Hackle: Grizzly.

AL RITT'S LIFE & DEATH CALLIBAETIS IS A FINE IMITATION of a *Callibaetis* spinner. The splayed wings imitate the wings of the real insect and help the pattern float on the surface. Spinner flies are often hard to track on the water, so Al added a wing post of fluorescent orange yarn; you can see this pattern under the poorest lighting conditions.

Callibaetis are part of the Baetidae family of mayflies. Although they are found throughout the United States, the largest concentrations are in the West. Look for *Callibaetis* in the slower sections of rivers and in ponds and lakes.

Although some *Callibaetis* range in hook sizes from 16 to 12, you'll find smaller *Callibaetis* at higher elevations.

ParaNymph

Hook: Regular dry-fly hook, sized to match the natural insects.
Thread: Golden olive 6/0.
Tail: Olive brown Z-Lon or a substitute.
Wing post: Fluorescent orange or lemon yellow calf-body hair.
Body: Natural hare's mask dubbing with plenty of guard hairs.
Hackle: Grizzly.

WHEN MAKING HIS PARANYMPH, TOM BALTZ, WHO IS A
right–handed tier, wraps the hackle counter clockwise using articulated
hackle pliers and then ties off the feather on top of the hook shank in front
of the wing post. He wraps the hackle so the concave side is facing up.

Tom also blends his own hare's mask dubbing. He trims the hair from
the ears and center of the mask, but not too much from the cheeks. He
blends the fur in a food processor, or he shakes it in a jar of water and then
places the material on a piece of newspaper to dry. The body of the fly, Tom
says, should be spiky, not smooth.

The ParaNymph is Tom's favorite dry fly. He uses this pattern when
fishing by himself and also when guiding in Pennsylvania, and it has caught
fish across North America as well as in Patagonia, New Zealand, and South
Korea.

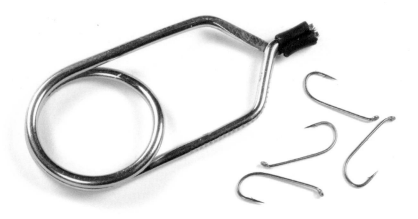

Flight's Fancy

Hook: Regular dry-fly hook, sizes 16 to 12.
Thread: Black 8/0.
Tail: Brown or ginger hackle fibers.
Tip: Gold tinsel.
Wings: Light mallard quill sections.
Body: Pale yellow floss.
Rib: Gold tinsel.
Hackle: Brown or ginger.

NOT ALL FISH-CATCHING DRY FLIES ARE TIED WITH FOAM
and rubber legs; the classics still catch their share of trout. Although you
won't find Flight's Fancy in the fly boxes of many of today's anglers, it
remains an essential pattern that will work on any stream or river.

Flight's Fancy, an English pattern, was named for a Mr. Wright, of Win-
chester, England, around 1885. The pattern quickly jumped the Atlantic to
the United States, and in 1912, Theodore Gordon, the father of American
dry-fly fishing, wrote, "Last week I renewed my acquaintance with a native-
born dry-fly fisher, who never read a book upon the subject, but picked up
his ideas upon the stream. He was troubled because he could get no more
flies of a pattern that he had found very killing. You may imagine my surprise when he said that it was called Flight's Fancy."

Closed-cell foam floats forever, and rubber legs give a fly a lot of lifelike
wiggling action, but nothing beats the grace and beauty of a pattern such as
Flight's Fancy. Even the name is great!

Scuddle Muddle

Hook: Turned-down-eye scud hook, sizes 22 to 10.
Thread: Tan 8/0.
Tag: Tying thread.
Extension fibers: Ginger hackle fibers.
Body: Ginger dry-fly dubbing.
Rib: Tying thread.
Wings: Ginger hackles.
Front hackle: Bleached elk.
Head: Clipped elk hair.

THE SCUDDLE MUDDLE IS ANOTHER OF AL AND GRETCHEN Beatty's original patterns. While they are best known for their outstanding dry flies, the Scuddle Muddle is an emerger. The Beattys also make terrific nymphs and streamers.

I have seen different versions of the Scuddle Muddle, so even the Beattys sometimes swap materials on their flies. For example, rather than elk hair, you can tie what they call the front hackle using deer hair. They also use a variety of colors for body dubbing to make patterns that imitate almost any emerging mayfly or caddisfly. If you wish to tie an extremely small Scuddle Muddle, you can even dispense with the dubbing and dress the body with just thread.

Loop-wing Dun— Pale Morning Dun

Hook: Regular dry-fly hook, size 16 or 14.
Thread: Gray 8/0.
Tail: Dun hackle fibers.
Abdomen: Gray dry-fly dubbing.
Rib: Brown tying thread.
Thorax: Gray dry-fly dubbing.
Hackle: Dun.
Wing: Gray polypropylene yarn.

THIS IS ANOTHER OF GARY BORGER'S GREAT PATTERNS on which he bends the first one-third of the hook up at a twenty-degree angle before tying the fly.

The looped yarn wing is a neat way to tie small- and medium-size mayfly dun imitations. This style of wing is easy to make. The fibers hold tiny air bubbles, so if the body slips beneath the water, the wing holds the fly close to the surface like an emerger or insect that has failed to emerge. A looped wing also creates a realistic silhouette and is easy to spot on the water. Try experimenting with white, orange, and pink yarn to increase the visibility of your flies. Switch back and forth, and see if the brightly colored wings put off the fish. Let me know how you do.

Mahogany Emerger

Hook: Standard dry-fly hook, sizes 20 to 12.
Thread: Dark brown 8/0.
Trailing shuck: Brown Z-lon.
Body: Stripped peacock herl, dyed brown.
Wing: Dun snowshoe hare foot fur.
Thorax: Brown Superfine dubbing

ACCORDING TO CONTRIBUTOR AARON JASPER, HIS Mahogany Emerger "is extremely durable and floats like a cork, even when presented in stream sections with turbulent surface currents."

The snowshoe hare foot fur, which is used for creating the wing of the fly, makes the pattern extremely buoyant. The Mahogany Emerger has a natural appearance when viewed from the bottom. The trailing shuck is very sparse, like the shuck found on the real insect. The stripped peacock herl used for wrapping the abdomen creates a slender, natural-looking body.

Fish the Mahogany Emerger, and any color variations you wish to tie, in both the fast and slow sections of your favorite trout stream. This is a fine choice when the real mayflies are beginning to hatch.

Opal X-Caddis

Hook: Tiemco TMC100, sizes 20 to 14.
Thread: Fifty denier, gel-spun thread.
Trailing shuck: Gold Z-lon.
Body: Opal Mirage tinsel.
Wing: Very fine deer hair.

IT'S SO REFRESHING TO ENCOUNTER A TIER WHO MAKES changes in another fellow's pattern and doesn't claim that he has created a new fly. Dennis Potter freely admits that his Opal X-Caddis is his take on Craig Mathews's great X-Caddis. The addition of the opal tinsel body makes it irresistible to the trout; Dennis says this fly is "ridiculously effective."

Both Craig and Dennis tie these flies in small hook sizes. To do this, you must use sparse amounts of materials. These patterns work well at the beginning of a caddis hatch when the natural insects are just beginning to pop through the surface film. Later in the hatch, when you see real caddisflies skating across the surface, you can switch to an Elk-hair Caddis or a Potter's Opal & Elk.

X-Fly Modular Green Drake

Hook: Regular dry-fly hook, size 10.
Thread: Black 8/0.
Abdomen: Tube Bodiz premade body.
Wings: Medallion Sheeting or a similar wing material.
Hackle: Teal and grizzly.
Head: Black dubbing.

THE X-FLY MODULAR GREEN DRAKE, WHICH IS COMMER-
cially produced by Rainy's, is tied using two unique fly-tying materials.

First, the abdomen, which is a Tube Bodiz, gives the pattern an amazingly lifelike appearance. Simply tie the Tube Bodiz to the hook and continue making the fly. The abdomen, which is quite sturdy, is hollow and also
adds flotation to the pattern.

The wings are clear Medallion Sheeting clipped into the shape of mayfly
wings. These wings add to the fly's realism and are very durable.

The green drake is a popular summer mayfly, and you will want to stock
up with imitations of this important and large insect. The X-Fly Modular
Green Drake is an ideal candidate for filling that end of your fly box.

Isonychia Comparadun

Hook: Tiemco TMC100, size 12 or 10.
Thread: Olive dun 8/0.
Tail: Dun hackle fibers.
Body: Grayish olive dry-fly dubbing, overwrapped with a stripped mallard quill.
Thorax: Grayish olive dry-fly dubbing.
Wing: Dark dun yearling elk

ON HIS HOME WATERS ON THE UPPER DELAWARE RIVER, tier Mike Romanowski says the *Isonychia* mayflies start hatching around the middle of May and continue until the pumpkins are ready for picking. During late spring and early summer, the "Iso's" have a distinct olive cast, and the stripped mallard quill over olive gray dubbing creates the perfect match. The *Isonychia* emergence really comes into its own in July and August, when most other hatches are slim.

Mike sometimes uses fifty denier, fly-tying thread. This allows him to create a very dense yet durable wing, so this pattern floats through the riffles and pocket water where the *Isonychia* live and hatch. Try using the darkest stripped duck quills (black quills are the best) for completing the body on this pattern.

Quill Gordon

Hook: Regular dry-fly hook, sizes 16 to 10.
Thread: Tan 8/0.
Tail: Blue dun hackle fibers.
Body: Stripped herl from the eye of a peacock.
Wing: Wood duck flank fibers.
Hackle: Blue dun.

THE QUILL GORDON HAS BEEN WRITTEN ABOUT MANY times over the decades, but there is no way I can write a book titled *101 Favorite Dry Flies* and not include this famous American pattern; it would be seeded high on any thoughtful angler's list of important floating imitations. How to write about the Quill Gordon in a couple of short paragraphs?

Theodore Gordon, who many consider the father of American dry-fly fishing, created this pattern in the late nineteenth century. Until the creation of the Royal Wulff, it's possible that the Quill Gordon was our most popular dry fly, and its influence has spread beyond fly fishing; there is a bed and breakfast called the Quill Gordon Inn, as well as a fictional detective named Quill Gordon.

Gordon made the body of the fly using a piece of stripped herl from a peacock eye. I might be wrong, but I don't think you'll find stripped peacock herl in any fly shop; you'll have to make your own. Simply pull a piece of herl between your index finger and the nail of your thumb; the nail will strip the flue from the quill. Or, spread the herl between the thumb and index finger of one hand, and remove the flue using a common pencil eraser.

Olive Snowshoe Baetis Spinner

Hook: Regular dry-fly hook, size 18 or 16.
Thread: Olive 8/0.
Tail: Medium dun Microfibbets.
Abdomen: Tying thread.
Wing: Light cream or bleached snowshoe hare foot fur.
Thorax: Natural snowshoe hare foot fur.

BAETIS MAYFLIES ARE WIDESPREAD ACROSS NORTH AMER-
ica. There are several species of Baetis, and in some locations they are one
of the highlights of the fishing season. The small spinners, returning to the
water to lay their eggs, can encourage surprisingly large fish to rise.

Ken Walrath used a synthetic material called Microfibbetts for the
splayed tails on his Olive Snowshoe Baetis. Another product you'll also find
in your local fly shop, called simply Mayfly Tails, is an ideal substitute. Or, if
you wish, you can use the bristles from a fine-fibered paintbrush.

The splayed wings imitate the appearance of a spinner mayfly lying
exhausted on the water.

Green Drake Fan Wing

Hook: Regular dry-fly hook, size 6.
Thread: Olive green 8/0.
Tail: Moose-body hair.
Body: Insect green floss.
Rib: Brown floss.
Wings: Mallard-flank feathers.
Hackle: Grizzly.

WE USE SEVERAL MATERIALS TO TIE THE WINGS ON MAYFLY dun imitations; hair, yarn, and feather fibers are among the most popular ingredients. Sharon E. Wright used mallard-flank feathers to fashion the wings on her Green Drake Fan Wing, and the effect is outstanding.

Feather fan wings look great; they give a fly an appearance of realism. They also help the pattern land upright on the surface of the water; the wings catch the air like a parachute, and the fly plops down in the correct position.

Practice tying fan wings on larger flies such as the Green Drake, and work progressively smaller as you gain experience. You will be limited by the size of the feathers you can find, but you should be able to work down to about size 12.

Crystal Wing Parachute Pheasant-tail and Adams

Crystal Wing Parachute Pheasant-tail
Hook: Curved-shank emerger hook, sizes 18 to 14.
Thread: Black 6/0.
Tail: Three ring-necked, pheasant-tail fibers.
Abdomen: Ring-necked, pheasant-tail fibers.
Rib: Clear monofilament.
Thorax: Peacock herl.
Wing: Pearl Crystal Splash.
Hackle: Brown.

Crystal Wing Parachute Adams
Hook: Regular dry-fly hook, sizes 18 to 12.
Thread: Gray 6/0.
Tail: Moose-body hair.
Body: Adams gray fine and dry dubbing.
Wing: Pearl Crystal Splash.
Hackle: Brown and natural grizzly.

THESE TWO FLIES DEMONSTRATE THAT YOU CAN ADAPT new materials to update older patterns. Here, the folks at the Spirit River Company have tied the wings on these two common parachute flies using their product, called Crystal Splash. The trout don't mind the change in materials, and these flies are easy to track on the water.

Look at the standard patterns you are already tying. Can you improve any of them using modern materials? Can you make changes in the bodies, wings, or other features? Don't go crazy; just make sensible substitutions and try your new creations the next time you go fishing. This sort of experimenting is fun, and it will keep your tying fresh and exciting.

CRYSTAL WING PARACHUTE PHEASANT-TAIL

CRYSTAL WING PARACHUTE ADAMS

Struggling Green Drake

Extended Abdomen
Base: Flymen Fishing Company Wiggle Shank.
Thread: Olive 8/0.
Tail: Moose hair.
Abdomen: Blue-winged Olive Superfine dubbing.
Rib: Hopper yellow 8/0 tying thread.

Thorax
Hook: Tiemco 2488, sizes 16 to 12.
Extended-body connection: 4X fluorocarbon tippet.
Wing: Black snowshoe hare fur from the back of the foot.
Thorax: Blue-winged Olive Superfine dubbing.
Hackle: Speckled badger or dark champagne.

THE STRUGGLING GREEN DRAKE IS AN UNUSUAL extended-body emerger imitation. Al Ritt ties the abdomen on a Wiggle Shank, a product of the innovative Flymen Fishing Company. Al then places a hook in the vise and attaches the abdomen to the shank; he leaves enough play so the abdomen moves freely. When fishing, the abdomen hangs down in the surface film while the thorax remains on the surface. The Struggling Green Drake does a fine job imitating an insect just breaking through the surface film and turning into a winged adult.

Use this design as a guide to creating imitations of other large, emerging mayflies—a Struggling Hexagenia comes to mind.

Harey Dun—
Blue-winged Olive and
Pale Morning Dun

Harey Dun—Blue-winged Olive
Hook: Daiichi 1100, sizes 22 to 16.
Tail: Olive Mayfly Tails.
Abdomen: Olive stripped quill.
Wing: Black snowshoe hare fur from the back of the foot.
Thorax: Blue-winged Olive Superfine dubbing.
Hackle: Grizzly, dyed olive.

Harey Dun—Pale Morning Dun
Hook: Daiichi 1100, sizes 18 to 14.
Tail: Medium dun Mayfly Tails.
Abdomen: Stripped quill, dyed pale morning dun.
Wing: Medium dun snowshoe hare fur from the back of the foot.
Thorax: Pale Morning Dun Superfine dubbing.
Hackle: Dun.

IT'S SURPRISING HOW MANY TIERS ARE TURNING TO snowshoe hare foot fur to tie the wings on their dry flies. It wasn't too many years ago that pattern designers were turning to new synthetic materials to fashion wings; maybe the large number of flies tied with snowshoe fur indicates that they are returning to natural ingredients.

Al Ritt is a master at the fly-tying vise; his patterns have a consistency you find only in the flies of an accomplished tier. Although the Harey Dun is not a parachute pattern, the fur wing will catch the air as the fly falls to the water, and it will land upright every time. The sparse tail and hackle, wrapped over the dubbed thorax, create the delicate impression of a real Blue-winged Olive on the surface film.

HAREY DUN—BLUE-WINGED OLIVE

HAREY DUN—PALE MORNING DUN

CDC X-Caddis

Hook: Regular dry-fly hook, size to match the natural insects.

Thread: Olive or brown 6/0.

Tail: Ginger Z-Lon.

Body: Natural hare's mask dubbing.

Underwing: Natural dun or brown cul de canard.

Wing: Natural deer hair.

Indicator: Fluorescent orange or pink cul de canard.

THIS IS A KNOCK OFF OF THE VENERABLE X-CADDIS, AND IS one of at least three X-Caddis variations in tier Tom Baltz's fly box. This fly ranks number two on his list of top-three dry flies, so you can feel confident it's a dandy.

The cul de canard underwing gives the fly a bit of bounce and life on the water, and the brightly colored indicator allows anglers "of a certain age" to follow it more easily in broken water. Tom uses only powder-type flotants on patterns containing CDC.

Don't hesitate trimming off the tail when trout are taking spent caddisflies; one summer, this altered fly worked quite well on the picky sippers feeding just off the boat ramp at Wolf Creek Bridge on the Missouri River.

Tying the CDC X-Caddis is not difficult. Either pluck CDC fibers off the feather stem by hand or roll the feather up with a CDC tool, fold, and tie on. Tie the deer hair over the underwing, and tie the CDC indicator on top of the deer hair with the tips to the rear, then fold back, and tie down. Wind a bit of dubbing over the bare thread at the head. Whip finish the thread behind the hook eye before trimming the butt ends off the CDC and deer hair.

Quick 'n EZY Parachute

Hook: Regular dry-fly hook, sizes 22 to 10.
Thread: Tan 8/0.
Tail: Ginger hackle fibers.
Body: Ginger dubbing.
Rib: Tying thread and dubbing.
Wings: Ginger hackles.
Hackle: Ginger.

AL AND GRETCHEN BEATTY TIE A WHOLE SERIES OF PARA-chute dry-fly imitations using their Wonder Wing technique. In this case, the reverse-hackle wings serve as the wing post, and they wrap the hackle around the base of the wings. The affect is outstanding.

Start tying the larger sizes—12 and 10—to imitate bigger drakes and similar mayflies; substitute colors to match the insects on your local waters. Work progressively smaller as you gain experience. It's hard to believe, but the Beattys tie the Quick 'n EZY Parachute as small as size 22. I hope to be as proficient at the fly-tying vise one day!

Parachute Floating Nymph—Dark Hendrickson

Hook: Regular dry-fly hook, size 16 or 14.
Thread: Brown 8/0.
Tail: Dark dun hackle fibers.
Abdomen: Brown dry-fly dubbing.
Thorax: Dark brown dry-fly dubbing.
Hackle: Brown.
Back: Brown ball of dubbing.

WHEN I ASKED ANGLING-AUTHORITY GARY BORGER TO submit a few of his favorite flies for this book, he asked, "Would you be interested in a floating nymph? I know it's not technically a dry fly, but you fish it at the surface. It's a really important pattern that catches a lot of fish."

When an expert such as Gary says he has a great pattern, we all need to listen.

Fish the Parachute Floating Nymph just as the trout are beginning to rise. You might not spot adult insects on the water, and the fish might not be breaking through the surface; look for swirls just under the surface—the obvious indication that the trout are feeding on the rising nymphs. Within minutes, the nymphs will be in the surface film, shedding their skins and turning into winged adults. The fish will follow them to the surface, and your Parachute Floating Nymph will be lying in wait.

Instead of the ball of dubbing, you can substitute a polypropylene yarn-looped wing. This is the type of wing Gary ties on his Loop-wing Dun. Follow the same tying instructions, but make the wing considerably smaller.

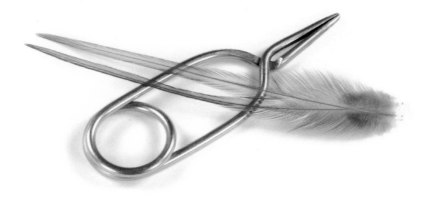

Egg-laying CDC and Elk Caddisfly

Hook: Standard dry-fly hook, sizes 20 to 12.
Thread: Tan 8/0.
Egg sac: Insect green superfine dubbing.
Body: Tan rabbit dubbing.
Collar: Dun cul de canard.
Wing: Coastal deer hair.

WITH RESPECT TO DRY-FLY IMITATIONS OF MOST AQUATIC insects, we should concern ourselves with three stages of development: the emerging nymphs or larvae, crawling through the surface film to turn into adults; the newly hatched, winged adults; and the mating males and egg-laying females. Many anglers are familiar with the spinner stage of mayfly development; this is when the insects return to the water to mate and lay their eggs and then fall exhausted to the surface. Did you ever stop to think that adult caddisflies also go through this stage?

Aaron Jasper used insect green dubbing to fashion the small egg sac on the end of the Egg-laying CDC & Elk Caddisfly. "Perhaps," he says, "it looks like an egg sac, or perhaps the fish just see it as a hot spot like on many of the newest nymphs."

Cul de canard, which is used as a collar, is the real magic of this pattern. The combination of the CDC and deer-hair wing makes the fly extremely buoyant.

Quill-bodied Hendrickson

Hook: Regular dry-fly hook, size 14.
Thread: Brown 8/0.
Tail: Grizzly, dyed tan, or Cree-hackle fibers.
Body: Grizzly, dyed tan, or Cree stripped-hackle quill.
Wing: Wood duck or mallard-dyed wood duck.
Hackle: Grizzly, dyed tan, or Cree.

FOR MANY TROUT ANGLERS ACROSS THE COUNTRY, THE hatch of the Hendrickson mayflies heralds the beginning of the real fishing season. The dainty mayflies ride the surface of the water, and the trout quickly spear this ready meal. The hatches usually occur in mid-May, but the timing shifts forward or back on the calendar by a week or two depending upon location and weather conditions.

With respect to weather, if you hear the Hendricksons are beginning to hatch on your local river, pray for an overcast sky and drizzle for the day you plan to fish. The wet weather prevents the insects from drying their wings and taking flight, and you will see more rising trout and enjoy better dry-fly fishing. If the sky is clear and there is a gentle breeze, the mayflies will quickly dry their wings and take to the air; as a result, you will probably see fewer rising trout, and the fishing might be a little slower.

The Quill-bodied Hendrickson is a Catskill inspired pattern that I have been tying for many years. I have outstanding success using it to catch Maine, landlocked salmon on my home waters. (I'm praying for a cool, overcast, and drizzly spring!)

X-Fly Parachute Adams

Hook: Regular dry-fly hook, size 16.
Thread: Black 8/0.
Abdomen: Tube Bodiz premade body.
Thorax: Gray dry-fly dubbing.
Wing post: White closed-cell foam.
Hackle: Brown and grizzly.

THIS SIZE 16 X-FLY PARACHUTE ADAMS IS ONE OF THOSE flies that makes me shake my head and say, "How'd they do that?" It is small yet perfectly tied, and it is ideal for matching most of the little, dun-colored mayflies you'll find on your local waters.

The abdomen of the X-Fly Parachute Adams is a small, gray Tube Bodiz. These premade bodies, which you can purchase at many fly shops, help in constructing bantam-weight patterns. The white, foam wing post creates a speck on the water so you can easily follow the fly.

Fish the X-Fly Parachute Adams using a long, fine leader and a three- or four-weight rod. Cast this pattern to rising trout, and you'll enjoy fine success.

Delaware Hendrickson Emerger

Hook: Tiemco TMC2488, size 14.
Thread: Dark brown 8/0.
Tail: Dark brown Antron.
Abdomen: Mahogany brown turkey biot.
Wing: Dark dun Hi-Vis yarn.
Thorax: Red quill Superfine dubbing.
Hackle: Grizzly, dyed tannish olive.

ACCORDING TO TIER MIKE ROMANOWSKI, "THIS IS PERHAPS the most effective Hendrickson imitation I have ever used."

The Klinkhamer design creates the illusion of an emerging dun, struggling to free itself from its nymphal shuck. One lucky angler, fishing this fly in the annual Delaware River One Bug Tournament, landed more than 120 inches (that's ten feet!) of trout in one day on this fly.

When tying the Delaware Hendrickson Emerger, try using the darkest turkey biots possible; they should be almost black at the base. Although Mike specifies tannish grizzly hackle, feel free to substitute with medium dun; this does not reduce the fly's effectiveness.

Mike did an outstanding job tying this pattern.

Batten Kill Badger

Hook: Regular dry-fly hook, size 12.
Tail: Badger-guard hairs.
Body: Dark muskrat fur dubbing.
Wing: Badger-guard hairs.
Hackle: Silver badger.

CATSKILL FLY-TYING AUTHORITY MIKE VALLA CREATED THE Batten Kill Badger in the late 1970s for fishing during the late evening on the New York State section of the Batten Kill, upstream from Greenwich, New York. Mike says that this pattern is easy to track on the water in the dim light. Even though it has a fairly realistic form, he says he did not tie it to match any particular natural insect; he calls it a "searcher" or "tempting" dry fly.

The white-tipped tail and wings, fashioned using badger-guard hair, look outstanding.

Adams Snowshoe

Hook: Regular dry-fly hook, size 16 or 14.
Thread: Black 8/0.
Tail: Black snowshoe hare foot fur.
Body: Gray snowshoe hare foot fur.
Wing: White or bleached snowshoe hare foot fur.
Hackle: Coachman brown and grizzly.

THIS FLY, TIED BY KEN WALRATH, IS ANOTHER PLEASANT surprise. This time he blended snowshoe hare foot fur and a classic design—the Adams—to create a very cool fly.

The Adams Snowshoe, featuring a tail, body, and wing all tied using the fur, floats high and dry over the roughest water. This pattern will bob along while other standard flies get sucked under the surface.

It seems like Ken is challenging us to think and experiment. Nothing requires us to remain hidebound to established pattern recipes. What other patterns can we improve using snowshoe hare foot fur?

UV2 Parachutes

Hook: Regular dry-fly hook, sizes 20 to 12.
Thread: White 8/0.
Tail: Hackle fibers.
Underbody: Pearl Flashabou.
Abdomen: Turkey biot.
Thorax: Fine & Dry UV2 dubbing.
Wing: Turkey flat feather.
Hackle: Rooster.

TIE UV2 PARACHUTES IN COLORS AND SIZES TO MATCH THE
adult mayflies on your local waters; this design lends itself to imitating almost
all small- to medium-size duns.

UV2 is a new line of products from the Spirit River Company. According to Spirit River, UVF is the fluorescent wavelength in bright colors we
see, and it allows fish to see flies and lures from great distances. UVR, which
stands for ultraviolet reflectance, is the UV light humans cannot see; insects
and animals, however, can see UVR. In fact, according to Spirit River, the
females of most species recognize the UVR signature of males. Spirit River
has developed a way to process materials with both UVF and UVR wave-
lengths, which they call UV2.

Spirit River recommends wrapping a base layer of pearl or silver Mylar
tinsel or white thread before wrapping UV2 dubbing or other material
onto the hook. Doing this, they say, allows the UV light spectrums to reflect
out of the pattern.

Is UV2 for real or just another form of hype? It's hard to tell. There is no
denying the fact, however, that many anglers believe adding chartreuse to
a streamer improves the fly's ability to catch fish. I believe this myself, and
Bob Clouser, the creator of the Clouser Minnow, is fond of saying, "It ain't
no use if it doesn't have chartreuse."

To this day, I have never seen anything in nature that is chartreuse.

Yarn Wing Caddis

Hook: Regular dry-fly hooks, sizes 18 to 12.
Thread: Black 8/0.
Body: Black dry-fly dubbing.
Hackle: Black.
Wing: Black polypropylene yarn.

GARY BORGER'S YARN WING CADDIS IS A SNAP TO TIE; I can't imagine anything easier. It also requires only a couple of ingredients: hook and threads (just like any fly), dubbing, polypropylene yarn, and a hackle. You'll find all of these materials in your neighborhood fly shop. Gary Borger sent a black version of this fly, but you can substitute colors to tie imitations of any caddisfly you find on the water.

Note that this is not a great pattern for skating across the surface; the Elk-hair Caddis and some other flies are better choices for more active presentations. The Yarn Wing Caddis rests lower in the water. What it lacks in this one category, it makes up for in its simplicity. Any new tier can make the fish-catching Yarn Wing Caddis.

Not Spent Spinner

Hook: Standard dry-fly hook, sizes 20 to 10.
Thread: Dark brown 8/0.
Egg sac: Sulphur orange Superfine dubbing.
Tails: Coq de Leon.
Body: Stripped peacock herl, dyed brown.
Wing: Cul de canard.
Thorax: Brown Superfine dubbing.

THE NEXT TIME YOU'RE ON THE WATER AND THE AIR IS FULL of spinner mayflies, catch a few of the swarming insects in your hat. Carefully examine the dainty insects, and you will probably see that a couple of them—the females—have brightly colored egg sacs on the tips of their abdomens. The Not Spent Spinner imitates this stage of mayfly development.

The sulphur-orange dubbing mimics the egg sac of a real mayfly, and the stripped peacock herl creates a slender abdomen. Cul de canard, used for the wings, makes the fly almost unsinkable; this is important because the majority of spinner falls last from early evening into the dark of night, and you might not be able to see whether your fly is floating or has become waterlogged and sunk.

Hi-Tie Sally

Hook: Regular dry-fly hook, size 12.
Thread: Yellow 8/0.
Wing: Elk hair.
Egg sac: Thread floss.
Body: Bright yellow or lime floss.
Hackle: Ginger.

YELLOW AND LIME SALLIES ARE COMMON STONEFLIES throughout much of the United States. Generally appearing in June, the mating flights of these small insects can generate mighty rises from some of the largest trout in the river.

Make the wing on this pattern using the "hi-tie" method. In this case, fashion the wing in three parts. First, wrap a small section of the body at the end of the hook shank and tie on a very small bunch of elk hair. Next, wrap the second body section and add a second bunch of hair. Finally, add the third sections of the body and wing. Take care not to crowd the hook eye; leave ample room to wrap a full, high-floating hackle collar.

Cream Comparadun

Hook: Tiemco TMC100, sizes 14 to 10.
Thread: Primrose 8/0 or gel-spun thread.
Tail: Cream hackle fibers.
Body: A double layer of yellow Krystal Flash covered with cream dry-fly dubbing.
Wing: Bleached yearling-elk hair.

THIS FLY NEEDS NO INTRODUCTION. THE COMPARADUN series of flies, popularized by Al Caucci and Bob Nastasi, has become world famous for its effectiveness for fooling selective trout.

Tier Mike Romanowski, who made this Comparadun, offered these tying tips.

"One area where the use of gel-spun thread has facilitated the tying process is in its application when tying hair flies. The use of fifty denier GSP thread has allowed me to almost double the amount of hair I use for the wings while eliminating the bulk associated with using such large quantities of material. Make sure the thread is heavily waxed, because it is pretty slippery stuff. When tying down the wing, make a few loose wraps and then gradually increase tension on subsequent wraps until you reach maximum pressure—*your* maximum, that is, because you never have to worry about breaking the thread. This results in a highly buoyant and durable wing that will keep its shape for the life of the fly.

"I've also taken a page out of the Dick Talleur's handbook and wrap a double layer of yellow Krystal Flash on the shank before applying the dubbing. The flash makes the body 'glow' when wet, and prevents the hook from darkening the dubbing."

Hock-wing Sulphur

Hook: Turned-up-eye dry-fly hook, your choice of sizes.
Thread: 8/0.
Tail: Light tan or cream guard hairs from a red fox.
Body: Blend of pale-yellow-dyed seal's fur dubbing (or a substitute) mixed with cream red fox fur dubbing.
Wing: Hock feather tips from a hen or rooster, natural or dyed dun.
Hackle: Light or medium ginger.

MIKE VALLA DESIGNED THE HOCK-WING SULPHUR FOR
fishing the Owasco Inlet in central New York State. The Owasco is a tributary of Owasco Lake, one of the smaller Finger Lakes. Rainbow trout
run the stream in the spring, and some fish hang around into May before
migrating back downstream to the lake.

The Hock-wing Sulphur gets its name from the two small feathers,
found on the hock (ankle) area of a chicken, used to make the wings of the
fly. Mike has never liked cut wings on sulphur imitations, and he says that
dry-fly hackle tips seem too narrow to simulate wings found on the natural
insects.

The body is seal's fur dubbing mixed with cream red fox fur. This
inspiration came from Jack Atherton's classic book, *The Fly and the Fish*,
which was published in 1951. Atherton favored the natural sheen of seal's
fur, but as he admitted, it's not an easy material to spin alone, so he blended
it with fox fur. Today, you will probably have to select a substitute for real
seal's fur.

Black's Lipstick Spinner

Hook: Light-wire, curved-shank emerger hook, sizes 18 to 12.
Thread: Size 6/0.
Abdomen: V Tube. (You can substitute with another brand of narrow-diameter tubing.)
Tails: Microfibbets or Mayfly Tails.
Thorax: Fine & Dry dubbing.
Wing post: Closed-cell foam post with a bright top.
Wings: 0.5-millimeter-thick, closed-cell foam, clipped to shape.
Hackle: Rooster.

BILL BLACK, THE HEAD HONCHO OF SPIRIT RIVER, INC., doesn't just sell fly-tying materials; he is also a good fly designer.

This pattern is Bill's Lipstick Spinner. To be honest, I didn't understand the name of the pattern until I took this photograph; the foam wing posts do look like tubes of lipstick.

The abdomens are small-diameter tubing with Microfibbets glued into the ends to create tails. The hackles, wing posts, and foam wings keep the flies floating on the surface of the water. The bright yellow tabs at the end of the posts make it easy to see these flies on the water.

This is another pattern you can tie in different sizes and colors to match the real spinner mayflies on your local waters.

Yellow Adams (Sort Of)

Hook: Regular dry-fly hook, size 14.
Thread: Tan or orange 6/0.
Wings: Grizzly hen-hackle tips
Tails: Coq de Leon or grizzly throat-hackle fibers.
Body: Light yellow rabbit fur with a bit of orange blended in.
Hackle: Dun Cree, barred rusty dun, golden grizzly, or light-barred ginger.

THIS IS A REALLY NICE PATTERN THAT SUGGESTS A CRANE fly, as well as various mayfly duns and spinners. It is a delicate change of pace for general dry-fly fishing. Use it during low water as an alternative to terrestrial patterns. This version is a little lighter in overall appearance than a traditional Adams and is a good fly for late spring, summer, and early fall fishing on either limestone or freestone streams.

If you don't have the hackles listed in the pattern recipe, use a light ginger and a grizzly hackle; wrap one feather at a time.

EZY Occasion— Double Magic

Hook: Down-eye scud hook, sizes 22 to 10.
Thread: Tan 8/0.
Tag: Tying thread with light blue dubbing.
Body: Ginger dubbing.
Rib: Tying thread with light blue dubbing.
Wings: Ginger hackles.
Hackle: Brown.

THE EZY OCCASION—DOUBLE MAGIC IS AN ADAPTATION of a Gary LaFontaine pattern called simply the Occasion. The major difference is that Al and Gretchen Beatty have added their Wonder Wings to the fly.

"The original Occasion was one of three similar emerger imitations that I remember," Al said. "It was a real killer pattern. We used to get together to fish with Gary, and we would use his flies and just catch a lot of trout."

The EZY Occasion—Double Magic is designed to ride with the body hanging down in the water, as seen in the photograph. The hackle holds the head and wings above the surface. This pattern mimics an emerger breaking through the surface and turning into a winged adult.

Olive CDC Caddisfly

Hook: Standard dry-fly hook, sizes 20 to 14.
Thread: Olive 8/0.
Body: Olive superfine dubbing.
Wing: Dun cul de canard.
Head: Dun cul de canard.

THE OLIVE CDC CADDISFLY IS VERY SIMPLE TO TIE YET IS AN extremely productive fly. The cul de canard, used to make the wing and head of the fly, makes it nearly unsinkable.

The origins of this style of pattern are more European than American. Rather than adding a lot of bells and whistles to their flies, many European tiers take a bare-bones approach, emphasizing the overall form of their patterns. The Olive CDC Caddisfly strikes the right posture on the water, and the cul de canard keeps it riding high and dry.

For making the head of the fly, Aaron Jasper inserted a cul de canard feather between the strands of the flat-waxed tying thread using a device called The Magic Tool. (Look for The Magic Tool in your local fly shop.) He then wrapped the thread and CDC on the hook as a collar. Switzerland's Marc Petijean created this nifty tying technique and The Magic Tool.

Transducer—Pale Morning Dun

Hook: Curved-shank nymph or caddis-larva hook, size 16.
Thread: Yellow 8/0.
Tail: Mottled hackle fibers.
Abdomen: Pheasant-tail fibers.
Rib: Narrow pearl Flashabou.
Head of nymph: Peacock herl.
Nymph legs: Mottled hackle-fiber tips.
Emerger body: Yellow dry-fly dubbing or tying thread.
Wing post: Fine hair of your choice.
Hackle: Light dun.

UTAH'S SAM SWINK CREATED THIS COOL PATTERN. THE Transducer is unusual in that it is really two flies in one. Check out the photos, and you'll see what I mean.

The first half of the fly is an imitation of a nymph; this part of the pattern hangs down in the surface film. The front portion of the Transducer is a bare-bones mayfly dun imitation: a simple body, wing post, and parachute hackle.

The Transducer is designed to mimic a mayfly emerging out of its nymph skin and turning into a winged adult.

This version of the Transducer is tied in the colors of a Pale Morning Dun, but you can substitute materials to tie imitations of all your favorite mayflies.

Sulphur Cripple

Hook: Tiemco TMC100, sizes 22 to 14.
Thread: Primrose 8/0.
Tail: Cream hackle fibers.
Abdomen: Sulphur turkey biot.
Wing: Two white hen-hackle tips.
Thorax: Sulphur orange Superfine dubbing.
Hackle: Pale yellow or cream.

THIS IS A VARIATION OF A FLY SHOWN TO TIER MIKE Romanowski by Bighorn-guide Bob Krumm more than twenty years ago. Since then it has become one of the few sulfur imitations he carries. The key to this fly's effectiveness is its ability to represent a cripple, dun, or spinner. Mike sets the wings slightly back on the shank so he can X-wrap the dubbing underneath the shank *after* wrapping the hackle. This pulls the hackle fibers up to the sides of the fly, resulting in a dense area of hackle on the sides of the body, providing superior flotation.

Don't worry too much about the position of the wings; you want this fly to look like a dying dun or spinner. It's tough to find biots that are light colored enough to imitate the abdomen of a sulfur, so Mike buys white biots and dyes them for about thirty seconds in yellow Rit dye.

Cahill Quill

Hook: Regular dry-fly hook, sizes 16 to 10.
Thread: Tan 8/0.
Tail: Ginger hackle fibers.
Body: Stripped herl from the eye of a peacock.
Wing: Wood duck flank fibers.
Hackle: Ginger.

THE LIGHT CAHILL (THERE IS A SEPARATE FLY PATTERN BY
that name) is one of our most dependable summer mayflies. In some areas,
the duns have a tendency to emerge throughout the day, and the trout never
seem to key in to them; in other locations, you might encounter a more
vigorous hatch that gets the fishes' attention.

There are many patterns designed to imitate the light Cahill insects, and
the Cahill Quill is certainly a member of that family. Mike Valla's rendition
of this important pattern is delicate and perfectly proportioned; use it as a
model when tying your own Cahill Quills.

A note about tying with stripped-peacock herl: although the body of the
finished fly has a lovely segmentation, the herl is not very durable. Place a
drop of cement on the thread underbody before wrapping the herl, or place

a drop of cement on the completed herl body. Either method increases the durability of the body.

Making Split Flank-feather Wings

There are a couple of ways to tie lovely Catskill-style wings. Wood duck feathers are more expensive that dyed mallard, so some tiers place one wood duck feather on the hook and then divide the fibers in half to create the two wings. Traditionally, tiers used two feathers placed back-to-back.

Since this information is going into a book, and it will live forever, I will use two real wood duck feathers. (Besides, I hunt ducks, and I'll collect more wood duck flank feathers this autumn.)

1. Place the two feathers together with the tips even. Strip the excess fibers from the bases of the feathers. Tie the bare stem to the top of the hook using two or three loose thread wraps. Draw the feathers toward the rear of the fly until the wing fibers are the proper length; keep the feathers on top of the shank while you work. Lock the feathers in place with several tight thread wraps.

2. Some tiers cut the butt ends even, but this will create a hump and perhaps an uneven finished body. I prefer cutting the butt ends of the feathers at different lengths. Later, when we wrap the thread to the end of the hook, this will create a more level underbody.

3. Pinch the wing fibers upright. Wrap a small dam of thread in front of the fibers to hold them up. Mike Valla, whose terrific flies you'll find in the book, prefers making a tall wing, and I follow his method; the height of the wing about matches the length of the hook shank.

4. Divide the fibers in half to create the two wings. Make several figure-eight wraps between the wings.

5. Wrap the thread to the end of the hook shank. We have a level underbody for making the rest of the pattern.

October Irresistible Caddis

Hook: Regular dry-fly hook, size 12.
Thread: Orange gel-spun.
Body: Orange deer hair.
Hackle: Brown.
Wing: Elk hair.
Antennae: Fine, brown monofilament.

THE CADDISFLIES OF THE GENUS *DICOSMOECUS*, WHICH
are referred to as the fall or October caddis, are considered one of the
West's caddis super hatches. The hatches of these large insects, which aver-
age about thirty millimeters long, are concentrated within a two- to three-
week period. The October caddis emerges in low, clear water and is most
active during the afternoon and early evening.

The classic Irresistible has an upright wing, a full-hackle collar, and a tan,
spun-and-clipped, deer-hair body; only accomplished tiers care to make this
sort of complicated body. The October Irresistible Caddis is a variant of this
older pattern, and it, too, will appeal to experienced fly tiers.

I recommend using fifty- or one hundred-denier, gel-spun thread for
making this pattern. Gel-spun thread is super strong and is perfect for spin-
ning deer hair and keeping bulk to a minimum. If you cannot find orange
gel-spun thread, use white gel-spun thread and swipe an orange permanent
marker on the last two inches of thread when tying the head.

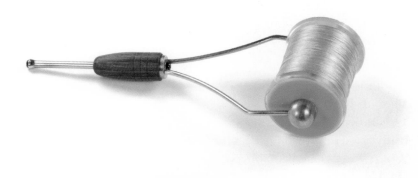

Bradley Special

Hook: Regular dry-fly hook, sizes 16 to 12.
Thread: Red 8/0.
Tail: Brown hackle fibers.
Body: Red squirrel dubbing, spun in a dubbing loop of red tying thread.
Wing: Wood duck flank fibers.
Hackle: Brown.

ACCORDING TO LEGEND, THE BRADLEY SPECIAL WAS
devised by Catskill-anglers William Chandler and William Bradley. Roy
Steenrod and Harry Darbee, two of the Catskill's most legendary tiers,
also claimed that William Chandler developed the famed Light Cahill. The
Dette family, longtime local tiers, added the Bradley Special to their lineup
of patterns they dressed for visiting anglers.

The Bradley Special is important, because it demonstrates using the
color of the thread to influence the appearance of the completed body;
if you look closely, you can see the red thread peeking through the body
dubbing. This effect becomes even more pronounced when the fly is wet.
Important note: consider using white thread if you do not want the color to
show up on the finished fly; white thread turns translucent when wet. Any
other color of thread, especially darker hues, will have a profound effect on
the completed pattern.

A.J.'s Hi-Vis Sulphur Emerger

Hook: Standard dry-fly hook, sizes 20 to 14.
Thread: Yellow 8/0.
Tail: Brown Z-Lon.
Body: Sulphur orange Superfine dubbing.
Thorax: White hackle.
Wing post: White Hi-Vis polypropylene yarn.

A.J.'S HI-VIS SULPHUR EMERGER HAS TWO KEY ATTRIBUTES: it is very easy to see at the end of long casts, and it floats extremely well.

The slender silhouette makes the fly appear very natural on the surface of the water, and it is an excellent choice when trout are taking emergers in the slower sections of a stream. In addition to this sulphur version, tier Aaron Jasper makes this simple pattern in several sizes and colors to imitate almost any emerging mayfly he encounters while fishing.

If your local fly shop doesn't carry Z-Lon, which is used to make the fly's trailing shuck, simply substitute with Antron or polypropylene yarn.

Woodruff

Hook: Regular dry-fly hook, size 16 or 14.
Thread: White 8/0.
Tail: Light ginger hackle fibers.
Body: Light green or lime green dubbing.
Wings: Grizzly hackle tips.
Hackle: Light ginger.

THE WOODRUFF IS ANOTHER UNUSUAL PATTERN THAT shows an overlooked side of tying in the Catskill tradition: spinners.

The splayed, grizzly hackle tips mimic the wings of a spinner mayfly. In the coloration of this pattern, tied by David Brandt, the Woodruff imitates a sulphur mayfly.

Chester Mills, of the famed William Mills & Son sporting goods house in New York City, originated this pattern in 1920. He gave the fly to fishing friend John E. Woodruff, who tested it on the upper Beaverkill. When word spread of the great success he was having with the fly, anglers clamored to William Mills & Son to purchase the pattern. As a result, Mills named the fly in honor of Woodruff.

According to David Brandt, it is possible that the original Woodruff was tied with upright wings, but Harry Darbee tied the fly with spent or semi-spent wings. Harry routinely offered the fly to his customers in the 1930s and 1940s.

Emerger Callibaetis

Hook: Curved-shank emerger hook, sizes 18 to 14.
Thread: Gray 8/0.
Tail: Mottled hen-hackle fibers and gray or tan polypropylene yarn.
Abdomen: Pale yellow turkey biot.
Rib: Tan, small D-Rib.
Wing: Grizzly hen hackles tied in reverse.
Thorax: Light brown Superfine dubbing.
Hackle: Grizzly.

YOU CAN'T TIE A LOT OF MATERIALS ON A SMALL HOOK, but this Emerger Callibaetis, designed by Idaho's Todd Smith, has everything a fly needs to fool a trout.

The two-part tail, made using hen-hackle fibers and short strands of polypropylene yarn, simulates an emerging nymph just crawling out of its skin. The pattern has ample hackle fibers to keep the head of the fly above the water. And the wings, which are reversed, small-hen hackles, ideally imitate the wings of a real mayfly.

Come to think of it, if you work carefully and plan ahead, maybe you *can* tie a lot of stuff to a small hook.

Cross Special

Hook: Regular dry-fly hook, sizes 16 to 10.
Thread: Brown 8/0.
Tail: Blue dun.
Body: Light fox-belly fur.
Wing: Wood duck flank fibers.
Hackle: Blue dun.

THIS IS ONE MORE CLASSIC CATSKILL PATTERN. THE FAMED Rube Cross, a fly-tying legend in that part of the country, created this pattern.

I am including it because I want to share a rare tidbit about tying the Catskill family of patterns.

It's a little-known fact—only members of the Catskill Fly Tyers Guild and serious students of that style of tying know it—that you're supposed to leave a very small piece of bare shank between the hook eye and the thread head of the fly. The old-time tiers used this space for tying flies to their gut leaders with a turle knot. Theodore Gordon said that the turle knot was best for attaching a fly to the leader, and Rube Cross followed his example and left this small space on his flies. Walt Dette followed their lead and also left this tiny piece of bare shank.

Mike Valla, who learned to tie flies from the Dettes and dressed this example of the Cross Special, told me that story.

X2 Caddis

Hook: Regular dry-fly hook, size 14 or 12.
Thread: Brown 8/0.
Trailing shuck: Amber Zelon.
Body: Green hare's mask dubbing.
Underwing: White Widow's Web or Zelon.
Wing: Elk hair.
Head: Natural rabbit dubbing.

NO BOOK ABOUT FAVORITE TROUT FLIES WOULD BE COM-
plete without including a Craig Mathews pattern. Craig operates Blue Ribbon Flies, in West Yellowstone, Montana. He also created the X Caddis, a
fly sold commercially by Umpqua Feather Merchants. According to Bruce
Olson, who oversees the selection of new patterns included in the Umpqua
catalog, the X Caddis remains one of their best-selling flies. The X2 Caddis
is Craig's updated version of that original pattern.

In addition to being an experienced fly-shop owner, talented fly designer,
and crackerjack angler, Craig is also a leading conservationist. He was one
of the driving forces behind 1 Percent for the Planet. In this program, busi-
nesses pledge to contribute one percent of their net profits to their favorite
environmental causes. Many fly-fishing manufacturers and retailers partici-
pate in 1 Percent for the Planet.

In 2013, *Fly Tyer* magazine gave Craig its annual Lifetime Achievement
Award for being a leader in the fly fishing industry, a fly designer, and a
protector of the waters we all love to fish.

J:son Mayflies

Dun 1
Hook: Short-shank, wide-gap, light-wire hook, size 10 or 8.
Thread: Size 6/0.
Tails: Microfibbets or fibers from a synthetic paintbrush.
Abdomen: Closed-cell foam.
Hackle: Rooster.
Wings: J:son Realistic Wing Material.

LET'S CONSIDER THESE UNUSUAL PATTERNS, CREATED BY Claes Johansson of a Swedish company called J:son, as our challenge flies.

Yes, they are designed for fishing! They are very durable, and when you study them closely, you will see that they require very few materials; in fact, except for the wings, many other flies in this book are tied using the very same ingredients.

J:son specializes in innovative flies, fly-tying methods, and tying tools. Claes Johansson, the head of research and development at J:son (I don't know of another fly-tying company with a similarly named position), is always looking for ways to create realistic patterns designed for real-world fishing.

The flies in the accompanying photos are all tied using thread, closed-cell foam, hackles, and dubbing; you'll find any of these ingredients in your local fly shop. Claes fashions the wings using his company's sheet wing material, but you could couple one of his terrific-looking abdomens with a wing of elk hair, cul de canard, or your favorite material. (Go to www. jsonsweden.com to see full instructions on how to tie these flies and many more. It might revolutionize the way you think about pattern design.)

I'm including the recipe for the large mayfly imitation Claes calls Dun 1, as well as photos of his emerger and spinner imitations. When I asked him what it's supposed to imitate, he said, "I don't know; maybe a drake. What do you think?" Pinning him down is impossible. Claes is too inventive, and his mind is always working; I don't believe he thinks in terms of "patterns."

And that's why I'm including the flies of J:son in this little book. I don't know if they'll catch on and become an essential part of our fishing kits, but they do point to the need for tiers to keep experimenting. Innovation—exploring new materials, tools, methods, and patterns—keeps our fly-tying fresh and interesting.

CHAPTER TWO

The Overlooked Flies: Midges, Damselflies, and More

Hornberg

Hook: Tiemco TMC100, size 10.
Thread: Black 6/0.
Body: Flat silver tinsel.
Underwing: Yellow calf-tail hair.
Wings: Mallard–flank feathers.
Cheek: Jungle cock.
Hackle: Grizzly.

I DON'T KNOW WHEN THE HORNBERG BECAME KNOWN AS a streamer, but Col. Joseph Bates includes this pattern in his book, *Streamers and Bucktails: The Big Fish Flies.* Okay, that was Bates's opinion, but I use the Hornberg as a dry fly.

Actually, the Hornberg was created by Frank Hornberg, a game warden from central Wisconsin, in the 1920s. He called it the Hornberg Special and designed it to imitate a caddisfly.

The Hornberg (Sharon E. Wright tied this version) also works very well in late spring and early summer during a damselfly hatch. On my local Maine trout ponds, when the damselflies fly across the surface of the water, the trout rise quickly and sharp shoot these flitting insects. I cast the Hornberg several feet ahead of a cruising fish and slowly twitch the fly across the surface, imitating an egg-laying, female damselfly. The trout quickly responds.

Crane Fly

Hook: Regular dry-fly hook, size 16 or 14.
Thread: Pale yellow 6/0.
Abdomen: Pale yellow beaver dubbing.
Wings: Light dun hen-feather tips.
Wing post: Gray McFlylon.
Thorax and legs: Ginger cul de canard.
Hackle: Light ginger.

CRANE FLY IMITATIONS ARE ONE OF THE MOST OVER-
looked group of patterns. Make no mistake, however, that the trout do feed
on these gangly looking insects.

Crane flies have very long legs and long, slender abdomens. Unlike most
insects, crane flies are poor fliers with a tendency to wobble in unpredict-
able patterns during flight. You'll often see them hovering over the water,
looking a little lost and flying without purpose. Adult crane flies feed on
nectar, or they do not feed at all; most species of crane flies exist only to
mate and then die.

North America has more than 500 species of crane flies, so you can bet
you will encounter these insects on your local trout stream.

Tie the hen–hackle-tip wings splayed along the top of the back. Tier
Dennis Charney makes the thorax and legs using cul de canard. The CDC
increases the buoyancy of the pattern, and according to Dennis, "Does a
great job imitating the spindly legs of the natural insect."

I.C.S.I. (I Can See It) Midge

Hook: Curved–shank emerger hook, size 20 or 18.
Thread: Golden olive 6/0.
Wing post: Fluorescent orange yarn.
Hackle: Grizzly.
Body: Muskrat-belly fur (in this fly, trapped on the Letort by Ed Shenk), finely spun onto thread.

THE I.C.S.I. (I CAN SEE IT) MIDGE SUGGESTS A NYMPH OR pupa just under the water surface and is particularly useful during any emergence of small mayflies, midges, and even tiny caddisflies on both lakes and rivers. Its origin predates similar-looking European patterns, and it has been a best-selling small dry fly in the Orvis catalog for many years.

A black-bodied version, designed to imitate a dark midge, has proven quite effective during *trico* spinner falls. Try other colors, too. The suggestion of a nymph or pupa stuck under the surface film holds a powerful attraction to trout. The first time this fly hit the water, a trout rose and sucked it in.

The post material on this pattern is a fiber-optic, synthetic yarn. Tie it onto the underside of the hook shank, pull the ends up each side of the shank, and post it with a couple of wraps of thread. Trim the post to length after wrapping the hackle.

Foam Damselfly

Hook: Regular dry-fly hook, size 12.
Thread: Blue or black 8/0.
Abdomen: Blue closed-cell foam damselfly body.
Thorax: Blue dubbing.
Wings: White polypropylene yarn.
Hackle: Grizzly, dyed blue.

DAMSELFLIES BEGIN EMERGING IN JUNE AND ARE PRESENT throughout the summer; you'll see them flying fast and low over the water. If you fish trout ponds, you'll often have damselflies land on your rod, line, and float tube. You'll often see male and female damselflies connected together while mating.

A good damselfly hatch is a memorable event; dozens of the large insects will be present on the water. Fishing a damselfly imitation, such as this simple Foam Damselfly, is also a unique event; it will be one of the largest dry flies you will cast during the season.

Even though a damselfly pattern is large, it does not have to be heavy. My Foam Damselfly is extremely lightweight; I regularly fish it using a four-weight rod and 5X leader. Spread a small drop of cement on each wing to stiffen the fibers; this prevents the wings from fouling around the hook when casting.

Black Gnat Snowshoe

Hook: Regular dry-fly hook, size 18 or 16.
Thread: Black 8/0.
Tail: Black snowshoe hare foot fur.
Body: Black snowshoe hare foot fur.
Wing: White or bleached snowshoe hare foot fur.
Hackle: Black.

SHOW ME A PIECE OF TROUT WATER THAT DOESN'T HAVE its share of little black insects flittering across the surface, and I'll show you a stream not worth fishing.

Whether they are small stoneflies, gnats, or midges, at some time or another, there will be a hatch of some sort of very small, black insect. And fortunately, as the insects get smaller in size, you can get away with using less precise imitations. Typically, you'll simply need a pattern that matches the size of the natural and makes a realistic impression on the surface of the water. The Black Gnat Snowshoe is the sort of diminutive fly that matches several types of insects.

Use this pattern when real gnats and midges are on the water. This is also a fine choice for when the small, black stoneflies are laying eggs; this often happens on balmy, late winter and early spring days, and it can result in some of the first rises of trout for the season.

Griffith's Gnat

Hook: Regular dry-fly hook, sizes 24 to 18.
Thread: Black 8/0.
Body: Peacock herl.
Hackle: Grizzly.

DO YOU NEED A SMALL DRY? I MEAN, A PATTERN SO SMALL
it's almost impossible to get the materials onto the diminutive hook? Then
the Griffith's Gnat might be the answer.

When tying a midge imitation, there is no reason to struggle making
an exact imitation; the fish won't be able to perceive all those complicated
parts. At most, the pattern should match the size of the natural insects and
imitate the dimpling of the legs in the surface film. These are the two key
features of the Griffith's Gnat.

George Griffith, one of the founders of Trout Unlimited, created the
famed Griffith's Gnat. One evening, while fishing the Benedict's Crossing
section of Vermont's Batten Kill River, the trout were rising to impossibly
small midges. I tried several small patterns with no success. I rummaged
through my vest and found a lonely Griffith's Gnat. I knotted the fly to the
end of my 7X tippet and caught several Batten Kill brown trout.

Thank you, Mr. Griffith!

Tying the Griffith's Gnat

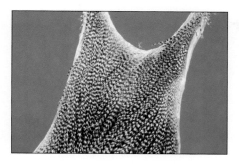

1. The tiny hackles at the base of a dry-fly cape are perfect for fashioning diminutive midge imitations such as the Griffith's Gnat.

2. Tie a hackle and piece of peacock herl to the hook.

3. Wrap the herl up the hook to form the body of the fly. Tie off and clip the remaining piece of herl.

4. Spiral wrap the hackle over the body. Tie off and cut the excess hackle tip. Whip finish and snip the thread.

CHAPTER THREE

Important Terrestrials: Inchworms, Grasshoppers, and Ants

Hot Legs Hopper

Hook: Regular dry-fly hook, size 8.
Thread: Tan 6/0.
Body: Yellow closed-cell foam colored with black permanent marker.
Rear legs: Hopper legs.
Front legs: Rubber legs.
Antennae: Extra-fine rubber legs.
Wing: Brown Bugskin.
Indicator: Pink polypropylene yarn.

CHUCK FURIMSKY, A LONGTIME FRIEND, DESIGNED THE
Hot Legs Hopper. Chuck founded the annual International Fly Tying Symposium more than twenty years ago, and he is the promoter of the national
string of fly-fishing carnivals called The Fly Fishing Show. Through these
efforts, I believe Chuck has done more than almost anyone to educate the
public about fly fishing and tying; every year, thousands of expert anglers,
as well as people who have never cast a rod or caught a fish, come to his
shows to improve their casting, discover new places to fish, and learn a few
fly-tying tricks.

Chuck has also run a successful leather-goods business, and he markets a
leather fly-tying material called Bugskin. He uses brown Bugskin to fashion
the wing on his Hot Legs Hopper.

Letort Hopper

Hook: 3X-long, dry-fly hook, sizes 18 to 10.
Thread: Yellow 8/0.
Body: Pale yellow superfine dubbing.
Underwing: Mottled turkey-wing quill.
Wing: Natural deer hair.

WHO SAYS A GRASSHOPPER IMITATION HAS TO BE COMPLI-
cated? The Letort Hopper, created by Ed Shenk more than fifty years ago, is
still a go-to pattern for many knowledgeable anglers.

Ed says he got the idea for this pattern while fishing Muddler Minnows
as grasshopper imitations. Those flies, normally fished as streamers, caught
trout. Shenk thought that a similar fly, substituting yellow dubbing for the
gold-tinsel body, would work even better. He called it the Letort Hopper.

The Letort Hopper is a simple, streamlined pattern. Even without the
usual grasshopper legs, it creates the right silhouette on the water and fools
trout. The Letort Hopper is a great grasshopper imitation for new tiers
who find more complicated flies too difficult to tie. And the Letort Hopper catches fish wherever fish eat grasshoppers. It is a fine addition to your
summer fly-fishing kit.

I.C.S.I. (I Can See It) Ant

Hook: Regular dry-fly hook, size 16 or 14.
Thread: Black 6/0.
Post: Fluorescent orange or lemon yellow calf-body hair.
Hackle: Grizzly.
Body: Black or brown rabbit-fur dubbing.

THE I.C.S.I. (I CAN SEE IT) ANT RANKS THIRD ON TOM BALTZ'S list of top-three dry flies. This current version is an evolution of a design the late Dr. Jack Beck, of Carlisle, Pennsylvania, gave to him.

During midday, when the hatches of aquatic insects lag, is a good time to try an ant imitation. Ants are ubiquitous and found anywhere a trout might live. Few bugs hold a more powerful attraction for trout during the temperate months from late March through November.

Fish your ant along the banks of large rivers and anywhere in medium- to smaller-sized streams. Orange or yellow wing posts are useful depending upon lighting conditions. This parachute ant also doubles nicely for a flying ant.

Wrap the hackle counter clockwise and tie it off on the side of the hook shank in front of the post. Try placing the post just in front of the midpoint of the hook shank. Spin the dubbing tightly on the thread and build the body "humps" in three layers.

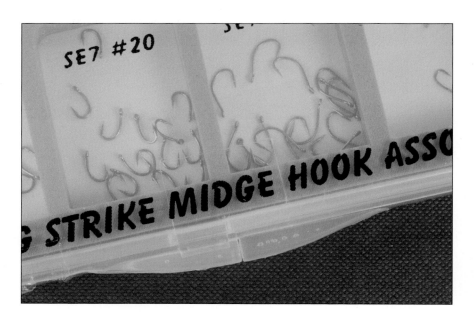

Parachute Ant

Hook: Regular dry-fly hook, size 14.
Thread: Black 8/0.
Body: Black dry-fly dubbing.
Hackle: Black.
Wing bud: White polypropylene yarn.

IN SOME PARTS OF THE COUNTRY, ESPECIALLY DURING late summer, ants become an important source of food for the trout. This is when you will want to have a small collection of ant imitations in your fishing kit.

Gary Borger prefers fishing with this unique Parachute Ant. In addition to the parachute hackle wrapped around the front section of the body, he adds a tiny wing bud of polypropylene yarn; you can see it peeking out of the bottom of the fly.

Sometimes ants fall onto the water and are available to the trout. Pay attention, however, for flights of ants. Some of the insects crash onto the water and will turn on the fish. Use a long, light leader, and tie on the Parachute Ant or one of the other imitations in this book. You will enjoy some memorable fishing to a unique form of "hatch."

Potter's Fat Head Moth

Hook: Tiemco TMC100, size 12 or 10.
Thread: Fifty denier, gel–spun thread.
Abdomen: Tan or cinnamon Superfine dubbing.
Rib: Opal Mirage tinsel.
Head and wing: Natural, dark elk hair.

DO YOU HAVE ANY MOTH IMITATIONS IN YOUR FLY BOX? IF not, then you might be missing out on some good fishing.

Moths and butterflies inhabit the riverbank from mid to late summer. Occasionally, one of these insects haphazardly lands on the water. Struggling to free itself and regain the air, it will attract the attention of the trout. Keep watching, and you might see a fish snatch this morsel.

Dennis Potter uses his Fat Head Moth from dusk until after dark from late June into August. He says this is a big-fish pattern. It certainly is an unusual terrestrial imitation that will bring a new, refreshing dimension to your fly fishing.

Grand Hopper

Hook: 2X-long dry-fly hook, size 8.
Thread: Tan 6/0.
Body: Closed-cell foam colored with permanent marker.
Underwing: Pearl Krystal Flash.
Wing: Tan feather placed on tape and clipped to shape. Add spots using a permanent marker.
Legs: Rubber legs.
Collar: Tan dubbing.
Eyes: Black pinheads.

GRASSHOPPERS INHABIT THE BANKS OF MANY RIVERS from the East to West Coasts during late summer and early autumn, and imitations of these important terrestrials populate the fly boxes of many anglers during this time of the season.

Many popular grasshopper patterns are tied using only hair and feathers, but they eventually become waterlogged and sink. With the acceptance of closed-cell foam as a fly-tying material, it is possible to create a grasshopper, and other patterns, that float forever.

Rainy's Grand Hopper is ideal for fishing wherever trout feed on hapless grasshoppers that fall or fly onto the water. Change body colors to create imitations of any grasshopper you find along the river.

Harvey Deer-hair Inchworm

Hook: 3X-long dry-fly hook, sizes 16 to 10.
Thread: Green 6/0.
Body: Bright green deer hair.

GEORGE HARVEY WAS ONE OF THE GREATEST ANGLERS OF
the twentieth century. I was pleased to meet this angling legend at the International Fly Tying Symposium. Mr. Harvey developed many fish-catching
patterns, and his Deer-hair Inchworm is one of his most unusual.

Many anglers have reported times when real inchworms were falling
into the water and sending trout into feeding frenzies; the fish quickly catch
on that the unprotected worms are something good to eat. Curiously, Harvey's solution to the inchworm-fishing challenge was to create a fly using
only spun-and-clipped deer hair. Does it look like an inchworm? Maybe
not, but the trout do like it.

Ed Shenk, who wrote about this fly when describing his favorite terrestrial imitations, recommends tying the Harvey Deer-hair Inchworm using
bright green hair.

CDC Foam Ant

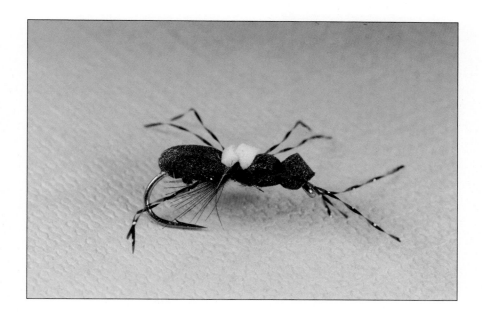

Hook: Regular dry-fly hook, sizes 18 to 12.
Thread: Size 6/0.
Body: Closed-cell foam.
Throat: Cul de canard.
Indicator: Yellow closed-cell foam.
Legs and antennae: Crystal Splash.

THE CDC FOAM ANT IS AN INTERESTING TAKE ON A common ant imitation. Fly bins across the country contain foam-bodied ant patterns, but the Spirit River Company has made a couple of additions you might want to consider for the ants you tie.

First, the throat of cul de canard improves the floatation of a foam-bodied pattern that is already unsinkable. The CDC helps the fly float a little higher than a standard ant pattern.

The legs and antennae, tied using Crystal Splash (you may substitute with Krystal Flash), is a worthwhile change. These appendages are easy to make, and they do not weigh the fly down.

Other than the yellow foam indicator, the pattern recipe specifies no colors. You might, however, encounter black or red ants, so choose materials in colors to imitate these common ants. And if you need some flying ants, simply tie your favorite wing material to the top of the pattern before adding the foam indicator.

Hyper Hopper

Extended body
Base: Flymen Fishing Company Wiggle Shank.
Thread: Hopper yellow 8/0.
Egg sac: Fluorescent orange Gator Hair.
Abdomen: Tan closed-cell foam.

Thorax
Hook: Daiichi 1280 or 1710, sizes 14 to 10.
Thread: Hopper yellow 8/0.
Extended-body connection: 4X fluorocarbon tippet.
Thorax: Tan closed-cell foam.
Legs: Rubber legs.
Underwing: Opal Mirage Flash.
Wing: Dark tan Widow's Web.
Hot spot: Fluorescent-orange Gator Hair.

AL RITT PULLED OUT ALL THE STOPS WHEN DESIGNING this fun grasshopper imitation. Still, if you study the Hyper Hopper closely, you'll see that any tier with moderate skills can make it.

Al tied the extended abdomen of the fly on a Wiggle Shank, a product of the Flymen Fishing Company. He attached the abdomen to the hook shank using 4X-tippet material before making the front section of the fly.

Al fashions the grasshopper's legs using rubber leg material. A piece of tan rubber leg makes the fly's two front legs. Each thigh of the back legs are three strands of rubber leg material left together. Al carefully glues a piece of small Centipede Legs to the end of the thigh to create an ankle.

The closed-cell foam body floats forever, and the synthetic wing dries with one or two false casts. This pattern will not sink even after catching several trout.

Letort Cricket

Hook: 3X-long dry-fly hook, sizes 18 to 10.
Thread: Black 8/0.
Body: Black Superfine dubbing.
Underwing: Black goose- or turkey-wing quill.
Wing: Black deer hair.

ED SHENK SAYS HE TIED THE LETORT CRICKET A COUPLE OF years after creating the Letort Hopper. He got the idea for his cricket imitation while watching that storied stream's trophy trout eating crickets and refusing his grasshopper. Although the patterns are similar in design, the Letort Cricket is black.

In some ways, the Letort Cricket has been more successful than the Letort Hopper. Ed says he caught a three-and-a-half-pound trout the first time he used the new fly. He also caught a Letort trout that measured twenty-seven and one-quarter inches long and, he estimates, weighed close to nine pounds using this pattern; that was the largest trout Shenk has caught on the Letort using a dry fly.

It's always more fun catching fish using your own flies.

Mr. Bill's Fly Ant

Hook: Regular dry-fly hook, sizes 18 to 10.
Thread: Size 6/0.
Body: Antron dubbing.
Wing: Wings & Things.
Legs and antennae: Crystal Splash.

SWARMS OF FLYING ANTS ARE PART OF THE MATING ritual of ants. Although the majority of winged ants are males, a few females are mixed into the swarm. If they survive, these females will become future queens and perhaps establish new colonies.

City and suburban dwellers fear the sight of flying ants because it's a sign that new colonies may be established, perhaps in their homes or apartments. For fly fishermen, however, flying ants are the sign of potentially good angling. Ants aren't born fliers, and some will crash into nearby streams and encourage the trout to feed. This happens during the heat of summer.

Mr. Bill's Fly Ant is a good, simple imitation of a winged ant. The legs, tied using Crystal Splash (you may substitute with Krystal Flash), splay on the water like the real insect. The simple wing is made using a material called Wings & Things (Medallion Sheeting is a suitable substitute).

Tie the Mr. Bill's Flying Ant in black and cinnamon to match the winged ants you find along your local trout stream.

Jassid

Hook: Regular dry-fly hook, sizes 24 to 16.
Thread: Black 8/0.
Body: Tying thread.
Hackle: Black.
Wing: Jungle-cock nail.

ED SHENK IS ONE OF THE LAST OF THAT FAMOUS GROUP OF anglers who raised the bar in American fly fishing in the middle of the twentieth century. Based in central Pennsylvania, Shenk, George Harvey, Charlie Fox, Vince Marinaro, Joe Humphrey, and their friends closely studied the trout living in the nearby limestone streams, and they designed imitations of the local insects. They wrote about their observations and findings and revolutionized the concept of match the hatch.

The Jassid is one of the unusual patterns that came out of their work. It was first covered in an article that appeared in *Outdoor Life* magazine in 1958. The Jassid is designed to imitate a leafhopper and is particularly effective during hot weather when the stream-bank foliage is full of these insects.

Add a drop of cement to the wing to prevent the jungle-cock feather from splitting when fishing the fly.

CHAPTER FOUR

Attractor Patterns: The Anti-imitators

Royal Wulff

Hook: 2X-long dry-fly hook, sizes 18 to 8. (The fly shown in the photograph was dressed on an Atlantic salmon dry-fly hook.)

Thread: Black 8/0 (Seventy denier).

Tail: Brown bucktail.

Body: Peacock herl and red floss.

Wing: White bucktail.

Hackle: Brown.

NO BOOK ABOUT FAVORITE DRY FLIES WOULD BE COM-
plete without the venerable Royal Wulff. This is undoubtedly the most
famous pattern created by the late Lee Wulff. Although he originally tied
this fly to fish for sea-run Atlantic salmon—yes, they really do snatch dry
flies from the surface of the water—the Royal Wulff has since been called
the unofficial state bird of Montana. All coldwater fish—trout, salmon, grayling, and more—will strike a high-floating Royal Wulff.

Built with the body of a Royal Coachman, the Royal Wulff has two
outstanding characteristics: a thick-hair wing and a bushy-hackle collar. The
wing makes the fly easy to spot on the water, and the hackle keeps the fly
afloat. These two features also make the pattern challenging to make.

Select fine bucktail when tying the wings on large Royal Wulffs. Some
tiers use calf-tail hair when making smaller versions of this pattern, but
these hairs are usually thick and slightly curled. Fine goat hair is a better
option for making the wings on small Royal Wulffs.

Use two or even three hackles for making the thick collar. Another
option is to use one of the extra-long saddle dry-fly hackles. Simply tie
the feather to the hook and make as many wraps as you wish to create the
heavy collar.

The Royal Wulff you see here, which was loaned to me by Lee's good
friend Ted Rogowski, was actually tied by Lee Wulff.

Ausable Wulff

Hook: Regular dry-fly hook, sizes 16 to 12.
Thread: Fluorescent orange 6/0.
Tail: Woodchuck-guard hair.
Body: Rusty orange, Australian opossum fur.
Wing: Calf-tail or calf-body hair.
Hackle: Cree, or grizzly and brown hackles.

YOU'RE ALREADY FAMILIAR WITH THE WULFF SERIES OF dry flies. Lee Wulff originally created these heavily hackled patterns for catching Atlantic salmon, but other anglers quickly downsized them to fish for trout. Fran Betters, a leading fly designer from New York's Adirondack Mountains, used Lee's formula—a thick tail, easy-to-see wing, and bushy hackle—to develop the Ausable Wulff.

The Ausable River, which flows through the Adirondacks, is a favorite destination for eastern trout anglers. The green drake hatch is one of the most important hatches on the river. The Ausable Wulff is great for matching a green drake; the body color might not be an exact match, but the size of this pattern attracts the fish.

The green drake hatch generally occurs during the first two weeks of June. Be sure to linger on the river until early evening for the spinner fall. During the spinner fall, the river seems to come alive with fish rising until well after dark. Continue casting your Ausable Wulff, and you will have a good chance of catching a trophy.

Quick 'n EZY Double Magic

Hook: Regular dry-fly hook, sizes 22 to 10.
Thread: Tan 8/0.
Tail: Ginger hackle fibers.
Body: Ginger dubbing.
Rib: Tying thread.
Wings: Ginger hackles.
Hackle: Ginger.

AL AND GRETCHEN BEATTY, OF BOISE, IDAHO, TIED THIS PAT-
tern called the Quick 'n EZY Double Magic. It features their technique
called Wonder Wings.

Wonder Wings are two hackles tied on in reverse. The fibers mimic the
veins in a mayfly wing. Wonder Wings create the silhouette of a real mayfly's
wings. The Beattys also make a caddisfly imitation with one Wonder Wing
tied flat over the back of the pattern.

Except for the Wonder Wings, I can almost see the influence of the
Catskill school of tying in the Quick 'n EZY Double Magic. The delicate,
slender body and perfect hackle remind me of many of those classic patterns; the wings, however, speak to the influence of more modern Western
tying techniques.

The Usual

Hook: Standard dry-fly hook, sizes 20 to 12.
Thread: Hot orange 6/0 (140 denier).
Tail, wing, and body: Natural snowshoe hare fur from the underside of the paw.

FRAN BETTERS WAS A LEGEND ALONG THE BANKS OF NEW York's Au Sable River. He opened one of the first fly shops in the United States, and he developed many great patterns. All knowledgeable anglers visiting the Adirondacks would stop to meet and chat with Fran at his Adirondack Sports Shop. I visited Fran's shop several times, and he was always sitting in a rocking chair behind the counter, his vise perched in his lap, tying flies. He was quick to share tips, discuss recent hatches, and relay fishing reports. Fran was inducted into the Fly Fishing Hall of Fame in 2008, and he passed away shortly after that.

Fran was not a "neat" tier; his flies typically had a disheveled appearance. Fran's patterns require few materials, and tiers with only modest skills can master his flies. The Usual is one of Fran's most enduring creations. It was originally designed as a general imitation of a Hendrickson mayfly, and you can select hook sizes and colors of materials to tie imitations of other mayflies.

Perhaps "materials" is too strong a word when describing the components of The Usual. This simple pattern requires only three ingredients: a hook, a spool of thread, and the fur from the foot of a snowshoe hare.

Snowshoe hare foot fur is curly and traps small air bubbles that keep The Usual afloat. Since the introduction of this pattern, other tiers have designed dry flies featuring this translucent and durable ingredient. Do not, however, become discouraged with the appearance of the flies you tie using this corkscrewed hair; they will look a little messy. The Usual, however, does catch a lot of trout.

Tying The Usual

1. Start the thread on the hook. Wrap a thread base on the shank. Clip a small bunch of fur from a snowshoe hare foot. Strip the underfur from the base of the bunch and set aside; we'll use it in a moment to complete the fly. Next, tie the bunch to the top of the hook with the tips pointing forward. Clip the butt ends at an angle and cover with firm wraps of thread.

2. Clip a smaller bunch of hair from the foot. Strip the underfur from the base of the bunch and set aside. Tie the hair to the end of the hook shank to make the tail of the fly.

3. Smear dubbing wax on the thread. Spin the underfur on the thread and twist into a noodle. Wrap the dubbing up the hook to create the body of the fly. Make a wrap of dubbing in front of the hair wing. Tie off the thread and clip. The thread commonly shows through the body of The Usual. This is not considered a polished pattern, but it does catch trout.

The Coyote

Hook: Partridge Bomber hook, size 2.
Thread: Brown 3/0.
Tail: Deer hair.
Body: Spun-and-clipped deer hair.
Hackle: Brown.
Wing: Deer hair.

WARREN DUNCAN, WHO CAME FROM NEW BRUNSWICK, Canada, remains a recognized leader in tying hair-wing Atlantic salmon flies. The Picture Province, which is the official fly of New Brunswick, and the Undertaker are two of his personal patterns.

This beautifully tied fly is called the Coyote. Although Warren made it for catching salmon, like the Royal Wulff, you can downsize it for trout fishing. In fact, the Wulff series of flies gave Warren the idea for the name of this pattern.

One day, while I was visiting his fly shop, called Dunc's, in Saint John, New Brunswick, Warren handed me a card with several of his flies pinned around the edges. Warren pointed to one of the flies and said, "See that one? That's the Coyote. There's a Wulff, so that's the Coyote. Get it?" With that he gave one of his hearty laughs that we all miss so much.

This is the first time the Coyote has appeared in print. And, just for fun, I am including a picture of Warren's take on the Royal Wulff; I believe this is another of his flies that has never been shown in a book or magazine.

Spirit of Harford Mills

Hook: Regular dry-fly hook, size 12.
Thread: Brown 8/0.
Tail: Badger-guard hairs.
Body: Light, dyed-olive rabbit fur and ginger hackle.
Wing: Grizzly rooster-hackle tips.
Hackle: Golden badger.

MIKE VALLA CREATED THE SPIRIT OF HARFORD MILLS circa 1975. The famous Spirit of Pittsford Mills dry fly, created by Stephen Belcher II, of Vermont, inspired it. Belcher's pattern, tied by Elsie Darbee, was featured in the color plates in A.J. McClane's book, *Fisherman's Encyclopedia*, where Mike first noticed it.

The Spirit of Harford Mills is named for the hamlet of Harford Mills, along Owego Creek in central New York State. The Owego was one of his favorite haunts; he had fished there since he was a boy. When Mike attended Cornell University—more years ago than he cares to admit—he would ride a bike to there from campus.

It is great to see the classic, Catskill style of pattern still used to commemorate contemporary thoughts and emotions.

Grizzly Wulff

Hook: 2X-long dry-fly hook, sizes 18 to 8. (The fly shown in the photograph was dressed on an Atlantic salmon dry-fly hook.)
Thread: Black 8/0 (seventy denier).
Tail: Brown bucktail.
Body: Green, wool yarn.
Wing: Brown bucktail.
Hackle: Grizzly.

LEE WULFF TIED THIS EXAMPLE OF THE GRIZZLY WULFF. LEE did not tie flies with the aid of a vise; he actually held the hook between the fingers of one hand and applied materials using his other hand. While it's relatively easy to understand wrapping thread, yarn, tinsel, and similar materials around a hook shank, imagine the challenges of mounting wing and tail materials. Try it sometime; it's quite a naughty problem.

Lee tied the Grizzly Wulff shown in the photograph for fishing for Altantic salmon, but you can make trout-size Grizzly Wulffs using smaller hooks. You can make the body of the Grizzly Wulff using green wool yarn as shown, substitute with another color, or use dubbing.

A lot of tiers run out of room on the hook when tying a Wulff pattern—the wing and bushy hackle take up a lot of space—but this problem is easy to solve. Divide the hook into two parts when tying a Wulff. The first half, which requires absolutely no more than two-thirds (or less) of the hook shank, contains the body of the fly. Wrap the hackle, which is the second major part of the fly, on the remaining one-third of the shank. Pay attention to these dimensions, and you will have ample room on the hook shank to tie the fly.

Egg-sucking Gnat

Hook: Daiichi 1280, sizes 12 to 8.
Thread: Orange 6/0.
Body: Peacock herl.
Rib: Grizzly dry-fly hackle.
Wing and head: Fluorescent orange deer hair.
Legs: Yellow and black rubber legs.

TIED ON 2X-LONG HOOKS, IN SIZES 12 TO 8, THE EGG-SUCK-ing Gnat doesn't remind me of a diminutive gnat. Colorado fly-tier Al Ritt created this fly as an attractor pattern.

Al is a guide who works the water flowing out of Rocky Mountain National Park. While he and his clients do encounter the local hatches, there are times when there is no insect activity, and they cast attractors to catch the resident trout. The Egg-sucking Gnat is a buggy-looking, easy-to-see fly that maintains its balance on the clear, flowing mountain water. The splayed rubber legs, spiral-wrapped hackle, and wing suggest—but do not exactly imitate—a stonefly or other large insect on the water.

Bomber

Hook: 2X-long dry-fly hook, sizes 16 to 12.
Thread: Size 8/0, color to match the body.
Tail: Deer hair.
Body: Rabbit dubbing.
Wing: Deer hair.
Note: Select materials in your choice of colors. Fran Betters dressed the Bomber *in white, brown, olive, and black.*

THIS PATTERN MIGHT BE FRAN BETTERS'S ANSWER TO THE Bomber tied for catching Atlantic salmon. Whereas the salmon Bomber has a complicated, spun-and-clipped deer hair body, Fran used dubbing to tie the body on his fly.

Like most of Fran's flies, his Bombers are a little scruffy, but they do catch fish. The Bomber is great for skating across the surface of the water and will generate explosive rises from trout and landlocked salmon.

These two flies were from an article Fran wrote about the Bomber for *Fly Tyer* magazine many years ago; he submitted these samples for the photography appearing with that piece. Although he preferred using more subdued colors, you can select bright colors for the wing—pink or hot orange—to increase the pattern's visibility in low-light conditions.

Bi-visible

Hook: 3X-long dry-fly hook, sizes 16 to 6.
Thread: White 8/0.
Tail: Three hackle tips.
Body: Three brown hackles.
Face: White or cream hackle.

THE BI-VISIBLE PROVES A THEORY I'VE HELD ABOUT DRY flies for many years. Fancy wings and other do-dads that remain above the water are designed to catch fishermen; the gentle dimpling of hackle tips and tail materials in the surface attract the trout.

The Bi-visible matches no insect yet imitates many. Perhaps the fish mistake it for a mayfly, caddisfly, damselfly, or some other insect. Who cares? It is what we consider an attractor pattern, and it does attract trout.

With respect to making the Bi-visible, one author pegs the degree of difficulty at level four, but he mustn't have much experience at the tying bench. The Bi-visible is a fairly straightforward pattern. Follow the accompanying tying instructions, and you'll quickly turn out fine Bi-visibles that will catch fish on your local waters.

Just a note before we tie the fly: some tiers include the tail in the Bi-visible, and others do not. I am adding the tail to match the fly in the main photograph.

Tying the Bi-visible

1. Wrap a layer of thread on the hook shank. Stack three hackles with the tips even. Measure from the tips to the spot where you will tie the feathers to the hook to create the tail; I like the length of the tail to equal to overall length of the hook. Brush the hackle fibers toward the base to expose the bare stems. Tie the feathers to the hook to make the tail.

2. Hold the hackle toward the end of the fly. Wrap one of the feathers two-thirds of the way up the shank. Tie off and clip the remaining piece of hackle.

3. Wrap the remaining two hackles—one at a time—two-thirds of the way up the hook. Rock each feather back and forth while working to prevent binding down the fibers of the previously wrapped feathers. Tie off and cut the excess pieces of hackle.

4. Tie a white or cream hackle in front of the body.

5. Wrap the face of the fly. Tie off and cut the surplus piece of feather. Whip finish and snip the thread.

Opal Wulff

Hook: Tiemco TMC100, size 12 or 10.
Thread: Fifty denier, gel-spun thread.
Tail: Moose-body hair.
Body: Opal Mirage tinsel.
Wing: Light gray EP Fibers or an equivalent.
Hackle: Brown.

DENNIS POTTER HAS ALTERED SEVERAL VENERABLE WULFF patterns, updating them with his own methods. For example, he substituted a synthetic wing for the standard-hair wing on this Wulff; Dennis used EP Fibers, which are usually considered a saltwater tying material, but you can use the ingredient of your choice. The wing holds its shape and has a great silhouette. And rather than dubbing, or the famous peacock herl and red floss found on the Royal Wulff, Dennis uses opal tinsel.

Wulff flies are usually used as attractor patterns, and the Opal Wulff fits right in. It is a great selection for fishing broken currents and pocket water.

Wemoc Adams

Hook: Regular dry-fly hook, size 12.
Thread: Brown 8/0.
Tail: Cree hackle fibers.
Body: Muskrat-fur dubbing.
Rib: Fine, gold wire.
Wing: Grizzly rooster-hackle tips.
Hackle: Cree.

THE WEMOC ADAMS, CREATED IN THE LATE 1970S AFTER fishing it on Willowemoc Creek in the Catskills, is Mike Valla's tweak of the common Adams dry fly. Mike does not claim that this fly is an entirely new concept. However, he uses what Eric Leiser used to call "Adams hackle," which is Cree. He adds fine, gold wire as a rib to help the muskrat-fur dubbing stay in place when fishing.

The fly was first featured in Mike's great book, *Tying Catskill Style Dry Flies,* and in his *Classic Dry Fly Box*; I have both well-thumbed volumes in my library.

Interestingly, Anne Lively, daughter of the late fly-tier Chauncy K. Lively, made a watercolor painting of the Wemoc Adams. Fly tying is a form of art, and it inspires art!

Searcher

Hook: Regular dry-fly hook, size 14.
Thread: Black 8/0.
Tail: Golden pheasant-tibbet fibers.
Tag: Red floss.
Body: Tying thread.
Wing: White or bleached snowshoe hare foot fur.

MOST PATTERNS TIED USING SNOWSHOE HARE FOOT FUR have a ragged, scruffy appearance. The material is unruly, so fly designers throw in the towel and use it to create disheveled-looking patterns. Ken Walrath's fly, the Searcher, is a pleasant surprise.

The Searcher has a trim tail, colorful butt, neat body, and perfectly wrapped hackle. The bright wings, made using snowshoe hare foot fur, are easy to spot on the water. Except for the wings, you might think this pattern came out of the Catskill tradition of fly tying.

As the name implies, this fly imitates no specific insect. Ken uses it as a general-searching pattern for exploring pocket water and other likely lies.

Crystal Wing Royal Wulff and Gray Wulff

Crystal Wing Royal Wulff
Hook: 2X-long dry-fly hook, sizes 18 to 12.
Thread: Red 6/0.
Tail: Elk hair.
Body: Peacock herl and red floss.
Wings: Crystal Splash.
Hackle: Dark brown.

Crystal Wing Gray Wulff
Hook: 2X-long dry-fly hook, sizes 18 to 12.
Thread: Gray 6/0.
Tail: Elk hair.
Body: Gray floss.
Wing: Crystal Splash.
Hackle: Medium dun.

THE WULFF SERIES OF FLIES, CREATED BY LEE WULFF, ARE some of our most popular patterns. Unfortunately, they are also a tad difficult to make; they're not the place to begin if you are a new fly tier. The bushy wings create bulk in the bodies, and tying the full-hackle collars is challenging. These versions of the Royal Wulff and Gray Wulff, sporting wings of a material called Crystal Splash, are easier to tie. The wings create less bulk on the hooks and leave more room for wrapping the hackle collars. If your local fly shop doesn't stock Crystal Splash, a product of the Spirit River Company, you can substitute with Krystal Flash.

CRYSTAL WING ROYAL WULFF

CRYSTAL WING GRAY WULFF

B.G. Dun

Hook: Regular dry-fly hook, sizes 16 to 12.
Thread: Gray 8/0.
Tail: Light dun hackle fibers.
Body: Stripped dun hackle quill.
Wings: Wood duck flank fibers.
Hackle: Grizzly and dun.

LEGENDARY FLY TIER AND GOOD FRIEND DAVID BRANDT originated the B.G. Dun. (I call him "legendary" because it will embarrass him.) "B.G.," he says, "is short for my pen name, Brooks Gordon—even though I don't have a pen yet."

According to David, the B.G. Dun represents no specific insect, yet it imitates many. He ties the fly in a range of sizes and shades. And although he prefers using real wood duck flank feathers for the wings, he has no objection to using mallard flank. With respect to using dyed mallard as a substitute, however, he says, "I don't like dyed mallard feathers because they don't feel the same as real wood duck."

Although this is a modern creation, the B.G. Dun is tied in the Catskill tradition.

Opal Trude

Hook: Tiemco TMC2312, sizes 16 to 10.
Thread: Red 8/0.
Abdomen: Opal Mirage tinsel.
Rib: Fine, gold wire.
Thorax: Peacock herl or peacock Arizona Synthetic Dubbing.
Wing: Light gray EP Fibers or an equivalent.
Hackle: Brown.

DENNIS POTTER, WHO OPERATES THE RIVERHOUSE FLY Company on the banks of Michigan's Ausable River, borrowed the Trude moniker for this pattern years ago; he was tying Trudes back then and got stuck looking for a name. It is mildly reminiscent of the hair-wing Trudes that were developed for use on the Henry's Fork water of the Snake River in Idaho.

This is another of Dennis's dry flies that use opal tinsel for the body. Even though this pattern rides high and dry, Dennis insists that the tinsel increases the fish-attracting properties of the pattern.

Grumpy Frumpy

Hook: 2X-long dry-fly hook, size 12
Thread: Red 8/0.
Tail: Brown polypropylene yarn.
Body: Yellow floss.
Back: Tan closed-cell foam.
Legs: Rubber legs.
Wing: White polypropylene yarn.
Hackle: Light brown.

WHAT IS IT ABOUT A FLY LIKE THIS THAT CONJURES THE word "fishy?" Maybe it's the sparse trailing shuck, the rubber legs, the full-hackle collar, or the easy-to-spot-on-the-water white wing. Whatever it is, when I first saw this fly, I knew I had to add it to my fly box.

In a couple of key areas, the Grumpy Frumpy reminds me of the famous pattern called the Quigley Cripple: the trailing shuck, forward-facing wing, and hackle collar. However, the addition of the foam back and legs and the change in the body and wing materials seem to make it an entirely new pattern.

Although a little fanciful, the Grumpy Frumpy serves as a fine imitation of an emerging mayfly or a mayfly that fails to successfully emerge. This version has a yellow body, but you can swap colors to tie tan, brown, and olive imitations.

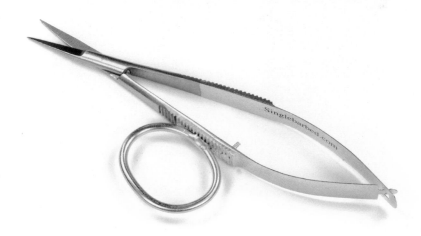

Royal Humpy

Hook: Regular or 2X-long dry-fly hook, sizes 16 to 12.
Thread: Red 8/0.
Tail: Moose hair.
Body: Red thread or floss.
Hump: Elk hair.
Wing: Elk-hair tips.
Hackle: Brown.

THE HUMPY IS A GREAT, CLASSIC DRY FLY YOU'LL FIND IN almost any fly shop. Al and Gretchen Beatty tied this example, so you'll find none better.

The trick to making the Humpy is to first tie the elk hair to the hook before wrapping the thread or floss body; the tips will point toward the rear-end of the fly. Next, wrap the body over the butt ends of the hair. Fold the hair over the top of the body to create the hump, and bend and pinch the tips upright to make the wings. Now you can wrap a full-hackle collar.

The Humpy is a terrific searching pattern for fishing fast currents and pocket water. The red body gives this version the name, Royal Humpy. Switch body colors—use dubbing, floss, peacock herl, etc.—to create your own versions of this timeless pattern.

Poly Humpy

Hook: Regular dry-fly hook, sizes 22 to 6.
Thread: Black 8/0.
Tail: Moose hair.
Body: Red floss.
Hump and wing: Gray polypropylene yarn.
Hackle: Brown.

MAKING A NICE FLY DOESN'T REQUIRE FEATS OF FLY-TYING strength or derring-do; you simply need to place quality materials on the hook in the proper order and proportions to create a durable pattern. If a step is too difficult, sometimes substituting a material simplifies things. A case in point is the Humpy.

The back and wings of the traditional Humpy, which is included in this book, are tied with elk hair. Manipulating the hair over the top of the hook and having the wings come out the correct length, is challenging. Al and Gretchen Beatty's simplified Poly Humpy solves this problem.

Rather than using elk hair, they select polypropylene yarn for the back and wing. The yarn back is easier to fashion, and you simply clip the wings off at the proper length after tying the fly. What could be easier?

Governor

Hook: Regular dry-fly hook, sizes 16 to 12.
Thread: White 8/0.
Tag: Gold tinsel.
Tail: Ginger hackle fibers.
Butt: Red tying thread.
Body: Peacock herl.
Hackle: Ginger.
Wings: Turkey.

I REMEMBER THE DAY I PICKED THROUGH DAVID BRANDT'S
fly boxes, looking for patterns for this project. David is a recognized authority on tying Catskill style dry flies, and he has an encyclopedic knowledge
of the region and the flies. I pointed to this pattern, called the Governor,
and remarked that I was unfamiliar with it.

"That's a very old one," David said, "but it's a dandy. It's also very unusual
in that it's not an imitation, but an attractor pattern."

Indeed, so much has been written about the classic Catskill imitations
of real insects—the Hendrickson, Light Cahill, March Brown, and all the
rest—that most anglers overlook the marvelous attractor flies originated in
that region.

This Governor, with its thick tail and heavy-hackle collar, will float high
and dry over the roughest currents.

EZY Kolzer

Hook: Regular dry-fly hook, sizes 20 to 6.
Thread: Black 8/0.
Tail: Ginger hackle fibers.
Body: Peacock herl or your choice of dubbing.
Body hackle: Brown grizzly.
Wings: Grizzly.
Front hackle: Brown grizzly.

"WHERE DID 'KOLZER' COME FROM IN THE NAME OF THIS pattern?" I asked Al Beatty.

"A guy named John Kolzer tied a dry fly by that name for fishing the McKenzie River. He was from the Pacific Northwest. I learned about it from a book that was published in the early 1950s. We've been tying our version—with the Wonder Wings, and we've lightened the color a bit—for about five years."

Al and Gretchen Beatty do tie perfect flies. The wings and spiral-wrapped hackle are without equal.

Whether used as an imitation or a searching pattern, the EZY Kolzer is one I am adding to my fly box.

Queen of Waters

Hook: Regular dry-fly hook, sizes 14 to 10.
Thread: Tan 8/0.
Tail: Ginger hackle fibers.
Body: Orange floss.
Rib: Gold tinsel.
Hackle: Ginger.
Wing: Mallard-flank fibers.

I AM INCLUDING THE QUEEN OF WATERS, SOMETIMES called the Queen of Water, for two reasons. First, the name of the fly gives our little collection of patterns a touch of class. Second, it highlights the "palmer" style of tying, a technique you can include in many of the flies you tie.

The name, Queen of Waters, hints to the British influence on this fly. Make no mistake, however, that it was once a very popular pattern in the United States, and American authors Theodore Gordon, Rube Cross, and George LaBranche all wrote about it. Note: do not confuse this pattern with a similar pattern, also called Queen of Waters, which is tied as a wet fly.

The palmer style of tying refers to the hackle spiral wrapped up the body. It improves the floatation of a dry fly and increases the buggy appearance of a wet fly. (The Elk-hair Caddis and Stimulator are other dry flies containing palmered hackles.) Catskill angler Rube Cross wrote that the term "palmer" comes from the palmer caterpillar, also known as the palmer worm.

That's a tidbit for conversation at your next fly-fishing cocktail party.

Royal Double Wing

Hook: Standard 2X-long dry-fly hook, sizes 8 to 14.
Thread: Black 6/0 (70 denier).
Tail: Green Antron yarn.
Tip (tag): Red floss.
Body: Peacock herl.
Body Hackle: Brown.
Wing: White calftail.
Butt Wing: Elk hair.
Hackle: Brown.

THIS ATTRACTOR FLY WAS DESIGNED BY FLY-FISHING LEGEND Gary LaFontaine. Although he said it was an attractor, which means it's not intended to imitate any specific insect, the Royal Double Wing would certain be a great choice to match a stonefly.

Curiously, LaFontaine tied this fly in twelve different color combinations to meet every lighting condition: orange for dusk, gray for overcast days, cream for early morning, yellow for midday, lime for fishing near streambank vegetation, and more.

Gary recommended the Royal Double Wing for fishing riffles near the middle of the day. Al and Gretchen Beatty, who supplied this sample of the pattern, call it "the ultimate attractor."

Since Gary LaFontaine developed the pattern, and the Beattys recommend it so highly, we should add it to our fly boxes.

NYMPHS AND WET FLIES

The Advantages of Fishing Wet

THERE ARE SEVERAL DISTINCT ADVANTAGES TO FISHING wet. No, I don't mean being soaked from the rain or from falling into the river. I mean that there are benefits to fishing with wet flies and nymphs. In fact, compared to fishing with dry flies, I dare say that you will usually catch more trout using subsurface patterns.

I love fishing dry flies to rising trout, but let's be real: most of the time the insects are not hatching and the fish are not rising. This doesn't mean that the trout are not feeding. They are simply eating the food they find below the surface of the water. And that's the rub for anglers—except in rare circumstances, it's impossible to see exactly what the fish are feeding on. This problem is even more challenging when we are fishing still waters and the trout are cruising far below the surface.

Successful anglers who consistently catch the most fish spend time deciphering the mystery of how trout feed subsurface. They learn about a trout's preferred foods and how it eats them. They use this hard-earned knowledge to refine their fishing tactics and design new fly patterns. The participants to the World Fly Fishing Championship are among the leaders in this studious approach to angling. Sure, controversy surrounds the idea of competitive fly fishing. But make no mistake: these anglers know how to catch large numbers of fish, and we can learn a lot from them.

Most of the new fishing methods and patterns coming out of the World Fly Fishing Championship involve nymphs and wet flies. I don't think this is because there are no new dry flies or streamers to create. It is because these anglers know that they will almost always catch more fish using small subsurface flies. They use this information to their advantage and so should we.

This little book contains 101 terrific wet flies and nymphs, spanning more than a century of fly-fishing history. Some of these patterns are well known, but others have never appeared in print. All are guaranteed to catch fish.

Enjoy these flies and discover the advantages of fishing wet.

David Klausmeyer

CHAPTER FIVE

Timeless
Wet Flies

Bergman Fontinalis

Hook: Regular wet-fly hook, sizes 10 to 2.
Thread: Black 8/0 (70 denier).
Tail: White, dark gray, and orange strips from duck or goose quill.
Body: Gray and orange wool yarn.
Hackle: Dark dun.
Wing: White, dark gray, and orange strips from duck or goose quill.

IN 1938, RAY BERGMAN PUBLISHED A BOOK TITLED *TROUT*. This fine book would anchor the angling libraries of fly fishers for many decades. There would eventually be several editions of *Trout*, and you can easily find a copy in a secondhand bookstore.

In addition to being chock-full of sound advice for catching trout, *Trout* included illustrations and recipes for several hundred wet flies. Fly tiers still enjoy making these patterns, and these flies still catch fish. If you are inclined to try your hand at dressing a few vintage flies, *Trout* will keep you very busy.

Ray Bergman really didn't design this pattern, called the Bergman Fontinalis; it was the creation of his friend, Phil Armstrong. "Fontinalis," of course, refers to the brook trout (*Salvelinus fontinalis*). Legend has it that once upon a time, the fins of small brook trout were commonly used as bait to catch larger fish. Classic wet flies such as the Bergman Fontinalis, Parmacheene Belle, Fontinalis Fin, Trout Fin—even the Royal Coachman—are supposed to imitate brook-trout fins.

I guess this was long before the catch-and-release ethic. Hey, don't blame me—I'm just reporting the story.

With respect to making the Bergman Fontinalis (Sharon E. Wright tied this perfect example of the pattern), the fly actually has two tails tied side-by-side, similar to the two wings of the fly. As a result, you will need six individual strips clipped from duck or goose quills; make each separate tail using three of the strips.

Cowdung

Hook: Regular wet-fly hook, sizes 16 to 12.
Thread: Orange 8/0 (70 denier).
Tag: Flat, old tinsel.
Body: Olive-orange rabbit dubbing. Some recipes recommend adding pinches of yellow and tan dubbing.
Wing: Cinnamon turkey.
Hackle: Brown.

WHAT CAN WE SAY ABOUT A FLY CALLED THE COWDUNG? Actually, quite a bit.

The name is not a comment about the color of the materials used in the fly, or some bit of odd, nineteenth-century humor. The Cowdung is actually an early attempt to match a terrestrial—or land-born—insect.

There are several early references to the Cowdung, but here we will refer to *The Sportsman's Gazetteer and General Guide: The Game Animals, Birds and Fishes of North America: Their Habits and Various Methods of Capture*, which was published in 1877. According to the authors, Charles Hallock and Henry M. Reeves, real insects called cowdung flies (they even give the scientific Latin name, *Scatophago stercoraria*, which you will readily find in an online search) were used as bait for catching trout. The larvae of the cowdung feed on the manure of cows, and the pupae hibernate in the ground. Upon emerging, some of the adult insects get blown onto nearby streams and become fodder for the fish. Anglers noticed how the trout readily fed on these insects and used what they thought was a matching fly.

By today's standards, the design of the Cowdung seems odd. We're used to seeing grasshopper, beetle, and ant imitations that look somewhat like real insects; fly designers add legs, wings, and antennae to create better forgeries. Although the Cowdung is tied in the colors of the natural insect, it is made and fished as a wet fly.

Before we leave the Cowdung, I should mention that there is also a fly called the Cow Turd. The Cow Turd was included in James Chetham's *Angler's Vade Mecum*, which was published in 1681. If you'd like to see an original copy of this historic volume, visit Chetham's Library in Manchester, England. Chetham's Library, which was founded in 1653 and is described as the oldest public library in the English-speaking world, has several copies of the *Angler's Vade Mecum*. The library describes the book as "A compendious, yet full, discourse of angling." How very British!

Parmacheene Belle

Hook: Regular wet-fly hook, sizes 14 to 6.
Thread: Black 8/0 (70 denier).
Tag: Silver tinsel.
Tail: Red and white hackle fibers or strips clipped from red and white goose quills.
Butt: Peacock herl.
Body: Yellow mohair, silk floss, or wool yarn.
Rib: Gold tinsel.
Throat: Red and white hackle fibers.
Wings: Red and white strips clipped from goose quills.

THE PARMACHEENE BELLE IS ONE OF OUR MOST FAMOUS wet flies. Even though it is relatively simple, it has just enough components that you will find several variations of this classic pattern.

For example, some tiers include the tinsel tag, but others do not. Some tiers make the tail using hackle fibers, while others marry together fine strips clipped from prime goose quills. The body was first tied using yellow mohair, but today tiers will use wool yarn, floss, or even rabbit dubbing.

A few tiers get their panties tied into knots over these differences, but I don't enter into those arguments. I'm interested in tying and fishing good flies, and the Parmacheene Belle still catches fish and is included in the catalogs of many commercial fly-tying companies.

Henry P. Wells created the Parmacheene Belle in 1876 in honor of the lake of the same name in Rangeley, Maine. Wells wrote an important fly-fishing book titled *Fly-Rods and Fly-Tackle*, which was published in 1885 and was even in the library of Theodore Gordon. The Parmacheene Belle was first mentioned in print, however, in 1883 in the book *Fishing With the Fly* by Charles F. Orvis and Albert Nelson Cheney. For more than 100 years, this beautiful little pattern has been included in fly-pattern books and studied in fly-tying classes.

Sharon E. Wright, a leading student of heritage flies and tying methods, tied this terrific example of the Parmacheene Belle using real mohair, which was used on the original pattern. It is particularly appropriate that Sharon dressed this pattern. Her great, great, great grandfather opened the first commercial sporting camp, Angler's Retreat, in the Rangeley in 1851. Her ancestor would be proud that she is preserving the Pine Tree State's outdoor sporting traditions.

Alexandra

Hook: Regular wet-fly hook, sizes 12 to 8.
Thread: Black 8/0 (70 denier).
Tail: Originally red ibis; you may substitute with red duck.
Body: Flat silver tinsel.
Rib: Small, oval, silver tinsel.
Throat: Black hen hackle fibers.
Wing: Peacock sword fibers.
Cheeks: Red ibis, but you may substitute with red duck.

THERE'S SOMETHING REGAL ABOUT A CLASSIC PATTERN
named Alexandra, and the wing, tied using peacock sword fiber tips, certainly fits the bill.

This lovely little fly, which was created sometime around 1860, was originally called Lady of the Lake: also not a bad name. There is some question
about who first tied the Alexandra—W. G. Turle or Dr. John Brunton—so
we'll leave the answer to history; suffice it to say that one of these gentleman
designed a beautiful, timeless pattern.

The Alexandra was created as a lake fly; we can infer this from the original name Lady of the Lake. Remember that in her book, *Favorite Flies and
Their Histories*, Mary Orvis Marbury devoted considerable space to the category of patterns called "lake flies." Today, we would call them stillwater
flies. In the late nineteenth century, most patterns, whether tied for fishing
moving waters or lakes and ponds, featured bright colors and looked like
nothing in nature. Today's anglers demand patterns that imitate nymphs, larvae, minnows, and other forms of natural fish forage—and thus are usually
dressed using drab colors.

The Alexandra is ideal for novice tiers interested in experimenting with
a classic fly for fishing, or who simply want to create and admire a lovely
pattern. Rather than using real ibis for the tail and cheeks—a material you
probably will not find in your local fly shop—substitute with narrow slips
clipped from a duck quill, dyed red. The tail and body are easy to make
using flat and oval tinsel, the throat is a small bunch of hackle fibers, and a
few strands of peacock sword fibers top off the wing of the fly. How simple
is that?

Watson's Fancy

Hook: Regular wet-fly hook, sizes 14 to 10.
Thread: Black 8/0 (70 denier).
Tail: Golden pheasant tippet fibers.
Body: Black and red floss.
Rib: Narrow, round, silver tinsel.
Throat: Black hackle fibers.
Wings: Duck quills, dyed black.

WATSON'S FANCY IS A CLASSIC ENGLISH PATTERN, AND you'll still find it in the fly boxes of a considerable number of anglers. I suspect the version you see here, with the tail tied using fibers from a golden-pheasant tippet feather and floss body, is the American variety; English tiers are apt to use a golden pheasant crest feather for the tail and seal's dubbing (or a substitute) for the body.

Golden pheasant tippet feathers come from the neck of the male bird. These lovely orange feathers have strong black bars on the edges. You'll find packages of these feathers, and even the complete golden pheasant necks, in your favorite fly shop. Select a smaller feather with a narrow, black band for tying the tail of the fly. Carefully strip a few fibers from the feathers, and tie the fibers to the hook to create the tail. Tie the butt ends of the tail fibers so that they extend to almost the hook eye to create a level underbody; this is essential for tying a smooth floss body.

Once upon a time, tiers used silk floss for making the bodies on patterns such as Watson's Fancy. Although you can still find silk floss, most tiers use flosses made of modern materials such as Rayon. These materials come in a rainbow of colors and are more durable than silk. Many English tiers, however, still use dubbing for making the body of this pattern.

Make the wings after adding the hackle fiber throat. The wings require two slips clipped from matching duck wing quills. Place the slips together between your thumb and forefinger. Pinch the wings to the top of the hook shank, and raise the thread up between your thumb and forefinger. Wrap the thread back down the other side of the hook between your fingers. Tighten the thread, and make another "pinch wrap." Remove your fingers to examine your work. If the wings are not directly on top of the fly, you can gently move them into position. Now you may wrap a neat thread head and complete the fly.

Yellow Sally

Hook: Regular wet-fly hook, sizes 14 to 10.
Thread: Black 8/0 (70 denier).
Tag: Flat gold tinsel.
Tail: Yellow hackle fibers.
Body: Yellow floss.
Rib: Flat gold tinsel.
Wing: Yellow duck or goose.
Hackle: Yellow hackle fibers.

YOU'VE HEARD THE ANGLER'S ADAGE: "BRIGHT DAY, BRIGHT fly; dark day, dark fly." It is easy to imagine that the Yellow Sally, which is a very old pattern, anchored the end of the fly box containing patterns for fishing on bright, sunny days.

Even though the Yellow Sally was first tied more than 100 years ago, you will still find it in many fly shops; it typically depends upon who in the store is responsible for purchasing flies. Younger anglers prefer patterns tied using a lot of rubber, foam, and flash, and this is often reflected in the flies they order. Many older anglers stick to the patterns that have withstood the test of time, and they'll offer at least a few flies such as the Yellow Sally.

The Yellow Sally is an excellent pattern if you'd like to try your hand at tying classic wet flies. Tying the tinsel tag and hackle fiber tail and wrapping the floss body and tinsel rib requires basic techniques. And you'll tie the wing using only two pieces clipped from matching duck or goose quills.

Note that the pattern recipe specifies using black thread. This is not entirely accurate. I usually follow the custom of listing the color of thread used to wrap the head and complete the fly, because stringing together a list of different threads would make the recipe cumbersome to read. However, on flies tied using light-colored ingredients, such as the yellow floss in the body of the Yellow Sally, make the fly using white thread and switch to black thread when tying on the wings and throat. If you do not follow this precaution when tying the fly, the color of the black thread will spoil the appearance of the body when then pattern becomes wet. It is also a good idea to wrap a layer of white thread on the hook shank before wrapping the floss body, so the color of the bronzed hook does not affect the color of the finished fly.

Blueback Trout

Hook: Regular wet-fly hook, size 10.
Thread: Black 8/0 (70 denier).
Tag: Red floss.
Tail: Black bear hair.
Body: Brown floss.
Rib: Flat gold tinsel.
Wing: Black, dark blue, and guinea fowl, married together.
Head: Peacock herl.

THE BLUEBACK TROUT IS CONSIDERED A RARE SPECIES OF char living in only a handful of remote Maine ponds. Because of its uniqueness, some anglers consider this fish an ultimate prize. I have caught only one blueback, and that was quite by accident.

One evening I was fishing a township in far-northern Maine, almost on the border with Canada. I was bobbing along in my float tube, kicking my way to shore before it became totally dark and dragging a fly behind me. All of a sudden the line went tight. After a minute, a lovely fish was flopping in the float tube apron; according to the scale, it measured a full 12 inches. I have caught many brook trout in this pond, but this fish looked different: few or no speckles and a steel-gray back. The light was failing, and I had never seen a live blueback trout, but I wondered if I was looking at one of these rare fish. The next morning, I described the trout to the lodge owner, and she instantly said that it was definitely a blueback.

Sharon E. Wright specializes in designing original streamers and wet flies. But, unlike many other tiers, she doesn't haphazardly blend materials and colors together to create new flies; a special person, thing, or event in her life inspires every one of Sharon's original patterns. Sharon tied a feather-wing streamer called the Blueback Trout to commemorate this special Maine fish, and she then tied this smaller wet fly.

Glory Girl

Hook: Allcock 1906M, size 7.
Thread: Black 8/0 (70 denier).
Tag: Light–green floss.
Tail: Moose body hair and a single, light–mottled pheasant quill section.
Body: Light–green wool.
Wing: Light–mottled pheasant quill.
Hackle: Light dun.

IT WAS MANY YEARS BEFORE HOOK MAKERS DISCOVERED how to make fine eyes on fish hooks. We take this part of hooks for granted, but turning and properly tempering the fine wire to create a strong eye was challenging. Before manufacturers perfected this technique, anglers attached flies to their leaders using snells.

A snell was a short piece of fine silk tied to the eyeless hook before making the fly. A loop was made on the other end of the snell, and the angler tied a small loop onto the end of his silk lead. He attached the fly to his line using a loop-to-loop connection.

Sharon E. Wright tied this Glory Girl, a pattern she dedicated to a dear friend, using a vintage Allcock hook and real silk gut. You'll often find similar patterns, made featuring snells, in old fly boxes; stop at your local flea market and you might discover a treasure of these flies.

There are generally two ways to tie the hackle on the front of a wet fly: as a collar or as a throat. A hackle collar entirely circles the hook shank, similar to a dry-fly hackle; the difference is that on a wet fly, you will use soft-fibered hen hackle, wrap the feather only two or three times around the hook, and stroke the fibers back when completing the thread head.

Tie the hackle throat on the bottom of the hook shank. The simplest method is to strip fibers from the feather and tie these opposite the wing. The more advanced technique for making the throat is to wrap a hackle collar and then stroke all of the fibers under the fly when tying on the wings or completing the thread head. Experiment with both methods to see which you prefer.

Telephone Box

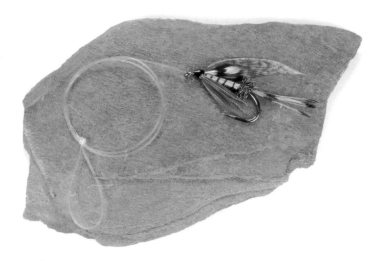

Hook: Regular wet-fly hook, sizes 14 to 10.
Thread: Black 8/0 (70 denier).
Tail: Golden pheasant tippet fibers.
Butt: Peacock herl.
Body: Orange floss.
Rib: Black floss.
Wing: Brown turkey tail.
Cheeks: Jungle cock nail feathers.
Hackle: Brown hackle fibers.

DR. EDGAR BURKE CREATED THIS PATTERN CALLED THE Telephone Box. In addition to being a fine angler and fly tier, Burke was also an accomplished artist and illustrator. He provided all of the colored illustrations of more than 250 flies in Ray Bergman's book, *Trout*. Even today, many tiers interested in classic wet flies consider *Trout* their Bible.

It's impossible not to see the influence of Atlantic salmon flies dressed with solid-feather wings in a pattern such as the Telephone Box; the golden pheasant tippet tail, peacock herl butt, and floss body are dead giveaways. The cheeks, tied using jungle cock nail feathers, are still common on many Atlantic salmon flies.

Jungle cock feathers puzzle new fly tiers. What are these feathers, and why are they so damn expensive?

Jungle cock nail feathers come from the neck of a male jungle fowl. Rather than the fibered feathers we call hackle that come from the necks of chickens, male jungle cock neck feathers are solid. The best grade of jungle cock neck pelt has the greatest number of feathers, the finest coloration, and very few or no "split" feathers; the majority of the nail feathers are solid.

Jungle cock nail feathers are expensive because jungle fowl are extremely difficult to raise in captivity. For example, one of the leading breeders of chickens for fly-tying feathers tried raising jungle fowl, but gave up because the birds were too temperamental. He said that they would accept food only from him and that he had to approach the birds' cages following the exact same path and procedure every day; the fowl, he said, would tolerate no deviation in the routine. In the end, he deemed the project commercially unviable, but he still raises his world-class chickens. The breeders who raise jungle fowl are specialists, and their feathers demand top dollar.

Toodle-bug

Hook: Regular wet-fly hook, sizes 14 to 10.
Thread: Black 8/0 (70 denier).
Tail: Gray mallard flank fibers.
Body: Blue floss and yellow wool.
Wing: Brown turkey tail.
Hackle: Brown.

MAINE'S SHARON E. WRIGHT IS QUICKLY GAINING A REPU-
tation as a leading authority on the history of New England streamers and
wet flies. And why not? Her output of magazine articles, classes and presentations, and flies—both classic and original patterns—is impressive. And
Sharon spends countless hours researching the topic; she is always visiting
a museum or historical society, or interviewing a senior fly tier. She shares
her passion for the Maine outdoors with her ancestor, Joshua Gross Rich.

In addition to opening the first sporting camp in the Rangeley region of
Maine in 1851, Rich was a prolific author, hunter, and trapper. In addition
to writing numerous magazine and newspaper articles chronicling Maine
wildlife, he supplied Harvard University with dozens of pelts for its natural
history collection. In fact, Sharon recently learned that he sent so many
skins to Harvard that the university had special labels printed with his name;
when they received another pelt from Rich, they simply attached a prepared label to the specimen. Many of these pelts are still in the collection of
the Harvard Museum of Natural History.

The Toodle-bug, which is a classic-style wet fly, was one of Rich's
favorite patterns. Although simple, the blue floss in the body makes it a
striking-looking pattern. Given Rich's vast experience in the Maine North
Woods, we can assume that the Toodle-bug, also called the Katoodle-bug,
is a real fish catcher.

Winter Brown

Hook: Regular wet-fly hook, size 16 or 14.
Thread: Orange 8/0 (70 denier).
Body: Three wraps of tying thread at the end of the body, and a blend of brown and maroon wool dubbing for the remainder of the body.
Hackle: Light Brahma hen hackle.
Head: Bronze peacock herl.

THE WINTER BROWN IS ANOTHER VERY OLD PATTERN that still catches trout. Even though it was first recorded in 1916 by Edmonds and Lee in the book *Brook and River Trouting*, it still teaches lessons about tying small wet flies and nymphs.

The recipe specifies starting the body using bare tying thread at the end of the hook shank and completing the body using sparse dubbing. This is a simple way to tie a slender abdomen and emphasize the color of the thread; the thread becomes integral to the color of the body. Study the pattern recipes in James Leisenring's important book, *The Art of Tying the Wet Fly*, and you'll find that the color of the thread was often supposed to show though the dubbing at the tip end of the fly. And why not? The tip of a small nymph is often different—generally slightly lighter—than the color of the rest of the body. A careful tier can replicate this difference in color using thread and dubbing.

To be truthful, the recipe for the Winter Brown specifies a barred, gray feather from the under coverts of a woodcock wing, with the lighter side of the feather facing forward. I typically shoot a couple dozen woodcock every hunting season, but I do not collect the feathers, and I suspect you also do not have woodcock feathers. Making a simple substitution, such as using a light Bramha hen hackle, yields a nice-looking fly that still catches fish.

Tenkara Wet Flies

Hook: Regular wet-fly hook or curved-shank emerger hook, sizes 16 to 8.
Thread: Size 8/0 (70 denier).
Body: Thread or dubbing.
Hackle: Wet-fly soft hackle.

TENKARA IS A FORM OF JAPANESE FLY FISHING THAT HAS captivated the imaginations of many anglers.

The tenkara style of fly fishing requires only a rod, line, and fly—there is no reel. The telescoping rods usually extend between eleven and fourteen feet long. The angler holds the rod high and dabs his wet or dry fly in likely spots on the water; at most, the angler makes short, slow casts. Due to the minimalist nature of the method, tenkara fly fishing is ideal for backpacking and other situations where you want to carry only a small amount of gear.

According to the website of Tenkara USA, "Tenkara flies (or '*kebari*') place less emphasis on imitation and more on the importance of their presentation and manipulation. The simple tenkara fly reflects a general tenkara philosophy: 'technique instead of gear.'" A tenkara angler might prefer one fly above all others and relies on correct presentation to catch a fish.

Check out this small selection of tenkara flies. They are very simple yet have just enough of the attributes that attract trout. The bodies are slender, they have no tails or wings, and the fibers of the finely wrapped hackles cant forward. When fishing the flies, the fibers bend back and stand out from the bodies, similar to the legs on real nymphs; they do not collapse against the hooks when drawn through the water.

You could tie many established wet-fly patterns in the tenkara style. For instance, you might tie a tenkara pattern with a body tied using flat tinsel, or perhaps wrapping pheasant tail fibers up the hook shank. Or, you could make the thorax of the fly using peacock herl and add a tail if you wish.

The point is to make a simple fly and rely on your technique and careful approach to the water to catch fish.

March Brown

Hook: Regular wet-fly hook, sizes 14 to 10.
Thread: Orange 8/0 (70 denier).
Hackle: Brown, mottled feather from the rump of a snipe.
Tail: Two fibers from the base of the hackle.
Body: Rabbit dubbing, dyed light red.
Rib: Fine gold wire or tinsel.

THE CLASSIC ENGLISH MARCH BROWN WET FLY IS A FINE example of designing a very simple pattern to match a real insect. The March brown is nothing more than thread, a dab of dubbing, a piece of wire or tinsel, and a feather; whip all these materials together, and you can create a lovely imitation of a real March brown. Cast the fly across-and-down stream to imitate a real insect struggling to the surface to emerge into a winged mayfly.

Some tiers specialize in tying classic patterns using authentic ingredients. For example, they will use real silk thread, not contemporary nylon thread from the local fly shop. And they will always strive to use the plumage specified in old-pattern recipes; in this case, the rump feather of a snipe. And, with respect to the March brown, for dubbing you would use fur from the nape of the rabbit's neck. I prefer, however, tying flies to catch fish, not impress fishermen.

Make the March brown using the orange thread you already have on your tying bench. For dubbing, buy a package of rabbit fur, dyed a very light red or reddish tan. And for the snipe feather, substitute with a Coq de Leon or Brahma hen hackle. This combination will create a terrific fly that catches trout.

Although the March brown is a traditional English pattern, it is dressed a little heavier than many other flies. Scale it up or down in size to match a wide variety of emerging mayflies.

Greenwell's Glory

Hook: Regular wet-fly hook, size 16 or 14.
Thread: Dark-olive 8/0 (70 denier).
Body: Tying thread.
Rib: Fine gold wire or tinsel.
Wing: Starling primary wing feather, bunched and split.
Hackle: Furnace.

IN TELLING THE HISTORIES OF THE FLIES IN THIS LITTLE book, as well as in *101 Favorite Dry Flies*, I must inevitably tell stories about myself and how I became a fly fisherman.

I purchased my first book about fly fishing and tying when I was about twelve years old. It was a reprint of the classic, *The Art of Tying the Wet Fly & Fishing the Flymph*, written by James Leisenring and Vernon Hidy, with an introduction by some guy named Ernest Schwiebert. I didn't know it at the time, but I possessed a book based on decades of research and streamside experience. Although he died more than half a century ago, Leisenring and his book continue echoing through the fly-fishing world.

We were living in Tulsa, Oklahoma at the time. No one in my family fly fished, and there was certainly no local fly shop, but I wanted to learn to tie and cast flies. It was a dark mystery, and I was determined to crack the code.

For example, the tying materials described in *The Art of Tying the Wet Fly*: what were they, and where could I get them?

Leisenring discussed something he called waxed fly-tying thread. I pondered this: thread with wax. Could I find or create a solution? The answer seemed simple enough.

I gathered together several spools of thread from my mother's sewing basket, a pot, and a box of paraffin. I melted the paraffin in the pot, and tossed in the thread. I let the spools swim in the steaming wax. After half an hour or so, I plucked the thread out of the paraffin with a spoon and set them aside to cool. As you can image, I had nothing more than spools of sewing thread caked with hardened wax.

I tried tying a few flies with the thread and sensed something wasn't right, but I didn't know what. I wouldn't discover the answer until years later.

Traditional English patterns, such as Greenwell's Glory, inspired much of what is written in *The Art of Tying the Wet Fly*. Fortunately, you can find almost all of the materials, or acceptable substitutes, at your local fly shop.

Baillie's Black Spider

Hook: Regular wet-fly hook, sizes 18 to 14.
Thread: Black 8/0 (70 denier).
Hackle: Glossy blue/black feather from a starling's back or lower neck.

THROUGHOUT THIS BOOK I HAVE SHARED THE FAVORITE flies of some very good anglers. They are all experienced and know how to catch fish. Few, I suspect, exceed the fishing prowess of James Baillie. You've never heard of him? Don't feel bad; he's been dead for many, many years.

W. C. Stewart first recorded Baillie's Black Spider in his book, *The Practical Angler*, in 1857. At the time it was known as the Stewart Black Spider, but it should have been called Baillie's Black Spider.

James Baillie was a professional fly fisher who supplied local restaurants and hotels with the fish he caught. According to legend, he supported his family this way and the Black Spider was key to his success. Later, Stewart wrote that this was his favorite fly.

Stewart tied the Black Spider using an unusual technique that made a very strong fly; we don't know if this was his idea or if Baillie taught him the method. Stewart started the thread in the middle of the hook shank, wrapped it toward the eye, and made a small thread head. He then tied in the hackle by the butt end. Next, Stewart twisted the feather and thread together, and wrapped the two to the middle of the hook. Finally, he separated the hackle from the thread and tied off and clipped the remainder of the feather. And remember: he did all of this without the aid of a vise, bobbin, or hackle pliers. You can make the same fly using these modern fly-tying implements, so it should go very easily.

Partridge & Orange

Hook: Regular wet-fly hook, size 16 or 14.
Body: Orange thread.
Rib: Fine gold wire or tinsel.
Hackle: Brown, mottled partridge back feather.

THE DECEPTIVELY SIMPLE PARTRIDGE & ORANGE IS ONE OF our most famous wet flies. Although of English origins, it has become the cornerstone in fly boxes of Americans who specialize in fishing small, sparse wet flies.

There are two styles of "soft hackles" in the United Kingdom. If the flies have wings, they are called North Country wet flies; if they do not have wings, they are North Country spiders. The Partridge & Orange, which does not have wings, is a North Country spider.

The hackle on a North Country spider is always tied in by the tip and wrapped twice around the hook. The slender body is tying thread; silk, of course, was used on older flies, but today you may substitute with your favorite brand of tying thread. If the body is dubbing, use natural fur. Some spiders have tails, and a few have heads of peacock or magpie tail herl. Rather than using the feathers of domestic poultry, hackles were usually partridge, red grouse, or some other game bird.

Typically, cast a wet fly across-and-down stream, and allow it to sink below the surface of the water. After a moment, the line will tighten and the fly will swing across the current; the fly must look like a swimming, struggling insect because a fish will often strike. If the fly seems to move too quickly, toss an upstream mend or two in the line to slow its progress. Remember, a wet fly is supposed to imitate an emerging insect, not a fleeing baitfish.

Partridge & Hare's Ear

Hook: Wet-fly hook, sizes 12 to 8.
Thread: Brown 8/0 (70 denier).
Body: Hare's ear dubbing.
Rib: Fine gold wire.
Hackle: Mottled partridge.

HERE'S ANOTHER PATTERN THAT HALES FROM THE ERA OF
Izaak Walton, silk lines, and rods made of greenheart. Times were gentle,
and so was the fishing. While most modern anglers believe that they have
an edge in fly design, largely due to our more comprehensive knowledge of
what fish eat and the great variety of available tying materials, we can still
learn a lot from our forebears. This Partridge & Hare's Ear wet fly, tied by
John Shaner, is a good example.

John is a master at tying and fishing older wet flies, and he often lectures
on the subject at major fly-fishing shows. When he plucked this pattern out
of his fly box, he called it the Partridge & Hare's Ear, but I suspect some call
it the Hare's Ear Soft Hackle. That's a quibble the fish wouldn't understand.

Note how sparse this Partridge & Hare's Ear is; it would do an excellent job of imitating a slender insect—probably a mayfly—ascending to the
surface. John used no more than a pinch of dubbing for the body, and extra-
fine gold wire, spiral-wrapped up the hook, create wonderful segmentation. When this sort of pattern gets wet, the wire stands out even more to
enhance the segmentation. And, true to form, John used no more than two
wraps of hackle to recreate the dainty legs of the real insect.

As simple as it looks, this is one of my favorite flies in this collection. It
is elegant, old, and will still catch fish.

Endrick Spider

Hook: Wet-fly hook, sizes 12 to 8.
Thread: Black 8/0 (70 denier).
Tail: Pheasant tail fibers.
Abdomen: Pheasant tail fibers.
Rib: Fine copper wire.
Thorax: Peacock herl.
Hackle: Brown partridge.

THE ENDRICK SPIDER IS ANOTHER OLD WET-FLY PATTERN. From what I can tell, it is of Scottish origin, but that's of no importance: it will catch trout everywhere.

John Shaner tied this fine example of the dainty Endrick Spider. Actually, because of the peacock-herl thorax, maybe it's one step larger than "dainty." It seems like more of an imitation of a small-to-medium sized emerging mayfly nymph, or perhaps a caddisfly pupa.

While we often think of using sparse wet flies and spiders as a form of fishing practiced only in the United Kingdom, nothing is further from the truth. Many knowledgeable North American anglers routinely use wet flies; the silhouette of an insect struggling to the surface often overcomes the instincts of the wariest trout.

American authors such as James Leisenring and Sylvester Nemes wrote about wet flies, and Dave Hughes and others carry on the tradition. These simple flies catch trout, and even novice anglers can quickly learn to use them. They are also extremely easy to tie, and by changing hook sizes and colors of materials, you can fill a fly box full of fish-catching patterns. Wet flies have been around for almost 200 years, and they will continue to be the cornerstones of many fly boxes.

Plover & Yellow

Hook: Wet-fly hook, sizes 18 to 12.
Thread: Yellow 8/0 (70 denier).
Body: Tying thread.
Rib: Fine gold wire.
Hackle: Plover.

THE WORD "DAINTY" HARDLY BEGINS TO DESCRIBE THIS small Plover & Yellow wet fly. This pattern, tied by John Shaner, using an economy of materials, will do a fine job imitating very small, emerging mayfly nymphs.

Generally speaking, traditional wet flies fall into two groups: those that follow specific recipes and those based simply on the combination of materials used in the patterns. Time-honored flies such as the Greenwell's Glory, Bradshaw's Fancy, and Coachman are defined patterns that often commemorate or refer to an individual angler or tier; deviate from their recipes and you have new flies.

The second family of flies is named for the materials used in their construction, typically the color of the body and type of hackle. The Plover & Yellow is one of these flies: the body is yellow thread and the hackle is plover.

Some tiers go to great lengths to be exact about naming patterns, but maybe the old-time tiers had it right: base the name of a fly on the materials you use to tie it. Think about an exchange between anglers on a river. One catches a large fish, and his pal calls out, "What fly are you using?"

"A Plover & Yellow," is the response.

"I don't have one of those. Will a Partridge & Yellow work?"

"Yes, that's close enough."

Such simple names are also a type of fly-tying shorthand. Any tier within earshot of this streamside conversation will know what fly to make that evening.

Montreal

Hook: Regular wet–fly hook, sizes 14 to 6.
Thread: Black 8/0 (70 denier).
Tag: Flat gold tinsel.
Tail: Red (scarlet) quill sections.
Body: Claret floss.
Rib: Flat gold tinsel.
Throat: Claret hackle fibers.
Wing: Mottled turkey.

PETER COWAN CREATED THE MONTREAL SOMETIME IN the mid-1800s. Cowan emigrated to Canada sometime in the 1830s and settled in Quebec's eastern townships. Cowansville, where Cowan served as sheriff, was named in his honor. We can only dream of the quality of the fishing where he lived at that time!

Cowan was a devoted trout angler, and he had great success catching trout on his fly. The popularity of the Montreal grew, and by 1850, it was being commercially produced in Canada. Samples of the Montreal were eventually sent back to the United Kingdom, where more professional fly dressers also began tying the pattern for catching both trout and Atlantic salmon.

Here we have the standard recipe for the Montreal, but there are many variations, including the Blue Montreal, Western Claret Montreal, Light Montreal #1, Light Montreal #2, Silver Montreal, Steelhead Montreal, and more. (There is a modern streamer pattern called the Montreal Whore, but it looks nothing like any of these flies.) I'll bet you could devise even more variations of the Montreal using the materials on your tying bench. So have fun and get creative!

Silver Doctor

Hook: Regular wet-fly hook, sizes 12 to 8.
Thread: Red 8/0 (70 denier).
Tag: Flat gold tinsel.
Tail: A golden pheasant crest feather and blue schlappen or a narrow strip clipped from a blue duck quill.
Tip: Red floss.
Body: Flat silver tinsel.
Rib: Oval silver tinsel.
Wing: Brown turkey; brown goose; guinea fowl; and red, blue, and yellow goose.
Hackle: Blue hackle fibers and guinea fibers.

IF THE WORM IMITATIONS FOUND ON OTHER PAGES IN THIS little book are the epitome of utilitarian patterns, then the Silver Doctor is simply fly-tying art. But this little gem of feathers does catch fish.

The Silver Doctor started life many decades ago as a full-dress Atlantic salmon fly. The Silver Doctor was first included in Mary Orvis Marbury's 1892 book *Favorite Flies and Their Histories*, and was categorized a salmon fly. However, three additional versions of the Silver Doctor were described by Marbury as lake flies. Many of the fancy freshwater patterns used in the late-nineteenth century were inspired by full-dress salmon flies.

Make no mistake, however: flies such as the Silver Doctor do catch fish. It is even still possible to find patterns such as the Silver Doctor in the fly bins of some older fly shops that still appreciate these classic patterns; of course, those flies might not be quite so elaborate and contain all of the bits of feathers and other materials.

The wings of the Silver Doctor are created using small slivers clipped from the feathers listed in the recipe. The pieces are then laid together and stroked. The strips actually cling together to create what is a called a "married" wing. Does this sound too complicated? Then tie the tail and body of the fly, and use dyed goat or some other fine hair for the wing. Select colors to match those found in the feather wing. This Hair-wing Silver Doctor is easier to make, equally beautiful, and will give you a taste of fishing with a classically inspired fly.

CHAPTER SIX

Nymphs, Larvae, Scuds, and More

Art Flick's March Brown

Hook: Mustad 7957BX or equivalent, size 12 or 10.
Thread: Orange 6/0 (140 denier).
Tail: Three ring-necked pheasant tail fibers.
Abdomen: Seal fur (or a substitute), dyed amber, mixed with fawn–shade red fox belly fur.
Wing case: Ring-necked pheasant tail.
Rib: A single thread of brown embroidery thread.
Thorax: Seal fur (or a substitute), dyed amber, mixed with fawn–shade red fox belly fur.
Hackle: Partridge.

IT'S IMPOSSIBLE TO WRITE ABOUT FISH-CATCHING NYMPHS and not mention the legendary Catskill fly tier, Art Flick. Although Flick lived and fished from the early-to-mid twentieth century, he is still a much-beloved figure in Catskill-angling circles; there is even a *Trout Unlimited* chapter named in honor of him. Art Flick Trout Unlimited meets monthly in Brookhaven, New York.

In 1947, Flick took the concept of match-the-hatch to new heights with his small book *Art Flick's Streamside Guide to Naturals and Their Imitations*. This book has gone through many printings and is still in print today; its contents and sound advice are timeless.

In addition to a healthy dose of Catskill-inspired patterns designed to match mayflies, stoneflies, and other important insects, the *Streamside Guide to Naturals and Their Imitations* offers specific dressings that imitate the nymphs found on the West Kill and Schoharie Creeks in the northern Catskills.

Flick's March Brown nymph is especially important, because he said this pattern was also a good match for the common Light Cahill mayfly nymph; both of these insects are members of the genus *Stenonema*. This pattern requires common fly-tying materials—be sure to substitute the seal's fur used for the body with one of the many available substitutes—and any tier with modest skills can make it.

Darbee's Stonefly Nymph

Hook: Mustad 9672, 79580, or an equivalent 3X- or 4X-long nymph hook, sizes 12 to 4.
Thread: Brown 6/0 (140 denier).
Tail: Two ring–necked pheasant tail fibers.
Abdomen: Seal fur (or a substitute), dyed amber.
Rib: Brown monofilament.
Wing case: Two split jungle cock eyes. Use the small, enamel section of the jungle cock eye for smaller hook sizes and longer eyes for very large hooks.
Thorax: Seal fur, dyed amber.
Hackle: Partridge or grouse.

I REMEMBER THE DAY WHEN CATSKILL FLY-TYING AUTHORITY and author Mike Valla submitted his article about the region's best nymphs. Mike thought it would be a great piece for *Fly Tyer* magazine, and I agreed. I was surprised, however, when I opened the package and examined the flies he sent.

The Catskill School of fly tying is best know for its sparse dry flies; I chronicle the histories of some of those patterns in the companion volume to this book, *101 Favorite Dry Flies*. Those dainty patterns could ride the surface like ballerinas. Mike's selection of subsurface patterns, however, contained some beefy flies; they looked tough enough to pull trout out of the roughest parts of a stream.

Harry Darbee's Stonefly Nymph is one of the patterns that caught my attention. It was obviously tied to imitate a golden stonefly, a large insect common to many streams through the Catskills, especially the Delaware River. Darbee utilized seal fur, dyed amber, for the abdomen and thorax for the pattern, but today you'll have to use one of the many seal fur substitute ingredients; you'll find these in any fly shops that stock materials for tying trout flies.

A lot of tiers create complicated patterns for matching large stoneflies; the great size offers a more generous platform for adding legs, antennae, and other features. Darbee's Stonefly Nymph is far simpler to make, and it's a great pattern for tiers possessing modest or intermediate skills. But don't be fooled by this fly's simplicity—it is a fine fish catcher.

Carrot Nymph

Hook: Mustad 9671 or equivalent, size 14 to 12.
Thread: Black 6/0.
Tail: Brown hackle fibers.
Abdomen: Carrot floss or dubbing.
Thorax: Black chenille.
Hackle: Dun hen soft hackle, clipped on the top and bottom.

RUBE CROSS REMAINS A LEGENDARY FLY TIER AMONG CATSKILL anglers. Living from 1896 to 1958, his flies and tying methods are still discussed and emulated. Other regional tiers who gained fame for their flies, such as the Dettes and Darbees, learned much about their craft from studying Cross's flies.

Although he was better known for his sparsely tied dry flies, like all master anglers, Cross also tied and fished nymphs. In his book titled *Tying American Trout Lures*, which was published in 1936, Cross contributed a small chapter devoted to nymphs where he described three very simple patterns. The Carrot and Black Nymph, which was more commonly called the Carrot Nymph, was one of these. In 1965, the Carrot Nymph, tied by Elsie Darbee, was included in A. J. McClane's important reference book, the *Standard Fisherman's Encyclopedia and International Angling Guide*.

Orange-bodied wet flies have always been favorite patterns. Rube Cross's Carrot Nymph is an easy-to-tie pattern that is a good choice if you want to experiment with an orange nymph or wet fly. Leave the full-hackle collar if you'd like to tie it as a dry fly, or trim the hackle on the top and bottom to create a pattern with the profile of a nymph.

Black & Yellow
Hard-back Nymph

Hook: Mustad 7957B, 7957BX, 3906, or an equivalent, size 12 or 10.
Thread: Tan, brown, or black 6/0 (140 denier).
Tail: Black hen hackle fibers.
Body: Yellow dubbing saturated with clear lacquer, pinched flat with needle-nose pliers. Paint the dorsal area with black lacquer.
Hackle: Black, trimmed on the top and bottom.

EDWARD RINGWOOD HEWITT (1867–1957) OWNED FOUR-and-a-half miles on the Neversink River in the Catskill Mountains. Hewitt used this amazing stretch of water as his laboratory for testing the large-hackled style of dry fly that would become known as the Hewitt Skater, and is sometimes called Hewitt's Neversink Skater or just the Neversink Skater.

In 1933, Hewitt's friend, John Alden Knight, who is primarily known for popularizing the Mickey Finn bucktail streamer and his *Solunar Tables*, used these waters to test a new flat-bodied nymph. Hewitt wanted a pattern that better matched the shape and color of natural insects found in the Neversink. Knight tied the new nymph using reddish-tan fox fur for the body, narrow oval, gold tinsel for the rib, and Rhode Island redrooster hackle for the tails and legs. Knight soaked the body in clear lacquer, allowed it to partially dry, and then squeezed it flat with pliers. He darkened the dorsal surface with some reddish-brown lacquer; today you can use a permanent marker.

The flat-bodied nymph fly is crude but effective, and has proved its worth. According to Catskill fly-tying historian Mike Valla, "The newfangled design gained acceptance by other fly anglers after Knight took seventy-four trout on the nymph during a Neversink red quill hatch."

You can easily use this tying method to create patterns to match other nymphs. This Black & Yellow Hard-back Nymph, for example, is a good fly for matching a smaller stonefly nymph.

Copper John

Hook: Regular or curved-shank nymph hook, sizes 16 to 12.
Thread: Brown 6/0.
Bead: Gold bead.
Tail: Brown goose or turkey biots.
Abdomen: Copper wire.
Thorax: Peacock herl.
Legs: Hen hackle fibers.
Wing case: Brown turkey, coated with a drop of epoxy.

ACCORDING TO THE FOLKS AT UMPQUA FEATHER MER-chants, the world's largest commercial fly-tying outfit, their best-selling fly is the Copper John.

"We tie and sell them by the tens of thousands," says Bruce Olson, one of the head honchos at Umpqua Feather Merchants.

John Barr, a terrific tier who lives in Colorado, created the Copper John only a couple of decades ago, but today you'll find it in the fly boxes of anglers around the world. The Copper John is a mainstay among guides who use it as a dropper tied 15 to 18 inches below high-floating stonefly and grasshopper imitations; if the trout don't take the dry fly, they often strike the tailing Copper John.

The Copper John is an ideal pattern for substituting materials. For example, I often use fine rubber legs for the tail and even the legs. You can substitute dubbing for the peacock herl used to make the thorax; this yields a far more durable pattern. And you can add a single strand of pearl Flashabou to the top of the wing case to give the fly a little extra sparkle; some tiers even swap Flashback tinsel material for the pheasant-tail wing case.

When making the Copper John, be sure to select beads and wire to match the size of hooks you are using. The best Copper John has the streamlined, svelte appearance of a real nymph. This is my version of the Copper John, with longer legs than what you'll probably find on the flies in your local fly shop; I prefer the look of these extended appendages.

Pheasant-tail
Cased Caddis

Hook: 3X-long nymph hook, sizes 14 to 8.
Thread: Green 6/0.
Bead: Clear silver.
Case: A section clipped from a pheasant or turkey tail feather.
Head: Your choice of bright-green wet-fly dubbing.

THIS IS ONE OF THE FLIES THAT MAKES IT WORTH BUYING this little book. After a considerable amount of time on the water—experimenting with a wide variety of cased caddisfly imitations—this simple Pheasant-tail Cased Caddis has become one of my favorite flies. Tie it and use it, and you *will* catch more fish.

Real caddisflies are common to almost all trout streams. Most anglers, however, don't realize that the fish eagerly eat cased caddisflies; these immature larvae, after all, live in houses built of bits of twigs, leaves, and sand. How can the fish identify them as something good to eat, and how do they digest the cases? Ah, the mysteries of nature!

Suffice it to say that trout *do* pick out cased caddisfly larvae from the rest of the material drifting in the current, and they happily feed on the feast.

The Pheasant-tail Cased Caddis is remarkably simple to tie: wrap fine lead wire on the hook for weight, wrap a section of pheasant tail feather two-thirds of the way up the hook to create the caddis case, and add a head of bright-green dubbing for the head of the larva peeking out of its home. I prefer using Ice Dub for the head of the caddis worm.

Pat Dorsey, a talented tier and guide who lives in Colorado, ties his Mercury Midges using silver-lined glass beads for the heads of his flies, so I added this embellishment to the Pheasant-tail Cased Caddis. This bit of sparkle seems to appeal to the fish.

If you wish to make a larger pattern, substitute the pheasant tail fibers for a section clipped from a brown turkey tail feather.

Rob's Caddis Pupa

Hook: Curved-shank pupa hook, sizes 16 to 10.

Thread: Brown or olive 8/0 (70 denier).

Abdomen: Rob's Realistic Body Wrap, color to match the natural insect.

Thorax: Rabbit dubbing, color to match the natural insect.

Legs: Partridge or mottled hen hackle fibers.

Wing case: Rob's Realistic Body Wrap, color to match the natural insect.

ROB LEWIS IS A TERRIFIC FLY TIER AND GUIDE WHO SPE-
cializes in fishing the Delaware River watershed, home to some of the largest trout in the Northeast. He is also one of the most entertaining tiers at
the winter East Coast fly-fishing shows. Rob always shows up with a table
full of his realistic patterns that are designed for real-world fishing.

Rob says this pattern is an imitation of a caddisfly pupa, and it would
certainly catch fish when the real caddis pupae are migrating to the surface
of the water to emerge into winged adults. But, this fly would also serve as
a fine caddis larva imitation; fished deep like a nymph, it will catch trout
laying or feeding near the bottom of the stream.

Rob makes the abdomen of his Caddis Pupa using an ingredient he calls
Body Wrap. Body Wrap, which you tie to the hook and wrap up the shank
to create a segmented-looking abdomen, comes in several lifelike colors. A
commonly available material such as Sow-Scud Back is a good substitute
for Body Wrap. The advantage of using either ingredient is that they do not
change color when wet; what it looks like in your vise is pretty much how
it will look when fishing.

Tie Rob's Caddis Pupa in a variety of sizes and colors to match the real
caddisflies in your local waters. You can even color the top of the abdomen
with a dark permanent marker to give your flies a more realistic two-tone
effect.

Rob's Caddis Pupa is a good choice as a dropper when fished with a
heavier nymph; the weighted fly will draw the lighter Caddis Pupa to the
streambed. You can also add a small bead to the head of the Caddis Pupa to
add weight to the fly.

Clouser Swimming Nymph

Hook: 2X-long nymph hook, sizes 10 to 4.
Thread: Fire-orange 6/0 (140 denier).
Tail: Dark-brown marabou or rabbit fur, and bronze Flashabou or Krystal Flash.
Body: Dark-rust rabbit dubbing.
Wing case: Peacock herl.
Legs: Brown or speckled brown hen hackle.

ALL FLY FISHERS KNOW THE CLOUSER DEEP MINNOW; WE commonly call it simply the "Clouser Minnow." Better yet, say "I caught this fish using a Clouser," and any fly fisherman will know what you're talking about. That simple pattern, featuring dumbbell eyes on top of the hook that force the fly to flip over when fishing, is perhaps the most famous streamer in the history of our sport.

Did you know that Pennsylvania's Bob Clouser has designed other types of flies? Clouser's Swimming Nymph is another of his classic patterns. And, just like with the Clouser Minnow, which jigs up and down when retrieved, the design of the Clouser Swimming Nymph maximizes fish-enticing movement and action.

The Clouser Swimming Nymph is simple to make, and I'm surprised it's not featured in more beginning fly-tying classes. The tail, which is either a small bunch of marabou or tuft of rabbit fur, and hackle-fiber legs give the fly a good swimming action. The body, which is simple rabbit dubbing, is easy to apply and adds to the fly's natural appearance.

The Clouser Swimming Nymph is an excellent, basic imitation of a medium-to-large swimming nymph. Tie this fly in a variety of colors—dark rust, dirty tan, brown, and olive—to match a wide variety of swimming nymphs. Although it works well in rivers and streams, it is also ideal for fishing in still waters; fish it deep with a full sinking line hours before an expected hatch or under just the surface when you spy feeding trout but there are no mature duns on the water.

In addition to catching trout, the Clouser Swimming Nymph is also considered an excellent carp pattern.

Vladi's Condom Worm

Hook: 4X–long streamer hook, sizes 8 to 4.
Thread: Fine monofilament.
Weight: Lead wire or a non–toxic subsitute.
Body: A condom.
Rib: 20–pound–test monofilament.

THIS IS ONE OF THE STRANGEST PATTERNS IN THIS BOOK. Even though it is very unusual, it is also an extremely useful fly. I learned about the Vladi's Condom Worm gradually, and it has become an important part of my fishing kit.

I had heard rumors that the master anglers participating in the World Fly Fishing Championship were using a pattern that imitated a worm. I was told that the fly was one of the keys in a new method of angling called European nymph fishing. This deadly technique requires using a rod measuring 10 to 11 feet long, only a few inches of fly line extending beyond the tip of the rod, and an extremely long leader. The angler typically fishes two or even three nymphs at the same time close to his position, sweeping the rod downstream almost matching the speed of the current. He moves slowly, covers the water thoroughly, and typically catches a lot of fish.

I was pleasantly surprised when Jack Dennis, one of our sport's most famous fly designers and businessmen—and coach of Team USA—introduced me to Vladi Trzebunia, the creator of the Condom Worm. We had a pleasant chat. Vladi eagerly explained how he ties and fishes his fly, and he gave me several samples, plus some other patterns he uses when fishing nymphs. Vladi gave me the Condom Worms you see here.

First, Vladi bends a standard streamer hook into shape. He wraps lead wire on the hump in the shank opposite the hook barb and point. The placement of the wire causes the fly to flip over when fishing, so it does not snag the streambed.

The body of the fly is formed using a pink condom wrapped up the hook shank. The Crown Skinless Condom comes in pink, and at least one online condom supplier mentions the fact that this product is used to tie flies!

How do I tie Vladi's Condom Worm?

I use a non-lubricated, Trojan-brand condom. Cut the unrolled condom into six pieces, much like a six-piece pie; when unrolled, you'll have six strips for tying at least six flies. I color the latex strips using a pink or tan permanent marker.

Vladi's Condom Worm is an ideal anchor pattern when using a multi-fly, nymph-fishing rig. The fly dives to the bottom and pulls the other patterns into the strike zone. The Condom Worm very rarely hooks the streambed, but it often hooks trout and even landlocked salmon.

Hare's-ear Nymph

Hook: Regular or 2X-long nymph hook, sizes 18 to 10.
Thread: Black or brown 6/0 (140 denier).
Tail: Hackle fibers or rabbit fur.
Abdomen: Rabbit dubbing.
Rib: Narrow gold wire or round tinsel.
Thorax: Rabbit dubbing.
Wing case: Turkey tail feather.

THE HARE'S-EAR NYMPH IS THE QUINTESSENTIAL NYMPH. This is one of the most popular patterns taught in fly-tying classes, and all trout anglers have a few copies of this fly in their fishing kits. It is a basic mayfly imitation that you can adapt to match almost any stream-born nymph. And, because it requires only a couple of common ingredients, it is also a very economical fly.

The basic material for making the body is rabbit dubbing, which you'll find in a variety of colors in fly shops. If you tie flies, select dubbing that contains a lot of long guard hairs; these fibers create the spiked legs on the fly. Regular rabbit dubbing, which comes from the body of the animal, contains guard hairs, but the variety typically called hare's mask dubbing works even better. Gray is the most popular color, but you may select other colors to tie imitations of any mayfly and small stonefly nymphs you might encounter; tan, brown, olive, and black are all excellent choices.

Novice tiers commonly use too much dubbing for making the bodies, which makes their finished flies too fat. Use just a pinch of dubbing to create a slender body that mimics the profile of a real nymph.

You'll also want to add weight to your Hare's-ear Nymphs so they break through the surface of the water and sink. Once upon a time, wrapping lead wire on the hook shank before tying the fly was the most common method of weighting this pattern, but today the Gold-bead Hare's-ear Nymph is very popular. The small bead adds weight and a dash of flash to this pattern, and many anglers swear that it catches more fish.

Fish the Hare's-ear Nymph—with or without a bead head—alone or as a dropper in a multi-fly rig. Choose pattern colors and sizes to match the real mayfly nymphs you are likely to encounter in your local stream.

Poxyback Stonefly

Hook: Long-shank nymph hook, sizes 18 to 6.

Head: Gold bead, size to match the hook.

Thread: Tan 8/0 (70 denier).

Tail and antennae: Sulphur-orange or tan turkey biots.

Underbody: Lead wire or a non-toxic substitute tied to the sides of the hook shank.

Abdomen: A sulphur-orange or tan turkey biot.

Thorax: A coarse nymph dubbing, such as angora or a substitute, golden stonefly.

Wing case: Turkey tail feather coated with a drop of epoxy.

Legs: Brown, mottled hen back feather.

Head: A coarse nymph dubbing, such as angora or a substitute, golden stonefly, colored on the top with a brown permanent marker.

CALIFORNIA'S MIKE MERCER IS ONE OF MY FAVORITE FLY designers, and the Poxyback Stonefly is one of his signature patterns. I don't know if Mike was the first tier to add epoxy to the top of a nymph wing case, but he certainly popularized this simple and effective technique.

First, you must select a bead to match the size of the hook. Once upon a time, fly-tying beads came in a limited selection of sizes. Today, beads—lead, brass, and tungsten—come in sizes to fit almost any hook you might wish to use. For this pattern, I tie on the biot antennae, clip the thread, remove the hook from the vise, and then slip the bead into place; the bead covers the base of the antennae and makes a neater-looking fly. I then place the hook back in the vise and continue making the pattern.

Tie a strip of lead wire or a non-toxic substitute onto each side of the hook shank to create a broad, level underbody. I tie on the wire and then coat the wire and thread wraps with superglue; this makes a rock-solid platform for tying the fly.

Use the Poxyback Stonefly as a model for creating imitations of many species of stoneflies. Select colors of biots and dubbing to match the stoneflies in your favorite waters.

Big Dave's
Stonefly Nymph

Hook: Partridge Czech Nymph Hook or your favorite brand of curved-shank nymph hook in your choice of sizes.

Head: Gold bead, size to match the hook.

Thread: Brown 6/0 (140 denier).

Tail and antennae: Brown turkey biot.

Abdomen: Golden stonefly Nymph Skin, colored with a brown permanent marker.

Thorax: Wapsi Life Cycle Dubbing, or a substitute, golden stonefly.

Legs: Brown, mottled hen hackle.

Wing case: Brown Medallion Sheeting or a substitute.

THIS IS ONE OF MY OWN PATTERNS: GIVE ME CREDIT IF IT catches fish for you, and blame me if it doesn't.

I use this beefy pattern to match large brown and golden stonefly nymphs; although often associated with our Western rivers, I encounter these insects from Southern Appalachia all the way to Labrador. Also, when fishing Alaska, I encountered healthy hatches of golden stoneflies. Wherever you have cold, clean water, you are apt to find stoneflies.

There are three varieties of Wapsi Life Cycle Dubbing: Nymph, Caddis, and Stonefly. I select Life Cycle Stonefly, which is a coarse variety of dubbing, when tying larger versions of this pattern, and switch to Nymph, or a substitute such as ordinary rabbit dubbing, when making smaller imitations. Wapsi Life Cycle Dubbing includes a dash of fine flash material that makes the fly stand out and attracts the attention of the fish.

I was introduced to Nymph Skin by English fly-tier Steve Thornton. Nymph Skin, which comes in a limited but important selection of colors, is a Latex product, and it will rot when exposed to the air over a long period of time. After wrapping the abdomen and coloring the back of the body with a brown permanent marker, coat the material with head cement. The cement seals the Latex so that it will not rot.

Medallion Sheeting, which I use for the wing case, is designed for making the wings on dry flies, but it also does an admirable job for fashioning wing cases on all styles of nymphs. You may, of course, substitute with any variety of wing-case material—even a strip clipped from a turkey.

Make no mistake: this is a heavy pattern. Select this fly when fishing deep pools or fast water where it is less likely to snag the streambed.

Tellico
Hare's-ear Nymph

Hook: Regular wet-fly hook, sizes 16 to 8.
Thread: Brown 6/0 (140 denier).
Tail: Ring-necked pheasant tail fibers.
Body: Tan rabbit dubbing.
Rib: Black 3/0 (210 denier) tying thread.
Back: Ring-necked pheasant tail fibers.
Hackle: Brown hen hackle.

TELLICO STREAM FLOWS THROUGH THE CHEROKEE National Forest, which lies south of the Great Smoky Mountains National Park in Tennessee. This region is home to some of the most beautiful trout streams you'll ever see, and over the years local tiers have created a host of fine fish-catching flies. As you might imagine, there is a pattern called the Tellico Nymph.

According to Don Kirk, who has chronicled the region's fishing for many years, the original Tellico Nymph has a yellow floss body, peacock herl rib, Guinea fowl tail, and turkey quill back. According to Kirk, Ernest Peckingbaug, an old-time fly tier who lived in Chattanooga, was the first to commercially offer the Tellico Nymph. That was many decades ago, and it remains a popular, simple imitation of a small stonefly nymph.

Al and Gretchen Beatty tied this version of the fly they call the Tellico Hare's-ear Nymph. Although their pattern maintains the general style of the original Tellico Nymph, they substitute with other ingredients to create a more durable fly. They use rabbit dubbing, rather than floss, for the body. And, they use tough, size 3/0 tying thread, rather than frail peacock herl, for the rib.

The tail on the Tellico Hare's-ear is the tips of a bunch of ring-necked pheasant tail fibers; they also use tail fiber for the back of the fly.

The Tellico Nymph, either the original or the Beattys' updated version, is a simple-to-tie imitation of a stonefly. It is still a basic pattern taught in the area's fly-tying classes. For experienced anglers like the Beattys to take notice of it, you know it catches fish!

Isonychia Nymph

Hook: 2X-long nymph hook, size 14 or 12.
Thread: Brown 8/0 (140 denier).
Tail: Ring-necked pheasant tail fibers.
Abdomen: Brown floss.
Gills: Cream Antron yarn.
Rib: Fine, clear monofilament thread.
Thorax: Peacock herl.
Wing case: Turkey tail feather.
Legs: Stripped hackle quills.
Back stripe: White 3/0 (210 denier) tying thread.

I AM INCLUDING THIS LOVELY PATTERN, CREATED BY expert-tier Floyd Franke, to demonstrate that you do not need to use a great deal of materials to design an amazingly real-looking fly. In fact, many of the "fishing realistics" in this book require deceptively few ingredients.

Floyd is an award-winning tier, an instructor at the Wulff School of Fly Fishing, and a leading force in the Federation of Fly Fishers Certified Casting Instructor program. He is also very active with the Catskill Fly Fishing Center and Museum, and the Catskill Fly Tyer Guild. And, as you can see from his Isonychia Nymph, he is a very inventive tier.

Although this pattern looks fairly realistic, Floyd uses materials you will find in any fly shop: floss, peacock herl, pheasant tail fibers, hackles, and a turkey feather. He makes the telltale stripe on the back of the nymph using a piece of white thread. How simple it that?

Isonychia mayflies are swimming nymphs found in many trout streams. The insects dart among the rocks and are available to the trout. In some areas of the country, *Isonychia* mayflies are called slate drakes.

I understand that the legs on this version of the Isonychia Nymph seem less than ideal for fishing. Rather than stiff hackle quill legs, substitute with a few brown hackle fibers tied on at the head of the fly. Also, rather than the accurate-looking wing case, you could fold a strip of turkey tail over the top of the fly, for a look that is similar to the wing case on a Hare's-ear Nymph.

But, you have to admire Floyd Franke's inventiveness and creativity. He tied a striking pattern using only a handful of materials.

Giant Salmonfly Nymph

Hook: Curved-shank nymph hook, sizes 6 to 4.

Thread: Black 3/0 (210 denier).

Tail: Black goose biots.

Abdomen: A strip cut from a bicycle inner tub.

Thorax: Tan Australian opossum dubbing.

Wing case: Bicycle inner tube, cut to shape.

Legs: Strips cut from a bicycle inner tube or black rubber legs.

Eyes: Red plastic dumbbell.

Antennae: Pheasant tail fibers, dyed black.

BOB JACKLIN'S GIANT SALMONFLY NYMPH IS ANOTHER PAT-
tern tied using a unique material; in this case, pieces cut from a bicycle inner
tube.

Bob Jacklin is a legend among fly anglers who visit the Yellowstone area.
He has been an outfitter for more than 40 years, a guide, and a masters certified fly-casting instructor. Bob started tying flies commercially in the early
1960s and still operates Jacklin's Fly Shop in West Yellowstone. In 2004, Bob
was inducted into the Fly Fishing Hall of Fame, located at the Catskill Fly
Fishing Center and Museum.

Pteronarcys californica, commonly called the salmonfly, is one of the most
spectacular hatches in North America. The jumbo nymphs live in a stream
or river for three years and are available to the trout throughout the season.
As the sun sets, the nymphs migrate to shore, where they crawl out onto
rocks, streamside vegetation, buildings, and even automobiles—anything
they can find—to shed their skins and transform into winged adults. Fishing an imitation such as Jacklin's Giant Salmonfly Nymph near shore during
this emergence is a particularly effective technique.

Because of the unique size of these insects and the ferocious rises from
the trout when the adult salmonflies return to the water to lay eggs, many
anglers plan their entire trips around this hatch. Depending upon where
you fish, the hatch can occur from late May to early July. To complicate the
timing, the hatch will progress to new sections on a river throughout the
weeks. Contact a local guide or fly shop for local hatching conditions.

Poxyback Green Drake Nymph

Hook: Curved-shank nymph hook, size 12 or 10.
Thread: Olive 8/0 (70 denier).
Tail: Ring-necked pheasant tail fibers.
Abdomen: Olive nymph dubbing.
Carapace over abdomen: Mottled turkey tail.
Rib: Small copper wire.
Gills: Olive ringed-neck pheasant aftershaft feather.
Thorax: Olive nymph dubbing.
Wing case: Mottled turkey tail, coated with a drop of epoxy.
Legs: Brown mottled hen back feather.
Head: Olive nymph dubbing.

TYING IMITATIONS OF GREEN DRAKE NYMPHS IS CHAL-
lenging; this is probably why most anglers use Woolly Buggers and similar
nondescript buggy patterns when the real insects are swimming to the surface. Yet, if you want to get the most out of a green drake hatch and catch
the maximum number of trout, you'll want to fish some sort of subsurface
pattern before the real insects pop to the surface.

Mike Mercer's Poxyback Green Drake is a superb imitation of a real
green drake. Yes, it's one of those more complicated patterns, but a tier with
intermediate-level skills should be able to make it.

Prominent gills along the sides of the abdomen are a key feature of a real
green drake nymph. Mike replicates gills on his fly using a single pheasant
aftershaft feather placed between the top of the abdomen and the carapace.
An aftershaft feather is a small, billowy plume at the bottom of a regular
feather. Other birds, such as grouse, have aftershaft feathers, so you can easily
substitute with what you have on your tying bench. The soft, marabou-like
fibers give the pattern a breathing, lifelike action in the water.

Note the proportions of Mercer's Poxyback Green Drake. The abdomen
comprises about two-thirds of the length of the body, which matches the
body proportions of a real green drake.

The only change I might make on this pattern is in the tail. Green drake
and *Hexagenia* nymphs have feathery tails. The tips of marabou feathers do a
fine job of imitating the tails of the real insects and give the flies additional
swimming action.

Prince Nymph

Hook: 2X-long nymph hook, sizes 20 to 12.
Thread: Black 8/0 (70 denier).
Tail: Brown turkey biots or hackle fibers.
Body: Peacock herl.
Rib: Fine, gold, round tinsel.
Hackle: Brown soft hackle.
Wing: Two white turkey biots.

A TIER NAMED DOUG PRINCE DEVELOPED HIS PRINCE
Nymph in the 1930s, and it has grown into one of our most popular subsurface patterns. According to Umpqua Feather Merchants, the Bead-head
Prince Nymph rivals the Copper John as their most popular pattern. "We
sell them by the tens of thousands," says Umpqua manager Bruce Olson.

The Prince Nymph, with or without a bead head, is a perfect pattern for
novice tiers. It requires only a handful of common materials that you will
find in any fly shop, and you can also use these ingredients to tie other flies;
there's no need to buy anything special to tie a Prince Nymph.

You can fish the Prince Nymph as a single fly, but a lot of anglers—especially guides—use this pattern as a dropper in a multi-fly rig. The dropper
is the second fly tied to a length of leader placed 12 to 18 inches above
the end, or "point" fly. Some multi-fly rigs have more than one dropper,
but casting such tackle is difficult; the multiple flies tangle easily, and you'll
spend considerable time untangling the fine strands of leader material.

Some say the Prince Nymph imitates a stonefly, but others say it mimics
a mayfly or caddisfly. It is probably more accurate to think of the Prince
Nymph as an attractor pattern that imitates no specific insect—or perhaps
it matches several!

Bead-head
Sparkle Pupa

Hook: Regular wet–fly hook, sizes 18 to 12.
Head: Gold bead.
Thread: Size 8/0 (70 denier).
Body: Antron dubbing.
Sheath: Antron dubbing.
Thorax: Cul de canard.

I REMEMBER RECEIVING A COPY OF GARY LAFONTAINE'S important book *Caddisflies* as a Christmas gift more than 30 years ago. For me, and countless other anglers and fly tiers, *Caddisflies* was a revelation. The research and thoroughness was impeccable; LaFontaine had set a new standard for writing about fly tying and fishing. Not since Ernest Schweibert's vast two-volume *Trout* had any author or publisher attempted so ambitious a project. But whereas *Trout* had that distinct Schweibert flare for storytelling—and sometimes bullshit—*Caddisflies* took a direct, no-nonsense approach to fly design and fishing.

Gary created his imitation called the Sparkle Pupa to mimic a real caddisfly migrating from the bottom of a stream or pond to the surface of the water. Gases build under the skin of the caddisfly to help it rise to the surface; the Antron sheath encapsulating the body of the fly imitates the gas-filled skin of the natural insect.

Whereas Gary wrapped lead wire on the hook shank to add weight to the fly he called the Deep Sparkle Pupa, today many tiers use a small metal bead.

A couple seasons ago, I added a thorax made of cul de canard. Whereas American tiers use high-floating cul de canard feathers to tie dry flies, European tiers include these feathers in many of their wet flies and nymphs. The fibers of the feathers contain hundreds of microscopic hooks that capture tiny air bubbles and add to the appearance that the skin of the fly is full of gas. The fibers also pulsate when stripping the fly through the water, giving the pattern a lifelike swimming action.

I fish the Sparkle Pupa, with and without a bead head, right before the hatch as real caddisflies are swimming to the surface of the water. The Beadhead Sparkle Pupa has also become one of my most important searching patterns when nothing is hatching and I am exploring the water for trout.

Poxyback Isonychia Nymph

Hook: 3X-long nymph hook, size 12.
Thread: Brown 8/0 (70 denier).
Tail: Brown ostrich herl fibers.
Abdomen: Brown nymph dubbing.
Carapace over abdomen: Pearl Flashabou.
Rib: Extra-small copper wire.
Gills: Ring-necked pheasant aftershaft feather.
Thorax: Brown nymph dubbing.
Wing case: Pearl Flashabou.
Legs: Brown hen back fibers.
Head: Brown nymph dubbing.

HERE'S ANOTHER IN THE POXYBACK LINE OF FLIES; YES, I really like the patterns created by Mike Mercer.

Mike has worked at the Fly Shop of Redding, California for many years. He's an authority on catching trout and steelhead. I had an opportunity to interview Mike a few years ago, and his enthusiasm for fly tying and fishing is contagious. After more than 30 years of fly tying, he still creates a couple dozen new patterns every year. His creativity is endless.

His Poxyback Isonychia Nymph contains the characteristic stripe down the back of the fly, just like the stripe on the real insect. Rather than thread, however, Mike uses a piece of thin, pearl Flashabou coated with a drop of epoxy. The flash from the material makes the Poxyback Isonychia Nymph stand out in the water and captures the attention of the fish. The pattern's realistic profile, along with a darting, swimming retrieve, seal the deal and get the trout to strike.

I like fishing any *Isonychia* nymph imitation using an intermediate sinking line or a line with a sinking tip. Cast down-and-across stream, let the fly settle in the water, and use a darting retrieve. This pattern and fishing technique works in waters containing large numbers of *Isonychia* nymphs, and it is also a good searching method when prospecting for trout.

Rubber-legged Copper John

Hook: Curved-shank larva hook, sizes 12 to 8.
Head: Medium orange metal bead.
Thread: Size 6/0 (140 denier).
Tail: Turkey biots.
Abdomen: Small wire.
Thorax: Hare "E" Ice Dub or a substitute.
Legs: Rubber legs.
Wing case: Flashabou, Flashback, or a substitute, coated with a drop of epoxy.
Collar: A small hen hackle.

THE CLASSIC COPPER JOHN WAS JUST THE BEGINNING IN AN entire series of patterns based on that simple design. Over the years, John Barr and others have altered that basic fly to create other fish-catching patterns. The Rubber-legged Copper John is a good example.

The Rubber-legged Copper John is an adaptable pattern. Trim the length of the legs to suit your needs and preferences. Umpqua Feather Merchant sells the lanky Rubber-legged Copper John you see here, but some tiers clip the legs a little shorter to more closely match the legs on a real nymph. Change body colors to match the stoneflies and large mayfly nymphs in your favorite trout stream—black, brown, olive, and tan—or use two colors of wire, wrapped simultaneously, to create a two-tone abdomen.

The wing case, made using wide Flashabou or Flashback material, gives the fly a little sparkle in the water, and the orange bead head reminds me of the "hot spots" now used on many modern European nymphs and larvae. Tiers who add hot spots to their flies insist that those patterns catch more fish.

If you wish, you may substitute rubber leg material for the turkey biot tail. Although the tail looks very lifelike, rubber is far more durable.

I think of the Rubber-legged Copper John as the big brother to the standard Copper John. Fish the Rubber-legged Copper John wherever you might encounter golden stonefly nymphs and similar meaty insects.

Shenk Cress Bug

Hook: Regular wet-fly hook, sizes 20 to 8.
Thread: Olive 8/0 (70 denier).
Body: Medium, olive-brown or gray fur dubbing.

WOW, WHAT A SIMPLE FLY RECIPE. CAN SUCH A NONDE-script fly really catch fish? You bet!

Ed Shenk specializes in fishing Pennsylvania's limestone spring creeks. These placid, weed-filled waters are loaded with cress bugs, which are sometimes called sowbugs. Ed designed this easy-to-tie fly to match a cress bug.

You will find cress bugs—or sowbugs—in waters across North America. They are a major source of food for tailwater trout throughout the Southeast. These small crustaceans are so important that there is a fly fishing and tying show called the Sowbug Roundup held every year in Mountain Home, Arkansas. Mountain Home is also the base for anglers who fish the White and Norfork Rivers, noted for containing world-record-sized trout.

Cress bugs cling to the weed in the stream or river, so you will want to fish your imitation deep and slow. Add a few wraps of narrow lead wire or a non-toxic substitute before tying the fly. Muskrat dubbing, with the guard hairs removed, is perfect for tying the Shenk Cress Bug. Apply the dubbing to the hook using a dubbing loop. Tie off and clip the excess piece of loop. Trim the top and bottom of the fly to simulate the flat profile of a natural cress bug.

It's hard to imagine a fish eating something so basic as the Shank Cress Bug. But the fish key in to these small crustaceans, and they eagerly suck in this fly. This is an especially good pattern for learning how to make a dubbing loop.

San Juan Worm

Hook: Regular or curved-shank nymph hook, size 12
Thread: Pink or tan 8/0 (70 denier).
Body: Pink or tan Ultra Chenille and dubbing.

I RISE IN DEFENSE OF THE SAN JUAN WORM AND SIMILAR patterns. Do they need an advocate? In the minds of some anglers, these aren't real flies. But then, once upon a time, "proper" fly fishing required casting only dry flies to rising fish. Fortunately, a few inquisitive anglers began looking under the surface of the water and explored the possibilities of designing and fishing subsurface patterns. Oh, those heretics!

It turns out that while we have busied ourselves creating all manner of nymphs and larvae imitations, the trout have been eating worms, and not the worms bait fishermen spear onto their hooks. The fish in some fisheries eat real, free-living worms!

There are many species of aquatic worms. They populate rivers across North America, and what I will call "earth worms" (sorry, I'm not a soil or worm scientist) can get into a stream when a mud or clay bank breaks off and slides into the water. The trout, not fools for passing up a tasty meal, feed on these worms.

The San Juan Worm was popularized on New Mexico's San Juan River. Some anglers consider the San Juan River—which is a significant tributary of the Colorado River—fly-fishing hallowed ground.

I am giving you the pattern recipe for the most basic San Juan Worm; there are many variations. The basic ingredient is Ultra Chenille that has been singed on the ends. Tie the length of chenille to the hook, and cover the tie-in point with a pinch of dubbing. Some San Juan Worms have copper or tan Ultra Wire wrapped on the hook shanks to add weight, or you can slip a metal bead onto the hook to give the fly extra heft.

Smerf Stonefly

Hook: Curved–shank nymph hook, sizes 10 to 6.
Thread: Black 3/0 (210 denier).
Tail and antennae: Goose or turkey biots.
Body: Your choice of nymph dubbing or yarn.
Rib: V-Rib.
Hackle: Webby saddle hackle.

IF YOU NEED A LARGE PATTERN TO IMITATE THE LARGEST stonefly nymphs in the river, the Smerf Stonefly, created by John "Smerf" Smeraglio, is an excellent choice.

There's a theory that the best flies suggest rather than imitate the features found on real nymphs. Why? According to the theory, the more we try to create a realistic-looking imitation, the easier it is for the fish to see through our deception. The legs and tails look correct to us, but to the trout, they lack the movement or some other trait they use to identify real food. And the larger the fly, the easier it is for the fish to spot a forgery. In other words, an artificial fly that closely matches the real insect looks more like a model drifting in the current rather than something good to eat. That's the theory, anyway.

I tend to agree with this point of view. A trout works largely off instinct, and the best fly possesses the features—legs, antennae, tails, and body shape—in the proportions, form, and color of the real insect. To a simple-minded trout with a brain the size of a pea, the Smerf Stonefly has all the appendages and shape the fish is looking for in a nymph.

The Smerf Stonefly is a dream to tie in smaller sizes; you can fill half a fly box in an evening of tying. The Smerf Stonefly is also a great choice for imitating salmonflies, big golden stoneflies, and other large nymphs. The Smerf Stonfly is the perfect point fly when fishing a multi-fly rig.

Dronestone

Hook: 3X–long nymph hook, sizes 10 to 6.
Thread: Dark-brown Monocord.
Head: Tungsten gold, copper, or black bead.
Abdomen: DMC embroidery floss.
Thorax: SLF Squirrel or SLF Prism Dubbing.
Appendages: Barred Centipede Legs or your choice of rubber legs.
Wing case: Natural-mottled or yellow-mottled Thin Skin.

NEW JERSEY'S AARON JASPER TURNED ME ON TO THE Dronestone in the first article he wrote for *Fly Tyer* magazine in 2010. In addition to being a talented author, Aaron is a guide, has appeared in a couple of top-notch instructional fly-fishing DVDs, and regularly demonstrates fly tying at major fly-fishing shows. Although only in his mid-30s, he is already making great waves and acquiring an appreciative following.

The Dronestone features an abdomen woven on the hook shank using two colors of embroidery floss. The effect is outstanding, and the technique is fairly easy to learn. Although it's beyond the scope of this book to demonstrate this tying method, you can find demonstrations of fly "weaving" on many websites. Spend an evening just learning the weaving technique to make flies with great-looking, segmented, dark-colored backs and light-colored bellies, just like the real nymphs.

Aaron uses Centipede Legs for the tails, legs, and antennae of the Dronestone. This material, similar to plain rubber legs, bends out of the way when a fish strikes and makes the fly more durable. For the wing case, you can substitute with a slip clipped from a turkey tail feather or your favorite wing case material.

Woven-bodied flies are a little more complicated to make, but the results are worth the effort. I spent a couple of evenings making the Dronestone, and I was pleasantly surprised how fast it is to construct the abdomen. You can then adapt the method to tying the bodies on mayfly nymphs and even caddisfly larvae; just select embroidery floss in colors to match the natural insects.

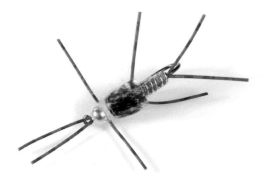

Gummy Stone

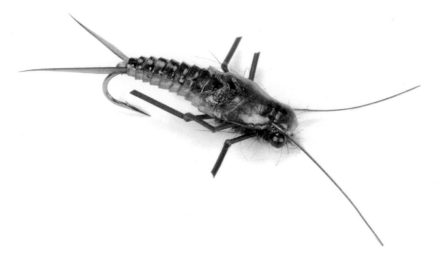

Hook: Tiemco TMC2487 or TMC200R, or your choice of sizes.
Thread: 3/0 (210 denier), color to match the body of the fly.
Tail: Turkey or goose biots.
Abdomen: Mother of pearl Sili Skin.
Thorax: Rabbit dubbing or a substitute.
Eyes: Monofilament dumbbell eyes, size of choice.
Wing case: Mother of pearl Sili Skin.
Legs: Rubber legs, or turkey or goose biots.
Antennae: Stripped hackle quills.

FLY TIER BLANE CHOCKLETT BURST ONTO THE FLY-FISHING scene about fifteen years ago with a series of amazing flies. Blane lives in Virginia and guides anglers to that state's best smallmouth bass and trout fishing. When he is not on the water, he is at his fly-tying vise designing new patterns. His first noteworthy creation, which won widespread acclaim, was the Gummy Minnow.

Blane fashioned the body of the Gummy Minnow using a soft sheet material called Sili Skin. This material comes in several flashy and lifelike colors, and yields realistic-looking and feeling flies. After the success of his celebrated baitfish imitation, Blane used Sili Skin to tie a variety of other patterns, including the Gummy Stone.

The Gummy Stone is a fat, juicy pattern that matches the largest stonefly nymphs living in a trout river or stream. Although it is large, it is surprisingly lightweight and easily managed with a typical five- or six-weight fly rod.

Blane fashions the abdomen of the Gummy Stone by wrapping a strip of Sili Skin up the first half of the hook shank. He makes the wing case using a stonefly wing case cutter offered by a company called River Road Creations. The wing case cutter is similar to a cookie cutter: lay the Sili Skin on a board, and punch out wing cases using the cutting tool. River Road Creations also produces cutters to make insect wings, frog bodies, and many more shapes out of Sili Skin, foam, and other soft materials. Look for River Road Creations tools in your local fly shop.

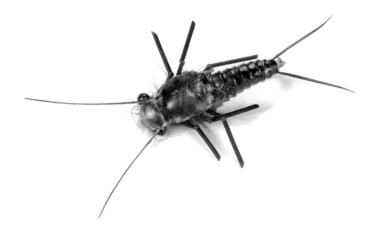

Thread Caddis Larva

Hook: Curved–shank scud or larva hook, sizes 18 to 12.
Head: Small black tungsten bead.
Thread: 6/0 (140 denier) or 3/0 (210 denier).
Rib: Fine wire.

I LIVE IN A SMALL TOWN ON THE COAST OF MAINE, A LITTLE more than an hour from Canada. Our town has a population of about 1,200; it grows by a couple hundred when the summer residents return.

I'm a member of our town's volunteer fire department. Yes, I have all the gear: boots, gloves, fire-resistant pants and coat, and helmet. We get together at least once a week to maintain the fire engines and train.

At one of our weekly meetings, one of the young firefighters—who is also a lobsterman—gave me a couple samples of small larvae and asked if I could tie some more for him. He said these were some of his favorite flies and swore that they catch plenty of fish.

"Sure, I've seen those flies, and I can tie them. You need maybe half a dozen?"

"No, just three or four—if that's okay," he replied.

Well, he didn't know it, but I typically tie flies by the half-dozen. There's no reason I do this—it's just my habit.

The samples he had were red, and although he was fishing them in a stream, I assume they were chironomid larvae imitations. Pattern books list many examples of this fly under different names, and they credit different tiers for designing the fly (if you could call wrapping plain thread on a hook a "design"). No matter: this simple pattern, which even the newest tier can make, is a snap to create.

In addition to red thread, you can switch to bright green, olive, or tan to make convincing caddisfly larvae imitations. For the rib, use fine copper or silver wire, or select olive, black, or brown Ultra Wire. After making a whip-finish and snipping the thread, I apply a drop of black fingernail polish to seal the knot and create a neat thorax.

I tied a dozen flies for my fellow firefighter: six in red and six in bright green. "What can I do for you in return," he asked. I told him that they were simple to tie and to forget about it.

A week later, my friend's pickup pulled into my driveway, he hopped out, and handed me a bucketful of fresh lobsters. We're more than even.

Natural Caddisfly Larva

Hook: Curved-shank scud hook, sizes 16 to 8.
Thread: Black 8/0 (70 denier).
Weight: Medium, flat, lead wire.
Back: Thin Skin.
Body: Hare's ear dubbing.
Rib: Fine monofilament thread.
Head: Black hare's ear dubbing.

DO YOU WANT TO BECOME A BETTER FLY FISHERMAN? DO you want to have a better understanding about what insects live in your local stream? Would you like to know what flies you should concentrate on tying and adding to your arsenal? Then spend some time using a simple seine.

Many fly shops and catalogs sell inexpensive insect seines in a variety of sizes. Select a fine-mesh seine that has two handles. The handles should be long enough that you can press the seine all the way to the streambed in a couple of feet of water. Most of the insects live across the entire streambed, so don't worry about sampling the deeper parts of the stream.

Select a section of the stream to sample. Face downstream and unroll the seine. Place the seine on the streambed, and lightly kick the sand and gravel to dislodge the nymphs and larvae. The insects will flow into the seine. Remove the seine from the water and count your catch. I'll bet you'll have at least a few free-living, non-cased caddisfly larvae.

You'll find examples of wormlike caddisfly larvae in almost all trout streams and rivers. Some of the best anglers in the World Fly Fishing Championship use almost nothing but imitations of these common insects; these flies are just that important. While some other anglers use them—especially experienced guides—these patterns seem to take up little space in many fly boxes. Why?

I think these flies are often overlooked because many novice and even intermediate-level anglers equate nymph fishing with using mayfly and stonefly nymph imitations; they don't think of larvae, at least in terms of fly fishing, as nymphs. But these insects are the immature form of caddisflies, and we use the same methods when fishing imitations. Often, when using a multi-fly setup, you might wish to use a caddisfly larvae with a mayfly or stonefly nymph, and see which pattern the trout prefer.

Aaron Jasper supplied these flies, appropriately called Natural Caddisfly Larva. Tie them in colors and sizes to match the real caddis larvae you find in your seine.

CDC & Hen

Hook: Regular wet-fly hook, sizes 16 to 10.
Thread: 8/0 (70 denier).
Head: Copper bead.
Tail: Turkey biots.
Abdomen: Fox squirrel dubbing.
Thorax: Cul de canard.
Hackle: Hen soft hackle.

THE FULL NAME OF THIS FLY, WHICH EXPERT ANGLER Aaron Jasper sent, is CDC and Hen Hackle Fox Squirrel. That's a mouthful, so I've shortened it to simply CDC & Hen.

Simple wet flies continue playing a vital role in fly fishing; I suspect wet flies are some of the first patterns new anglers learn to use. Even during a hatch when trout are feeding on adult insects on the surface of the water, you will still catch fish—perhaps in greater numbers—casting wet flies.

Most wet flies have little weight added to their construction; at most a little wire is wrapped on the hook shanks before tying the flies. The CDC & Hen hackle, however, sports a bead head. Given the heft of the fly, I think it's probably a copper-colored tungsten bead. The bead will force the fly to settle well below the surface at the end of the cast. When the line tightens, the CDC & Hen will rise through the water column like a real insect struggling to the surface.

Use your favorite five- or six-weight rod when fishing patterns such as the CDC & Hen. I prefer using a floating line and long leader so I can quickly change to a dry fly when the fish begin rising.

I refer to the cul de canard feather, wrapped behind the hackle collar, as the thorax, but you could also think of it as a second hackle. I list it as the thorax in the recipe to clarify where it sits on the hook shank. The CDC fibers will trap air bubbles when casting and imitate the small air bubbles generated under the skin of an emerging insect.

Tie the CDC & Hen in a variety of sizes to match the real mayfly nymph and caddisfly pupae in your local waters.

Medusa

Hook: Daiichi 1120, size 10.
Thread: Red 6/0 (140 denier).
Tail: Red or pink Ultra Chenille and Flex Floss.
Body: Pearl Sili Skin.
Over body: EZ Shape Sparkle Body.
Antennae: Red or pink Ultra Chenille and Flex Floss.
Head: 3/32-inch tungsten bead.

THE MEDUSA IS A CRAZY LOOKING YET INGENIOUS AND very productive pattern. The Medusa was created by North Carolina's Dave Hise for catching trout in run-off conditions, and it came to my attention while editing an article for *Fly Tyer* magazine about favorite flies for catching carp. Freshwater carp have become the latest craze in fly fishing, and many of the flies used in that sport started as trout patterns.

Hise crafted the Medusa as a radical San Juan Worm variant designed for catching trout in high, run-off conditions. The color is great, and all those appendages give the fly great wiggling action in the water.

The Medusa, sporting a heavy tungsten bead head, is an ideal point pattern when fishing a multi-fly rig. The heavy Medusa quickly pulls the other patterns, tied to your leader as droppers, down the water column and into the strike zone. Sometimes the fish will strike those other flies, but many times they will eat the Medusa. And, of course, you can also fish the Medusa as a single fly.

Tie the Medusa in hot pink, red, and tan. Use it in any waters where San Juan Worms and similar patterns catch fish. It's a fun fly that will add a new dimension to your fly tying and fishing.

Christmas Caddisfly Pupa

Hook: Tiemco TMC2457, size 8.
Thread: Red 8/0 (70 denier).
Head: Black tungsten bead.
Abdomen: Red and green Ultra Wire.
Thorax: Emerald-green and red Ice Dub.
Antennae: Wood duck flank fibers.

GEORGE MACIAG, OF ALLENTOWN, PENNSYLVANIA TIED THIS
unusual pattern called the Christmas Caddisfly Pupa. But is it so unusual?

I think George's fly raises an interesting question: What if we designed
flies using the forms of natural insects—nymphs, larvae, and pupae—using
colors typically found on attractor patterns? Would these flies catch fish?

There's no denying that chartreuse is one of the most popular colors for
tying streamers and baitfish imitations, even though this color does not exist
in nature. And the legendary Bob Clouser, the designer of the Clouser Minnow, is fond of saying, "It isn't any use if it doesn't have chartreuse." (Secretly,
I've often thought that I should replace all of the nymphs in my fly box with
patterns tied in chartreuse. They'd probably catch more fish.)

And then along comes Maciag's Christmas Caddis.

The Christmas Caddis is sort of a Royal Coachman in the shape of a
caddisfly pupa. It has a winning form, and the colors certainly make it stand
out, much like every other attractor pattern. It seems to me that the Christmas Caddisfly Pupa features the best of both worlds: the correct shape and
colors that will catch the eye of a trout.

Here's a challenge: Tie several of your favorite nymphs or wet flies
designed to match real insects in natural colors, and then tie several of the
same patterns in red, chartreuse, and colors you would not find in nature.
Fish both types of flies, and see how they work. Does one dressing attract
more trout than the other? Wouldn't you like to know the answer to this
question?

Bactrian Worm

Hook: Tiemco TMC2457, size 6.
Thread: Red 6/0 (140 denier).
Body: Small or medium, red Ultra Chenille.

PETER ELKIN IS A TALENTED SOUTHERN FLY TIER WHO IS an expert at fishing for carp. Peter turned me on to a number of carp patterns, including the Bactrian Worm. In addition to using this pattern to catch carp, this fly is also a killer on trout.

Carp are omnivorous predators with an appetite for benthic and land worms. San Juan Worms aren't new to the fly-fishing scene, and along with various egg patterns, they are often referred to as "junk food" flies, implying that they are perhaps too simple for serious fly anglers. In any event, variations of the venerable San Juan Worm, and even bright egg patterns, are deadly for feeding carp under many conditions. I modify typical San Juan Worms by adding several humps or loops to the flies—hence, the Bactrian tag. This additional bulk makes the fly more visible in silted water. It also slows the sink rate. I like to think that by increasing the mass of the fly's body, carp, notorious for ejecting flies before the hook-set, tend to "gum" this pattern a little longer. Don't hesitate to experiment with body color; while red is a standby, there are times when fluorescent or hot pink, orange, or chartreuse produce strikes. The Bactrian Worm is a perfect dropper pattern when fishing tandem flies. You can add a small bit of lead wire or a small bead to increase the sink rate.

Hot-top Czech Nymph

Hook: Scud hook, sizes 14 to 8.
Weight: Medium, flat, lead wire.
Thread: Black 8/0 (70 denier).
Back: Speckled Thin Skin.
Body: Hare's ear dubbing.
Rib: Fine monofilament thread.
Hot spot: Hare's ear dubbing in the fly, and Loon Hard Head on top of spot.
Head: Black hare's ear dubbing.

HERE IS A TERRIFIC CADDISFLY IMITATION. AS THE NAME implies, anglers using the new Czech nymph-fishing methods created it. They fish long rods and leaders, and caddisfly patterns are among their favorite flies.

Although it looks fairly realistic, it is actually quite easy to tie using materials you'll find in almost any fly shop. If you do not have Thin Skin for the back, substitute with a strip clipped from a plastic freezer bag or even a turkey tail feather.

The participants to the World Fly Fishing Championship pioneered the use of "hot spots" on their nymphs and larvae patterns. A hot spot is a bright, contrasting color that makes a fly stand out in the water. Although a hot spot makes the pattern look less natural, anglers who have added them to their patterns swear they catch more fish.

You can make hot spots using a wide variety of materials: beads, thread, chenille, and floss. The spot on the Hot-top Czech Nymph is made using dubbing and a drop of colored Loon Hard Head on top of the back. Angler Aaron Jasper recommends tying the Hot-top Czech Nymph in brown, tan, olive, or any other basic colors that match the real caddisflies living in your neighborhood trout stream, and adding hot spots to increase the effectiveness of the completed patterns.

Iced Cased Caddis

Hook: Standard nymph hook, sizes 16 to 10.
Head: Black nickel bead, size to match the hook.
Thread: Brown 8/0 (70 denier).
Abdomen: Peacock Ice Dubbing.
Rib: Small copper wire.
Thorax: Insect-green Ice Dubbing.

HERE'S A NEAT LITTLE, EASY-TO-TIE CASED CADDISFLY larva imitation. A lot of cased caddis patterns are made using dull-colored materials, but the body and head of the Iced Cased Caddis are tied using Ice Dubbing. This bright, flashy material makes the pattern stand out in the water and is surprisingly effective at attracting trout. Do the fish eat the fly because they think it's a real caddis larva, or do they strike because it has the correct shape and looks interesting? Who cares?! The Iced Cased Caddis does catch fish.

The bead head adds weight to the fly and makes it sink quickly into the strike zone along the streambed. Although this specific pattern was tied using peacock Ice Dubbing for the body—the cased portion of the imitation—and insect-green Ice Dubbing for the head of the insect, you can use brown Ice Dubbing for the case and light tan for the head. Tie the Iced Cased Caddis in a variety of colors and sizes, and experiment with these flies on your favorite trout stream.

The beauty of the Iced Cased Caddis is that they are inexpensive and easy to tie; a couple packages of dubbing will yield a few dozen flies. And, because they are so simple, you can fish them close to the bottom and not worry too much if you lose a few of them. As a wise angler once said, you're not fishing nymphs and larvae correctly if you don't lose an occasional fly.

Sparrow

Hook: 2X- or 3X-long wet-fly hook, sizes 14 to 4.
Thread: Size 6/0 (140 denier), your choice of color.
Tail: Pheasant or grizzly rump feather.
Body: Dubbing or chenille.
Hackle: Ring-necked pheasant rump feather.
Head: Ring-necked pheasant aftershaft feather.

JACK GARTSIDE, WHO HAILED FROM BOSTON, CREATED many terrific fish-catching flies. Jack received his first fly-tying lesson from baseball legend Ted Williams, and after many decades of innovative tying, he was inducted into the Fly Fishing Hall of Fame. Although Jack's base was in the heart of New England, he traveled far and wide in search of good fishing. He was also a prolific author and tied flies at most of the major East Coast fly-fishing events.

Jack also had a great sense of humor. He would often hang a poster of himself behind his tying table at the fly-fishing shows. In the photo, Jack was wearing a jacket and tie, and a cigarette dangled from the side of his mouth. His head rested on the fingers of his right hand, and a drink was sitting in the foreground. Art Scheck, who edited *Fly Tyer* magazine many years ago, said the photo reminded him of Noël Coward.

Sadly, Jack passed away in 2009, but his great flies live on.

Jack devised the Sparrow while visiting Montana's Madison River. He said he wanted to create an impressionistic pattern that could look like a number of things but nothing in particular. In the original Sparrow, Jack used a blend of rabbit, squirrel, and Antron dubbing for the body, but you may substitute with your favorite dubbing to match the size of fly you are tying. On this Sparrow, the tier used a bright, synthetic dubbing. The hackle and head give the Sparrow terrific swimming action in the water.

According to Jack, when a friend saw a pile of the completed flies, the gentleman said they looked like a flock of sparrows, and the name stuck.

Bitch Creek

Hook: 4X-long streamer hook, sizes 12 to 8.
Thread: Black 6/0 (150 denier).
Tail: White rubber legs.
Body: Black or brown, and orange or yellow Ultra Chenille.
Legs: Brown hackle.
Antennae: White rubber legs.

THE BITCH CREEK STONEFLY NYMPH IS A MODERN CLASSIC pattern. The great George Grant, a legend among Montana fly fishers, once said that the origins of the pattern are a mystery, and to my knowledge, no one is sure who created this fly. Grant contended that the Bitch Creek fly was designed in Montana, but Bitch Creek begins as two small creeks that flow out of the Teton Mountains in Wyoming, meet near the border of Wyoming and Idaho, and become a tributary of the Teton River, which is in turn a tributary of the Henry's Fork of the Snake River. One wonders if the Bitch Creek fly wasn't really created in Idaho?

Of course, where the Bitch Creek fly was designed does not matter; it is important to us because it catches fish.

The body of the fly is woven using two pieces of Ultra Chenille; the light-colored material goes on the bottom of the hook to create the belly, and the dark chenille is placed on top to make the back. Select colors of Ultra Chenille to match the large stonefly nymphs in your favorite waters. The rubber legs used to form the tails and antennae make the pattern very durable; they bend out of the way when a trout eats the fly.

While you can use the Bitch Creek to match a stonefly nymph, many anglers use the fly as a general searching pattern. It has the general form of a stonefly, but given the multi-colored body and appendages, the trout might just as easily mistake it for some other form of food.

Red Squirrel Nymph

Hook: Mustad 9671, sizes 12 to 8.
Thread: Brown 6/0 (140 denier).
Tail: Body hair from a red fox squirrel.
Body: Red fox squirrel dubbing.
Rib: Fine gold tinsel.
Hackle: English partridge.

IT'S HARD TO TALK ABOUT GOOD FLIES FOR CATCHING
trout and not mention Dave Whitlock's great patterns. The Red Squirrel
Nymph is one of his best, and it has become a favorite of many anglers.
If you're an experienced fly tier, making the Red Squirrel Nymph will
be easy; if you're fairly new to tying, but have completed a basic fly-tying
course, then you have all the skills necessary for completing this fish-
catching pattern.

Dave Whitlock is a legendary fly tier and angler. He has written many
articles and books, is a fine artist and illustrator, and has been inducted into
the Fly Fishing Hall of Fame. Dave is also one of the friendliest and warmest
people you could ever hope to meet.

While many wet flies are sleek, the Red Squirrel Nymph has a fuller
profile. I suspect the fly's beefy silhouette and orange-brown coloration
suggest a stonefly nymph to the trout. Even though it might perform well
as a nymph, most anglers fish it using the classic across-and-down stream
approach, and swing the fly through the water using a tight line.

Rather than the hackle collar, some tiers make the collar using red
squirrel body hair placed in a dubbing loop. They spread a small amount of
hair in the loop and then wrap the material around the hook. This creates
an even fuller appearance that certainly imitates a nymph. This technique,
however, requires an entire squirrel shin and is a little difficult to perform.
Wrapping a hackle around the hook is far easier, and the fly is just as durable.

Microstone

Hook: Curved-shank nymph hook, sizes 14 to 8.
Thread: Black 6/0 (140 denier).
Head: Black tungsten bead.
Tail: Brown, mottled Centipede Legs or rubber legs, and a tuft of Antron yarn.
Abdomen: Tying thread, black floss, or black Micro Tubing.
Rib: Gold wire.
Thorax: Black Ice Dubbing or a similar material.
Wing case: Black Thin Skin.
Collar: Black Ice Dubbing or a similar material, wrapped behind the bead.

NOT ALL SUCCESSFUL STONEFLY IMITATIONS ARE COMPLI-
cated. Vince Wilcox's Microstone is a model of simplicity, yet it contains all
the elements that attract the attention of the trout.

The splayed tails and legs make the pattern stand out in the water. The
two-tone abdomen creates very realistic segmentation. The bead head and
wire rib add enough weight to draw the fly quickly to the bottom. And, like
most of my favorite flies, the Microstone is simple and inexpensive to tie,
so I can fish it close to the streambed with confidence. If I snag and lose a
couple of flies, I can quickly make more.

Tie the Microstone in black, brown, and golden stone colors. Make the
pattern in smaller sizes to imitate larger species of mayflies. If you need a
slightly heavier fly, tie the abdomen using two pieces of Ultra Wire, such as
black and gold, or brown and yellow. Tie the tag ends to the hook and wrap
the wires simultaneously up the shank; the pieces of wire should lay neatly
together to create a segmented body. This solid fly will sink quickly to the
streambed.

Whether using one or two strands of wire, make sure the tag ends extend
from the base of the tail to the back of the bead head. This will create a level
underbody so you can tie a neat fly.

Buggy Stone Nymph

Hook: 4X–long streamer hook, sizes 12 to 8.
Thread: Brown 6/0 (140 denier).
Tail: Brown goose or turkey biots.
Body: Brown dubbing.
Rib: Brown Larva Lace or Swannundaze.
Wing case: Brown turkey tail feather.
Antennae: Brown goose or turkey biots.

THIS PATTERN REMINDS ME OF SOME OF THE STONEFLY imitations featured in the aptly-named book *Stoneflies*, written by Carl Richards, Doug Swisher, and Fred Arbona. That volume, which came out in 1980, has withstood the test of history; the classics live forever.

In *Stoneflies*, the authors demonstrate how to tie an imitation that emphasizes the shape of the body, the tail and antennae, and the wing case; prominent legs were not a part of the pattern. I generally take great pains to add legs to my stonefly imitations, but the silhouette of the Buggy Stone Nymph is very convincing and is ample to fool most trout.

Select angora or a similar shaggy dubbing for the body. If you want to stick with a commercial brand readily available in realistic-looking colors, consider using Mercer's Buggy Nymph Dubbing (how appropriate for this pattern) or Wapsi's Stonefly Life Cycle Dubbing. In addition to dark brown, tie the Buggy Stone Nymph in black and gold. If you wish to tie an imitation of a golden stonefly, make the body using golden-yellow dubbing and brown Larva Lace for the rib—this combination creates excellent segmentation.

When making the body, it's not enough to just wrap dubbing up the hook shank. Note the naturally tapered silhouette; this is key to the effectiveness of the fly. Wrap any lead weighting wire on the front two-thirds of the shank to create a tapered underbody. And place only a fine pinch of fur in the dubbing loop near the base of the tail.

If the individual wing pads are too difficult to make, substitute with a single strip of turkey tail feather folded over the top of the thorax.

Brassie

Hook: Curved-shank scud hook or a regular wet-fly hook, size 20 or 18.
Thread: Black 8/0 (70 denier).
Body: Ultra Wire.
Thorax: Peacock herl.

HERE IS A CLASSIC RED BRASSIE; THIS IS A FAVORITE PATTERN of thousands of fly fishers. It mimics a tiny chironomid larva.

Although this specific example does not have a bead head, many tiers add a bead to give the fly a little more heft so it sinks quickly. This is especially helpful if you fish the Brassie in still waters. Some knowledgeable anglers fish trout ponds using extremely long leaders so their flies dangle just above the weed line; sometimes a leader will measure up to 30 feet long. A tungsten bead speeds the decent of the fly. Our Brassie would be ideal for fishing closer to the surface as the insects are emerging to turn into winged adults.

Although red is a popular color, use anodized Ultra Wire, which you'll find in almost any fly shop, to tie Brassies in other colors; black, olive, or brown are also effective.

If you wish, you may add a very short tag of pearl Krystal Flash as a wing bud. And, in addition to a black bead head, use a silver or white bead to imitate the gas bubble on the head of a real emerging chironomid larva.

The Brassie is a standard pattern, but the recipe is not written in stone. Subtle variations yield a wide variety of fish-catching flies.

Cosseboom

Hook: 2X-long wet-fly hook, sizes 14 to 8.
Thread: Red 8/0 (70 denier).
Tag: Flat, silver tinsel.
Tail: Yellow floss.
Body: Yellow floss.
Rib: Flat, silver tinsel.
Wing: Gray squirrel tail hair.
Hackle: Lemon yellow.

WHAT, YOU MIGHT WONDER, IS THE COSSEBOOM DOING IN a collection of wet flies and nymphs? After all, it was originally created as a hair-wing Atlantic salmon pattern. Who cares? When tied in smaller sizes, it and many other simplified salmon flies catch trout, bass, panfish, and other species of fish.

You might insist that we toss out the Cosseboom. But then, should we also strike the Royal Coachman—which is also tied a streamer—from our list? We could go on and on in making these sorts of judgments. But doing so would miss the point: when scaled to the right sizes, many patterns make splendid wet flies.

I suspect that at least part of the history of fancy wet flies originates in tying Atlantic salmon patterns. How else do you explain the use of exotic materials and fancy colors? Flip over to the pages about the Silver Doctor; that pattern would be at home on a trout pond or a salmon river.

When prospecting for native trout, I sometimes use attractor patterns. These are flies that represent nothing in nature, but encourage a fish to strike out of anger, territoriality, curiosity, or some other fishy instinct. This small, yellow Cosseboom—there are many color variations of this fly—is an ideal attractor pattern. Get a good book about Atlantic salmon or steelhead patterns, and you'll have dozens of candidates for tying trout and panfish wet flies.

High Lake Larry

Hook: Bent–shank scud hook, size 14.
Thread: Blue and brown 6/0 (140 denier).
Abdomen: Tying thread.
Rib: Gunmetal-blue and silver Ultra Wire.
Thorax: Poul Jørgensen SLF Dubbing, electric blue.
Hackle: Brahma hen hackle, brown.

IT'S SUCH A PLEASURE TO INTRODUCE A YOUNG AND gifted tier, and it's a double pleasure when it is a talented young woman.

Erin Block is just beginning to make waves in the fly-fishing world. She has already made her own split-bamboo fly rod and is the author of a book titled *The View From Coal Creek*. Erin is also a terrific fly tier, and she is a pattern designer for Umpqua Feather Merchants.

Erin grew up in Nebraska and moved to Colorado some years ago. She's taken to her new home, and enjoys hiking, fishing, and a variety of other outdoor sports.

High Lake Larry is a fine example of one of her original patterns for fishing Alpine lakes and ponds. The fly is an ideal blend of traditional and modern materials. It is understated yet would stand out in a crowd of wet flies. It is perfectly and delicately tied and would catch trout anywhere.

Brahma hackles come from a Brahma chicken. This breed was developed in the United States from large chickens imported from China. It was the principal meat bird in the US from the mid-1800s until about 1930, and it is still considered a fine winter egg layer. Fly tiers use the beautiful, mottled feathers of brown and buff Brahma chickens to tie dry and especially wet flies. A high quality Brahma hen cape—the pelt from the neck of the bird—is one of the best bargains in fly tying. Brahma hen hackles are a fine substitute for English partridge: the Brahma cape typically has more feathers, and the quills are usually much stronger.

Erin tied the hackle of the High Lake Larry using a Brahma hen hackle.

Bird's Nest

Hook: 2X- or 3X-long wet-fly hook, sizes 16 to 8.
Thread: Size 8/0 (70 denier).
Tail: Wood duck flank fibers.
Abdomen: Australian opossum dubbing.
Rib: Fine copper wire.
Thorax: Australian opossum dubbing.
Legs: Wood duck flank fibers.
Collar: Australian opossum dubbing.

FLY TIER AND ANGLER CAL BIRD OWNED A FLY SHOP IN SAN Francisco in the 1940s and 1950s. In the late 1950s, he created a new pattern called the Bird's Nest. This fly is designed to imitate a caddisfly pupa for use on the Truckee River. Since the invention of the Caddis Sparkle Pupa and other, more realistic patterns, the Bird's Nest is now considered more of an attractor fly, yet it is still extremely effective at catching trout.

Many fly recipes change over time. For example, the original pattern for the Bird's Nest called for a dubbing blend of Australian opossum and dyed coyote, but you may tie a very fine fly using only opossum. The traditional Bird's Nest, which we see here, is tied in tan, but you can also tie the fly in cream, brown, or olive to match a wide variety of caddis pupae.

The best Bird's Nests have a shaggy, ratty appearance. The dubbing fibers catch small air bubbles to match the appearance of emerging caddisflies. After tying the fly and snipping the thread, lightly pick out the dubbing using a bodkin.

Although this fly was first designed for fishing in California, it works wherever you find caddisflies. The Bird's Nest is also a fine imitation of many small mayflies, and of course, you can also use it as a searching pattern when no hatching insects are visible.

Bethke's Pink Squirrel Nymph

Hook: Scud hook, sizes 16 to 12.
Head: Small gold bead.
Thread: Pink 6/0 (140 denier).
Tail: Pearl Krystal Flash.
Body: Hare's ear or squirrel dubbing.
Rib: Fine red Ultra Wire.
Collar: Pink Ultra Chenille or Ice Dubbing.

ALTHOUGH A GROWING NUMBER OF ANGLERS ARE ADDING hot spots of pink and other bright colors to their nymphs—flip through the pages of this book to find examples of these flies—we've known for a long time that flashy flies work best during the winter. The fish have slowed down, and it sometimes takes a slightly brighter fly to encourage them to strike.

John Bethke, a fly designer from Wisconsin (the anglers in that part of the country know about fishing during the winter) created the Pink Squirrel. It's a pattern that works for trout, steelhead, and even panfish, and it's popular throughout the Midwest and Rocky Mountains. Bethke, who has taught fly fishing at the University of Wisconsin-LaCrosse, wanted a pattern that would sink quickly and stand out in the flow. In addition to the heavy bead head, place several wraps of .020-inch lead wire or a non-toxic substitute behind the bead before tying the fly. This weight makes the Pink Squirrel descend through the water column very quickly to where the lethargic winter trout are lying.

At first blush, the Pink Squirrel looks like an imitation of a caddisfly pupa, but it was not designed to imitate any specific insect. Think of the Pink Squirrel as an attractor pattern, and use it whenever you are searching the water for fish during the winter or any other time of the year.

Edwards's Cased Caddisfly Larva

Hook: 3X–long wet–fly hook, sizes 10 to 6.
Thread: Bright-green or tan 3/0 (210 denier).
Body: Deer hair or dubbing.
Head: Tying thread.
Legs: Partridge or coq de Leon hackle fibers, or the butt ends of pheasant tail fibers.

I AM A GREAT ADMIRER OF OLIVER EDWARDS'S FLY patterns. Oliver, who lives in England, is a leading proponent of what are sometimes called "fishing realistics." These are flies that closely match the real foods trout eat, yet the patterns require only common tying materials and are surprisingly easy to make. If you want to learn more, be sure to read his groundbreaking book, *Oliver Edwards' Flytyer's Masterclass*. Don't be overwhelmed by the word "masterclass." Any tier with intermediate-level skills can make the flies, and it also offers a lot of great ideas for novice tiers.

Oliver tied this Cased Caddisfly Larva, and you will be surprised just how easy it is to make. First, wrap the hook with lead wire or a non-toxic substitute. Start the thread near the end of the hook shank, and make a large dubbing loop. Clip a large bunch of deer hair, clean out the fuzzy fibers at the bottom of the bunch, and spread the hairs in the loop. Spin the loop closed; this will create a long brush of deer hair. Wrap the loop two-thirds to three-fourths of the way up the hook, tie off and clip the excess piece of loop, and temporarily tie off and snip the thread. Next, use heavy tying scissors to cut the hair close to the shank to create the caddis case.

Restart the thread on the hook after making the caddis case. Wrap the thread between the case and hook eye to make the head of the caddis larva, and tie on your choice of legs. Finally, here's a neat trick: when you're ready to tie off the fly, first color about three inches of thread with a brown permanent marker. When you wrap the thread, the brown marker creates the nose of the caddis worm!

Play around with these ideas, and you'll quickly discover how easy it is to make the Cased Caddisfly Larva.

Bead-head Stonefly Nymph

Hook: 2X-long nymph hook, sizes 16 to 12.
Head: Small, gold bead.
Thread: Yellow 8/0 (70 denier).
Tail: Yellow goose or turkey biots.
Abdomen: Pale-tan rabbit dubbing with the guard hairs removed.
Rib: Fine, copper or brown Ultra Wire.
Back and wing case: Pale-cinnamon turkey.
Thorax: Pale-tan rabbit dubbing.
Hackle: Pale-ginger hen hackle.
Collar: Pale-tan rabbit dubbing with the guard hairs removed.

IT'S EASY TO BECOME CAPTIVATED BY LARGE STONEFLY nymph imitations; they're easy and fun to tie, and they look nice lined up in a fly box. But, you should also carry a selection of patterns to match small stonefly nymphs. Spend time collecting insects in your favorite trout stream, and you'll find nymphs in hook sizes 16 to 12. On some rivers, these insects are very common, and the fish key in to them.

Rather than scaling a large stonefly imitation down to sizes 16 to 12, it is often simpler to select a pattern that has the key attributes of a stonefly, yet is easier to tie. The Bead-head Stonefly Nymph, which is a fairly generic fly, is a good example. Make this pattern in pale yellow, brown, and dark gray to match almost all small stoneflies.

For example, what anglers call yellow and lime sallies are commonly found flittering across the surface of the water during midsummer early in the evening. Fish a fly such as the Bead-head Stonefly Nymph earlier in the day when the hatches reach their peak. Remember that stoneflies do not emerge in the flowing water like mayflies and caddisflies, but crawl out of the water onto rocks and streamside vegetation to turn into winged adults. You can use a nymph during the height of the swarm and catch fish, but the trout are really keying in to the flying stoneflies that fall onto the water to lay their eggs.

Pregnant Scud

Hook: Bent-shank scud hook, size 14 or 12.
Thread: Olive 8/0 (70 denier).
Bead: Orange glass bead.
Body: Light-olive Sow-Scud Dubbing.
Shellback: A strip clipped from a plastic freezer bag.
Rib: 5X clear monofilament.

ANDREW PULS, WHO WAS A GUIDE IN MONTANA, FIRST
called my attention to the Pregnant Scud. Other than a few dry-fly imitations that have small egg sacs tied to the ends of their abdomens, I had never
heard of a fly designed to imitate an egg-laying insect or crustacean. The
Pregnant Scud is a unique pattern.

According to Andrew, who earned his masters degree as a fisheries biolo-
gist, there are sound reasons for tying the Pregnant Scud. Scientific research
has demonstrated that orange segmented scuds suffer increased predation
from trout, probably due to the crustaceans' increased visibility in the water.
The orange bead in the middle of the body of the Pregnant Scud mimics a
scud that is either full of eggs or has become infected by a parasite.

The Pregnant Scud works especially well when you need a pattern containing a dash of flash or when fishing heavily pressured water. The fly has
a unique, realistic look that most other anglers overlook. It will give you an
advantage when fishing waters containing real scuds.

Wapsi Fly offers a wide variety of glass fly-tying beads; look for these in
your neighborhood fly shop. If your favorite fly-tying emporium doesn't
stock glass beads, head to your local discount retailer or craft store; these
stores always stock glass beads in various sizes and colors.

Aftershaft Scud

Hook: Curved-shank nymph hook, sizes 16 to 12.
Thread: Olive 8/0 (70 denier).
Tail: Gray, hen saddle hackle fibers.
Body: Olive Sow-Scud Dubbing.
Legs: A Hungarian partridge or pheasant aftershaft feather.
Shellback: Olive Larva Lace Dry Fly Foam or a substitute.
Rib: 5X clear monofilament.

OVER SEVERAL DECADES OF FLY FISHING, I HAVE BECOME convinced that movement—a natural swimming or sometimes struggling motion—is the most important attribute of a good subsurface pattern. Try explaining the fish-taking ability of a Woolly Bugger. It's said that the fly imitates a leech, but I have never seen a leech full of bristly legs. The Woolly Bugger catches fish because the marabou tail and spiral-wrapped hackle create great fish-enticing action when drawn through the water. It's not that hard to understand.

The Aftershaft Scud also has good swimming action in the water. The aftershaft feather, taken from the base of a partridge or pheasant body feather, huffs and puffs when the fly is slowly stripped through the water. The feather fibers make the fly seem alive, and the trout love it.

When tying the Aftershaft Scud, the aftershaft feather is placed between the body and shellback of the fly. The shellback protects the frail quill of the feather and makes the pattern quite durable. Here we see the olive Aftershaft Scud, but you can also tie the pattern in gray and light tan. Fish the pattern around weed beds containing real scuds.

Clearwater Callibaetis

Hook: Regular wet-fly hook, size 12.
Thread: Olive 8/0 (70 denier).
Tail: Pheasant tail fibers.
Body: Light-olive Ice Dubbing or a substitute.
Rib: Fine copper wire.
Back and wing case: A very small bunch of pheasant tail fibers.
Legs: Mallard flank fibers, dyed yellow.

THE STILLWATER CALLIBAETIS IS A PATTERN BY BRIAN Chan and Philip Rowley, two of Canada's best fly designers. In 2014, they were awarded a *Fly Tyer* Magazine Lifetime Achievement Award for their work.

Callibaetis, which belong to the Baetidae family of mayflies, are found in many trout ponds and lakes. They are prolific and provide an almost constant source of food for the fish. Although most anglers go armed with dry flies for matching the hatching duns, they will catch more trout using matching nymphs or subsurface emergers before the hatch. The *Callibaetis* hatch can start as early as April on low-elevation lakes and continue through October, so it pays to always carry a selection of matching flies: nymphs, emergers, and duns.

Baetidae nymphs are strong swimmers and can rise to the surface quickly. Whether you use this fly or another imitation, employ a stripping retrieve, and hang on!

Although the color of most Baetidae nymphs match the lake bottom and are usually shades of brown, Brian and Phil tied this Clearwater Callibaetis in a light olive. And, to brighten the pattern even further, they selected Ice Dubbing for the body. This fly stands out in the water and is very visible to the trout, and they love it.

The Stillwater Callibaetis is an especially fine fly for beginning tiers possessing basic fly-tying skills.

Woolly Worm

Hook: Regular or 2X-long wet-fly hook, sizes 10 to 6.
Thread: Black or olive 6/0 (140 denier).
Tail: Soft hackle fibers or marabou tips.
Body: Peacock herl or narrow chenille.
Hackle: A hen body feather.

THE CLASSIC WOOLLY WORM, A PATTERN THAT HAS EXISTED for many decades, is the Woolly Bugger's little brother. If you've ever taken a beginning fly-tying class, you must have made at least one—perhaps both— of these patterns. Suffice it to say that if you can tie one of them you'll be able to tie the other, and you'll be set to catch a barrel full of fish.

The Woolly Worm is a loosely defined, adaptable pattern. Tie it in your favorite colors: tan, olive, brown, black, yellow, and chartreuse all work well. You can use hackle fibers for the tail or substitute with the soft tips of a marabou feather; the marabou gives the fly additional swimming action in the water. Many tiers use chenille for the body, but three or four strands of peacock herl wrapped up the hook for the body give the Woolly Worm a nice radiance.

The Woolly Worm looks like nothing in nature (the same can be said of the Woolly Bugger streamer), yet it is very buggy. And the soft hackle fibers and tail give it a terrific swimming action. It must look like some sort of swimming or emerging nymph to the fish.

I know a lot of advanced anglers look down their noses at the lowly Woolly Worm, and they are missing out on the fish-catching potential of a time-honored fly.

Skunk Caddis

Hook: 2X- or 3X-long wet-fly hook, sizes 12 to 8.
Thread: Black 6/0 (140 denier).
Body: Skunk tail hair.
Rib: Copper wire.
Hackle: Black soft hackle.

THE SKUNK CADDIS IS ONE OF THE MOST UNUSUAL PATTERNS
in this little collection of favorite flies.

The two-tone, black-and-white body is tied using the hair from the
tail of a striped skunk. Really! No, I'm not suggesting that you find a dead
skunk in the middle of the road—that would stink to high heaven. (Fans
of the old Dr. Demento syndicated radio show will get that reference.) If
you look hard, however, you might find skunk tails at a fly shop. What's the
source of these tails?

Believe it or not, but some trappers target skunks for two reasons. First,
fur buyers will purchase skunk pelts for a few dollars apiece. Second, skunk
musk is an important ingredient for lures used to attract and catch other
fur-bearing animals such as martens and fishers. A seasoned trapper will
blend a concoction of ingredients, like spoiled fish and raw meat, and add a
dash of skunk musk. He'll place a dash of this lure close to his trap to attract
his quarry. Inevitably, the tails from the trapped skunks are sold (of course
they are first cleaned and processed), and some make their way onto fly
tying benches.

If you can't find a skunk tail, you can tie a very similar-looking Skunk
Caddis using bucktail, dyed black, and natural-white bucktail. The wire rib
protects the hair—skunk or bucktail—from breaking when fishing the fly,
and the soft-hackle collar gives the pattern fine swimming action.

Pheasant-tail Nymph

Hook: 2X-long wet-fly hook, sizes 22 to 10.
Thread: Fine, copper wire.
Tail: Pheasant tail fiber tips.
Abdomen: Pheasant tail fibers and copper wire.
Rib: Fine, copper wire.
Thorax: Peacock herl.
Wing case: Pheasant tail fibers.

DOES THE RECIPE FOR THE PHEASANT-TAIL NYMPH SEEM repetitive? It is: Almost the entire pattern is tied using a small slip of fibers clipped from a ring-necked pheasant tail feather.

Frank Sawyer, an English river keeper, created this popular and extremely utilitarian pattern. The pheasant tail fibers, used for the tail, abdomen, and wing case, give the pattern a realistic mottled-brown coloration. Sawyer twisted the pheasant tail fibers and the wire together and wrapped the two up the hook to create the abdomen of the fly; the wire strengthens the frail pheasant fibers. Sawyer also used the wire as a substitute for thread. He even used the wire to wrap the head of the fly.

Today you'll find a number of variations of the Pheasant-tail Nymph. Most commonly, rather than twisting the pheasant fibers and wire together before wrapping the abdomen, the fibers are wrapped about halfway up the hook shank and then the wire is wrapped up the hook as a rib. I prefer this method because it gives the finished fly a more segmented appearance. Most tiers also make the "PT," as it is often called, using thread; I also prefer using thread. And finally, like on most contemporary nymphs, your neighborhood fly shop probably carries Bead-head Pheasant-tail Nymphs. Adding a bead is a simple way to add weight and a dash of sparkle to this fine fly.

Rather than using peacock herl for the thorax, you can substitute with hare's mask dubbing. The guard hairs in the material do a fine job of imitating the legs on a real nymph. I prefer using dubbing for the thorax to increase the realism of the pattern.

Micro Mayfly

Hook: Regular nymph or wet-fly hook, sizes 20 to 14.
Head: Copper or other metal bead, size to match the hook.
Thread: Size 8/0 (70 denier), color to match the fly.
Tail: Ring-necked pheasant fibers.
Abdomen: Flashabou.
Rib: Small, copper wire.
Thorax: Your favorite brand of nymph dubbing for tying smaller flies.
Wing case: Mottled turkey tail feather, coated with a drop of epoxy.
Wing case stripe: Flashabou.
Legs: Ring-necked pheasant tail fibers.
Head: Your favorite brand of nymph dubbing for tying smaller flies.

OVER THE PAST TWENTY YEARS OR SO, SUBSURFACE IMITA-
tions have gotten progressively smaller to match the real insects living in our
favorite waters. There's nothing more impressive than looking in a fly box
filled with small nymphs and wets; they look like tiny soldiers lined up for
inspection. Mike Mercer's Micro Mayfly series of flies are fine examples of
these diminutive patterns.

I did not recommend colors for the materials listed in the pattern recipe;
select any that meet your fancy. Mike prefers brown, olive, yellow, and even
ruby. However, you can just as easily tie Micro Mayflies in black, tan, and
any other color.

The Micro Mayfly is a bright pattern, and the flash is designed to attract
the attention of the fish. Mike uses Flashabou for the slender abdomen
and folds a single piece of narrow Flashabou over the top of the wing case
before applying a drop of epoxy. There is a theory that the flash in the wing
case mimics the air bubble in the wing case of a real emerging-mayfly
nymph, and many fly designers now incorporate this feature in some of
their best patterns.

If you prefer duller flies with less flash, simply substitute floss or tying
thread for the Flashabou in the abdomen. You could also make the abdomen using a stripped hackle quill or turkey biot. Experiment with colors
and materials, and have fun!

Big Dave's Caddisfly Pupa

Hook: 2X-long wet-fly hook, sizes 12 to 8.
Thread: Brown 6/0 (140 denier).
Abdomen: Nymph Skin, colored with a permanent marker.
Rib: Brown 3/0 (210 denier) tying thread.
Thorax: Hare "E" Ice Dub or squirrel dubbing.
Legs and antennae: English partridge or coq de Leon hen hackle.
Head: Pheasant aftershaft feather.

THIS IS ANOTHER ONE OF MY PATTERNS. I GOT THE IDEA for this fly while bobbing along in a float tube early one evening just as the sun was setting below the horizon. Large caddisflies were scampering across the surface of the water, and the trout eagerly attacked the meaty morsels. While enjoying the fast dry fly action, I noticed the empty pupal shucks floating in the surface film. It occurred to me that if I had used an appropriate imitation before the hatch, I could have enjoyed a couple more hours of excellent fishing. Returning home, I set about tying a large caddisfly pupa.

I thought the new fly should have a couple of important attributes. First, it should have the general silhouette of a real caddisfly pupa. Second, due to its large size, I thought the abdomen should have proper segmentation. And finally, I like a fly tied with materials that make it look alive in the water.

Making the body using Nymph Skin or a similar material gives the abdomen a lifelike shape. Wrapping the Nymph Skin up the hook shank creates a segmented appearance, but I also wrap a piece of stout thread over the body as a rib to enhance the segmentation. And finally, the head, legs, and antennae give my Caddisfly Pupa a lifelike, pulsating action.

I fish the Caddisfly Pupa a couple of hours before the expected hatch using an intermediate-sinking line; I'm exploring for trout feeding on the rising pupa. If I get few or no strikes, I switch to a fast-sinking line and fish the fly deeper in the water column. When I see swirls but no trout breaking through the surface of the water, I change to a floating line. Finally, when I see adult caddisflies on the surface and actively feeding fish, I will change to some sort of caddis dry fly.

Bead-head Royal Coachman

Hook: 2X-long wet-fly hook, size 12 or 10.
Thread: Red 3/0 (210 denier).
Tail: Golden pheasant tippet fibers.
Body: Peacock herl and red tying thread.
Wing: White marabou.
Collar: Brown, English partridge, or coq de Leon hackle.

THE ROYAL COACHMAN HAS BEEN TIED AS A WET FLY, DRY fly, and, of course, there's the Royal Wulff, which has been called the unofficial bird of Montana. In the book *101 Favorite Dry Flies*, I included a photo of a Royal Coachman—or maybe it is an extra-heavily dressed Royal Wulff—tied by Canada's Warren Duncan for catching Atlantic salmon; that is one of the bushiest flies I have ever seen.

The Bead-head Royal Coachman is my version of this iconic pattern. This pattern is one of my go-to searching flies when fishing for local brook trout. While it's dandy for fishing streams, it is also a fine choice when exploring trout ponds.

The bead gives the fly a bit of flash, but more importantly, the Bead-head Royal Coachman settles into the water and comes alive when you tighten the line. I strip the fly through the water, and the fish eagerly strike.

The purpose of the bead head on this fly is obvious, but I believe the white marabou wing is the key to the pattern's success. The soft marabou huffs and puffs in the water with lifelike swimming action. The soft-hackle collar adds to the swimming action.

I also know the white is important, because when fishing waters with smaller trout, I will feel a lot of tugs but hook fewer fish. The trout seem to grab the wing and miss the sharp hook, the lucky devils.

This Bead-head Royal Coachman actually came from my fly box, and I'll put it back for my next fishing trip.

Bead-head
Ovipositing Caddisfly

Hook: Regular or 2X-long wet-fly hook, sizes 14 to 10.
Head: Small, black bead.
Thread: Size 8/0 (70 denier).
Abdomen: Goose or turkey biot.
Thorax: Rabbit dubbing with the guard hairs removed.
Underwing: Rabbit dubbing with the guard hairs removed.
Wing: Medallion Sheeting or a substitute.
Legs: Partridge hackle fibers.
Antennae: Two long, fine hairs.

STUDYING FLY PATTERNS FOR TROUT, ESPECIALLY WET
flies and nymphs, often requires some knowledge of entomology. No, you
don't have to study as though you are going to take a test in bug Latin, but
you should become informed about the basic stages of the lifecycles of
aquatic insects.

In *101 Favorite Dry Flies*, we spend time talking about patterns that match
the egg-laying stages of mayflies and stoneflies. I mention experiences when
the fish seemed most interested in eating imitations of mayfly spinners and
egg-laying stoneflies. If you didn't have the right flies, you would catch far
fewer trout. Of course, those patterns were dry flies.

Some species of caddisflies remain on top of the water when laying eggs,
and you'll often see them skittering and hopping on the surface. Other species, however, actually break through the surface and swim *down* the water
column to lay their eggs. What an extraordinary thing!

For example, *Glossosoma* caddisflies are some of the most common caddisflies in California's Sierra Nevada Mountains. About an hour after sunset,
the insects return to the water to lay their eggs. The insects actually shroud
themselves in tiny air bubbles for the trip underwater. This is when they are
most available to the trout.

The Bead-head Ovipositing Caddisfly is a great pattern for matching
Glossosoma and similar caddisflies. Fish it similar to a wet fly. If you wish to
add the air bubble, rub a small amount of powder dry-fly floatant on the
pattern; the heavy bead will force the fly under the water, but the floatant
will create a realistic-looking air bubble.

October Caddis Wet Fly

Hook: Curved-shank nymph hook or a 2X-long wet-fly hook, size 8 or 6.
Thread: Orange 8/0 (70 denier).
Body: Light-orange rabbit dubbing with the guard hairs removed, or your favorite brand of wet-fly dubbing.
Rib: Pearl tinsel.
Hackle: Partridge.
Head: A pheasant aftershaft feather.

HMM, HOW DID THE OCTOBER CADDISFLY GET ITS NAME?

Of course: it hatches and is of greatest importance to fly fisherman during the month of October. Actually, you will find the October caddis on the water from late September through early November. Although they do not emerge in great numbers, these insects do provide fine fly-fishing action during a time of the season when few other insects are hatching.

Dicosmoecus caddisflies are most common in the Pacific Northwest. Although I have occasionally found imitations of this insect in the Northeast, it is my impression that they ended up in those fly shops by mistake. The October caddis is far better known in British Columbia, Washington, Oregon, and northern California.

In addition to hatching during the fall, the October caddis is a rather large insect; it is certainly bigger than many other caddisflies. Tie the October Caddis Wet Fly—and your favorite caddis dry fly—in hook size 8 or 6. Cast it across-and-down stream, and fish the fly like any other wet fly. The trout will mistake your pattern for an emerging caddisfly pupa.

Use the October Caddis Wet Fly as a basic design for creating other caddisfly pupa imitations. Tie the pattern in other sizes and colors to match almost all of the emerging caddisflies you encounter wherever you fish.

Montana Stone

Hook: 3X- or 4X-long nymph hook, sizes 10 to 4.
Thread: Black 6/0 (140 denier).
Tail: Two black, brown, or olive spade hackle tips or hair.
Abdomen: Black, brown, or olive chenille.
Thorax: Yellow, orange, or olive chenille.
Hackle: Black, brown, or olive.

THE MONTANA STONE IS A TERRIFIC PATTERN FOR
beginning fly tiers, but you'll also find it in the boxes of many experienced
anglers.

The Montana Stone is a stylized imitation of a large stonefly nymph.
While it was first used in Montana, you'll find huge stoneflies across the
United States and Canada. It's a little-known fact, but some of the huge
stoneflies living in Labrador's trout rivers rival stoneflies found anywhere.
Although generally not thought of as nymph-fishing waters, I have used
stonefly imitations on Labrador's Eagle River with excellent results.

The most common Montana Stone is tied with a black abdomen and
yellow thorax; the fly tied with an orange thorax is also fairly common. But
you can tie a wide variety of stonefly imitations using the pattern's simple
design: brown, olive, or some combination of colors to match the insects
living in your favorite waters.

Some tiers use spade hackle for the tails of the Montana Stone. These
are the feathers on the edges of a dry fly cape. The fibers are rather stiff, and
they make durable tails. You can also strip a small bunch of fibers from a
spade hackle for making the tail on a small nymph or dry fly.

Remember that the Montana Stone must sink. Wrap lead wire or a non-
toxic substitute on the hook shank before making the body of the fly.

Hot-belly
Pheasant-tail Nymph

Hook: 2X-long wet-fly hook, sizes 20 to 12.
Head: Gold bead.
Thread: Brown 8/0 (70 denier).
Tail: Pheasant tail fibers.
Abdomen: Pheasant tail fibers.
Rib: Fine gold wire.
Thorax: Ice Dubbing.
Wing case: Pheasant tail fibers.

YOU CAN GIVE NEW LIFE TO OLDER PATTERNS USING modern fly-tying materials. In this case, we have a classic Pheasant-tail Nymph spruced up with a brightly dubbed thorax.

Flip through the pages of this book and you'll find patterns sporting "hot spots." The hot spot is a bright color in the fly that is supposed to attract the attention of the trout. While most flies with hot spots are new patterns, you can add a hot spot to a Pheasant-tail Nymph or most of our other favorite patterns.

Ice Dubbing is a synthetic material. While this example of the Hot-belly Pheasant-tail Nymph has a pink thorax, Ice Dubbing also comes in purple, red, chartreuse, yellow, and other colors; use any of these to create a variety of Hot-belly Pheasant-tails.

The trick to tying a Pheasant-tail Nymph—a Hot-belly or the classic pattern—is how you apply the tail fibers to the hook. The tail, abdomen, and wing case are not separate pieces; make all of these components using one small bunch of fibers. Tie on the short tail of the fly using only the tips of the fibers. Tie on a piece of wire for the rib and then wrap the fibers up the hook to create the abdomen. Next, wrap the rib. Brush the butt ends of the fibers back and make the fly's thorax. Finally, pull the fibers over the top of the fly to fashion the wing case. This method requires far fewer materials, and it is easier than tying on new bunches of tail fibers to fashion each component of the fly.

Get Down Worm

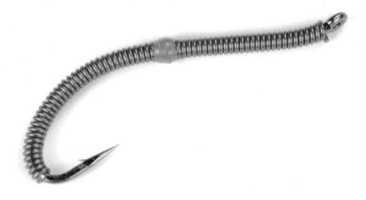

Hook: Curved-shank nymph hook, size 8 or 6.
Thread: Red 8/0 (70 denier).
Body: Red Ultra Wire and red Loon Hard Head.

WHEN I STARTED WRITING THIS LITTLE BOOK, IT DIDN'T occur to me that there are so many worm imitations; the few in this collection only scratch the surface of what is available. The San Juan Worm might be the most famous worm pattern, but anglers across North America and throughout Europe are discovering that trout eat fake worms; we won't discuss fishing with real worms.

Oh, what the hell: I have to tell you a story about myself and worms. When I was very young—about eight years old—my first business was selling worms next to a state highway in Terre Haute, Indiana. I would dig worms in the backyard and put them and fistfuls of dirt in Styrofoam coffee cups. I set up a small table next to the highway and erected a sign advertising my product. As I recall, one gentleman stopped and bought a cup of my worms. He never returned for more worms, so maybe they didn't catch fish. I'll never know. (Almost half a century later, I'm still in the worm business, although now they have no slime.)

I also spent some years living in East Tennessee. The tailwaters in that region are prime for using worm imitations. As the banks of the major tailwaters break off (you'll also see this on the White River in Arkansas), the real worms become readily available to the fish. I saw few worm patterns in the fly boxes of anglers back then, but today they play an important role in successful tailwater-trout fishing.

The Get Down Worm requires little more than a hook and some wire. I added the thread if you'd like to tie off the ends of the body; I would do this, but many tiers simply wrap the wire tight against the hook shank. Make the bulbous section in the middle of the body using Loon Hard Head or a similar product.

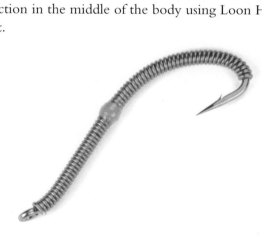

Flying Circus Caddisfly

Hook: Bent-shank emerger hook, sizes 10 to 8.
Head: Gold bead.
Thread: Size 6/0 (140 denier).
Abdomen: Ostrich herl.
Rib: D-rib.
Thorax: Ostrich herl.
Antennae: Pearl Krystal Flash.
Hackle: Coq de Leon.

THE FLYING CIRCUS CADDISFLY WAS ORIGINALLY TIED FOR catching Midwest Great Lakes salmon and steelhead. But as its reputation spread, anglers dunked this pupa imitation in their local trout streams with good results.

I've seen two versions of the Flying Circus Caddisfly: one was bright and the other orange. Here we have the orange fly. I have not recommended colors in the pattern recipe, because I think you should tie this fly in a variety of colors to match almost any caddisfly pupa: black, tan, brown, olive, and gray.

When making the abdomen of the Flying Circus, tie the tag butt end of the D-rib along the entire top of the hook shank to create a level underbody. If you tie the tag only halfway up the shank, there will be an unsightly hump in the middle of the abdomen. Spiral wrap a long piece of ostrich herl up the hook shank, and then wrap the D-rib between the herl. This completes a great-looking abdomen. Select a darker piece of ostrich herl for tying the fly's thorax.

Fish the Flying Circus as real caddisflies begin appearing and the trout are swirling just under the water, feeding on the emerging insects. You can also fish this fine fly in any situation where you might use the LaFontaine Sparkle Pupa; the Flying Circus Caddisfly is a good substitute for that pattern.

Kaufmann's Stonefly

Hook: Tiemco TMC300, sizes 10 to 2.
Thread: Size 6/0 (140 denier).
Head: Medium gold bead.
Tail: Goose or turkey biots.
Body: Your favorite shaggy nymph dubbing, such as Wapsi Lifecycle Stonefly Dubbing.
Rib: D-rib.
Legs: Rubber legs.
Wing case: Turkey tail feather.
Antennae: Goose or turkey biots.

YOU WOULD THINK THAT A LARGE STONEFLY IMITATION would be the perfect platform for adding all sorts of realistic parts, but Kaufmann's Stone, which is one of the most popular stonefly imitations, proves that it might be best to keep things simple.

Randall Kaufmann developed Kaufmann's Stone. Randall owned the legendary Kaufmann's Streamborn fly shops in Washington and Oregon, and wrote several highly respected fly-tying books and many magazine articles. Kaufmann is also a leading fly designer; this is only one of his fine patterns.

Tie Kaufmann's Stone with and without a bead head. It is customary to pack this pattern with lead wire or a non-toxic substitute for fishing fast-flowing western rivers and deep pools. Although I hate losing a fly, Kaufmann's Stone is easy and inexpensive to tie, so I fish it in the strike zone near the streambed without worrying about snagging the bottom.

Select colors to match a wide variety of large stonefly nymphs. The black Kaufmann's Stone is very popular, but also tie this pattern in brown and golden yellow. When tying the body, take care to wrap a tapered abdomen to match the silhouette of a real stonefly.

Any tier who has completed a basic fly-tying course will quickly learn to make Kaufmann's Stone and be ready to catch more trout.

Vladi's Czech Nymph

Hook: Curved-shank nymph or caddis hook, sizes 12 to 8.
Head: Gold bead.
Thread: Tan 6/0 (140 denier).
Abdomen: Embroidery thread.
Rib: Copper wire or narrow, pearl Flashabou.
Thorax: Rabbit dubbing.

FLIP THROUGH THE PAGES OF THIS LITTLE BOOK, AND
you'll see a pattern called Vladi's Condom Worm. That fly rocked the
fly-fishing world some years ago because of its ability to catch fish, and
the fact that it is tied using a real condom. European fly-fishing champion Vladi Trzebunia gave me those Condom Worms, as well as the Czech
Nymphs you see here. Vladi is given credit for helping to popularize the
style of angling called Czech nymph fishing, and I want you to see more of
his patterns.

Sometimes this style of fishing, in which a string of flies is drifted through
the water very close to the angler, is called Polish nymph fishing, and I
believe one or two other countries also claim it as their own. Regardless of
where it originated, it catches trout, landlocked salmon, and grayling everywhere. Today, many manufacturers offer rods and lines specifically designed
for Czech nymph fishing, and there are growing number of books, videos,
and websites devoted to the topic. I have spent a considerable amount of
time learning the technique (although there really isn't much to learn) and
have used it across the United States and Canada with great success.

Vladi wrapped lead wire in the middle of the hook shank to make a
tapered underbody. He then tied a woven abdomen, which creates a fantas-
tic two-tone effect. Although I might use a dark-colored dubbing for the
thoraxes, Vladi prefers tan dubbing.

Vladi's Czech Nymphs are realistic looking and very effective. They are
also slightly large and easy to tie.

Two-bead
Prince Nymph

Hook: 2X- or 3X-long nymph hook, sizes 12 to 6.
Beads: Large gold beads.
Tail: Brown goose or turkey biots.
Abdomen: Peacock herl.
Rib: Round gold tinsel.
Wing: White goose or turkey biots.
Hackle: Brown soft hackle.

HAVE YOU EVER SEEN FILM FOOTAGE OF TROUT LIVING IN streams? It's amazing how these creatures can survive in the strongest currents. If you watch closely, you'll see that the flow close to the streambed is actually quite moderate. The friction of the moving water against the rocks and debris slows the water so fish can survive and thrive. Sometimes a group of trout will even huddle behind a small boulder or log and dart out to catch food being swept downstream.

The challenge for us is to reach these fish in heavy flowing water.

This Two-bead Prince Nymph takes the bead-head concept a step further. This fly is very heavy and will sink like a stone. I have seen two beads used on a variety of nymphs. All of these flies sink quickly into the strike zone.

Two-bead flies are specialized patterns for fishing fast-flowing water. Keep in mind that they spend much of their time dragging on or close to the bottom. As a result, you will occasionally snag the streambed and lose a few flies. The Prince Nymph is fairly easy to tie using commonly available materials, so it won't break your heart if you lose a couple of them while fishing. Choose other easy-to-tie patterns when tying extra-heavy, two-bead flies.

Stryker's Golden Stonefly

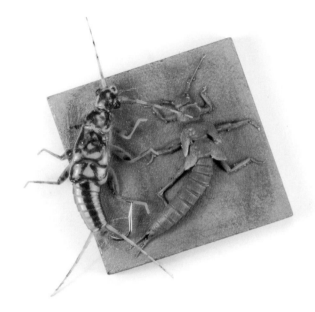

Hook: Curved-shank nymph hook, size 4.
Thread: Tan 6/0 (140 denier).
Tail: J:SonSweden Silicone Tails.
Abdomen: Nymph Skin, Real Skin, or a similar material.
Thorax: Rabbit dubbing or your favorite nymph dubbing.
Wing case: Nymph Skin, Real Skin, or J:SonSweden Realistic Wing Material.
Legs: J:SonSweden Realistic Nymph Legs.
Eyes: Black bead chain.
Antennae: J:SonSweden Silicone Tails.

WOW, WHAT A PATTERN! NEW YORK'S SCOTT STRYKER nailed this imitation of a large golden stonefly nymph. And, best of all, he created it using an economy of materials you might find in a fly shop.

Scott ties a wide variety of typical patterns that he sells for the usual price of a couple dollars apiece, as well as super-realistic flies that appeal to collectors. This fly, which is very durable for fishing, costs $25. While that might seem like a lot of money for a "fishing fly," have you seen the price of some plugs and lures? Today, some mass-produced plugs cost even more than that, and they're cast into dark, gnarly lakes full of snags. While you still might shy away from spending so much for a fly, Scott is proving that we can tie realistic flies designed for real-world fishing.

Several of the ingredients in this pattern come from a Swedish fly-fishing company called J:SonSweden. The legs and antennae are silicone, so they are very flexible and will not break while fishing. Scott did a wonderful job of coloring this pattern, and the proportions are outstanding.

Although I might not ever make and fish such a fly, Stryker's Golden Stonefly is the sort of pattern that gets me excited to return to my tying bench. I want to experiment with new materials and tying methods, and I want to tinker with my own patterns.

Safet's Isonychia

Hook: Curved-shank or regular nymph hook, sizes 18 to 10.
Thread: Brown 6/0 (140 denier).
Tail: Brown hackle fibers or opossum fur.
Abdomen: Stripped quill, colored with a brown permanent marker.
Thorax: Brown dubbing.
Back and wing case: A feather coated with GOOP.
Legs: Brown hackle fibers or opossum fur.

SAFET NIKOCEVIC IS A FASCINATING FELLOW. DURING THE
day he restores pianos at the Steinway & Sons factory in New York City.
He is also a black belt karate instructor. And, as if that isn't enough, he is an
inventive fly tier.

This book contains a couple of other examples of *Isonychia* imitations.
What's so different about Safet's Isonychia? He has designed a really unique
way of creating the back and wing case on this pattern and many of his
other flies.

Safet purchases long pieces of ribbon at the craft store: brown, tan, and
other natural colors. He then glues small feathers—hen hackles and various
flank feathers—to the ribbon using Household GOOP. This common glue
is flexible and waterproof, and the feathers maintain their mottled coloration. Safet glues dozens of feathers to the ribbon in one sitting, and then sets
the material aside to dry. Later, when tying flies, he'll select a ribbon and set
of glued feathers to match the color of the pattern.

It's easy to clip the wing case to shape from a feather. Tie the wing case
to the pattern and complete the fly. A real *Isonychia* nymph has a stripe down
its back, which is simulated using the quill of the feather. Safet's Isonychia
is remarkably easy to make, and you can change hook sizes and colors of
materials to imitate a wide variety of mayfly nymphs.

Little Black
Caddis Larva

Hook: Curved–shank caddis hook, size 10 or 8.
Thread: Tan 8/0 (70 denier).
Body: Latex.
Rib: Tying thread.
Legs: Tan soft hackle.

THE NAME LITTLE BLACK CADDISFLY ACTUALLY REFERS TO
the color of the adult insect, not the immature larva.

I learned this from inventive fly-tier Safet Nikocevic. He has a large
board containing dozens and dozens of fish flies pressed into the foam. It
seemed like he had imitations of almost every conceivable aquatic insect
that would catch the fancy of a trout. My eye caught the pale-orange Little
Black Caddis Larva, and Safet explained the fly and how to tie it. The Little
Black Caddis Larva imitates a *Chimmara aterrima* larva, which is indeed pale
orange.

Safet's Little Black Caddis Larva is extremely easy to make and requires
very few materials: a hook, thread, latex, and a soft hackle are all that is
needed. Safet wraps latex up the hook to create the entire body of the fly.
A couple of wraps of hackle makes the legs, and he pulls the latex back to
create the wing case. A single strand of thread pulled over the top of the
fly and held in place with a thread rib creates the telltale stripe of the real
insect. Like all of Safet's patterns, the Little Black Caddis Larva is simple and
effective.

The Little Black Caddis Larva is an ideal dropper pattern when fishing
a multi-fly rig. Select a heavier fly for the anchor, and tie the Little Black
Caddis Larva about 12 inches from the end of the leader. The anchor pattern will dive to the body, pulling the Little Black Caddis Larva with it.

Green Sedge Larva

Hook: Curved-shank caddis hook, size 10 or 8.
Thread: Brown 8/0 (70 denier).
Body: Latex.
Rib: Tying thread.
Legs: Brown soft hackle.

I DEFY YOU TO NAME A HEALTHY TROUT STREAM THAT does not contain some form of green caddisfly larvae. These immature insects live among the rocks and stones of every trout stream and river around the world. If you're serious about nymph fishing, you'll want to have a selection of green caddisfly imitations.

Once again, Safet Nikocevic has created an easy-to-tie pattern that requires an economy of materials. On this fly, however, he colors the abdomen with a green permanent marker and shades the thorax area using a brown marker. Because the pattern is so easy and inexpensive to tie, you can fish it close to the streambed or around debris without fearing snags and the loss of a few flies.

As with some of the other patterns in this book tied using latex, you will want to coat the body with Softex or a similar material. Natural latex will rot when exposed to the air, so you will want to seal the material after tying the fly. Although the body of an unprotected fly will last for a couple of years, if you only occasionally fish, you do not want to open your fly box one day and discover that any of your flies have deteriorated.

Apple Caddis Pupa

Hook: Curved–shank emerger hook, size 8.
Thread: Tan 8/0 (70 denier).
Abdomen: Latex.
Leg and antennae: Tan cul de canard and frayed ribbon.
Thorax: Tying thread.

THE APPLE CADDISFLY (*BRACHYCENTRUS APPALACHIA*) IS A popular hatch in the Delaware River Valley and other local waters. Depending upon water levels, you'll run into this hatch from the first of May until the middle of June, so go prepared with a selection of matching pupa and adult imitations.

Safet Nikocevic's Apple Caddis Pupa is a fine imitation of this small, size-16 insect. You might be tempted to fish a pupa pattern just under the surface during the full-blown hatch, thinking you'll catch a few extra trout, but many anglers claim they actually catch fewer fish using this method. Why? Perhaps there is too much competition for your fly among the natural insects, or perhaps the fish simply key in to the adult caddisflies scurrying across the surface.

On the other hand, fishing a pupa caddisfly deeper a few hours before the hatch definitely produces trout. Even though we do not see them, the insects are turning from larvae in to pupae, and begin drifting with the current. The fish quickly key in to this drifting buffet and will readily strike your fly. This is a good time to fish the Apple Caddis Pupa using a sinking-tip line and long leader. Cast the fly down-and-across stream, let it sink, and gradually draw the line tight. The fly will sink under the surface during the drift and begin rising when you tighten the line. Or, fish the Apple Caddis Pupa even deeper as a nymph; it's a splendid dropper when paired with a heavier anchor fly.

Hook-up
Hellgrammite

Hook: Tiemco 200R, Dai-Riki 270, or similar; a 3X-long, curved-shank nymph hook, size 6 or 4.

Thread: Black 3/0 Monocord.

Tail: Black ostrich herl.

Abdomen: Black wool yarn and black ostrich herl.

Back: Black Thin Skin.

Rib: Black size A Monocord or small Ultra Wire.

Thorax and legs: Black rabbit fur in a dubbing loop.

Head: Black wool yarn.

FLY FISHERS SPEND A GREAT DEAL OF TIME TALKING ABOUT mayflies, stoneflies, and caddisflies, so that we sometimes overlook some of the most interesting varieties. Hellgrammites, also called Dobson flies, are certainly fascinating creatures.

Okay, let's be very specific: the hellgrammite is the larval stage of this insect, and the Dobson fly is the adult. Perhaps this bit of confusion is one of the reasons anglers overlook them. It was years before I knew the two were actually the same insect.

Hellgrammites only thrive in clean, well-oxygenated water and are a good indicator of a potential trout habitat. The adult Dobson flies lay their eggs on overhanging branches and rock ledges. The eggs hatch, and the immature hellgrammites fall into the water, where they live and grow for up to three years. The hellgrammites eventually emerge into adult Dobson flies, and this amazing lifecycle is repeated.

Although hellgrammite imitations are considered prime patterns for catching smallmouth bass, they are important but overlooked trout patterns. Because they are large, you can pack them with weight and easily fish them close to the streambed or in heavy flows.

Here is another pattern designed by New York's Greg Heffner. Greg ties heavy weighting wire to the sides of the hook shank, which causes the hook to flip over when fishing. With the point on the top, you are less likely to snag the streambed. The soft rabbit fur in the thorax gives his Hook-up Hellgrammite swimming action in the water.

Hook-up Stonefly

Hook: Tiemco 200R, Dai-Riki 270, or similar; a 3X-long, curved-shank nymph hook, sizes 8 to 4.
Thread: Brown 3/0 Monocord.
Tail: Amber or brown goose biots.
Abdomen: Brown and yellow Swannadaze or D-Rib, or dubbing.
Back and wing case: Natural-oak mottled Thin Skin.
Thorax: Dubbing to match the local stoneflies.
Legs: Brown rabbit fur in a dubbing loop.
Antennae: Amber or brown goose biots.

WE'VE EXAMINED SEVERAL IMITATIONS OF GOLDEN STONEFLY nymphs. These are common insects, and they also populate the fly boxes of most anglers. Work at becoming an accomplished nymph fisherman, and it will pay dividends.

Here are two versions of Greg Heffner's golden stonefly. They are designed to ride with their hook points on top, so they are ideal for fishing close to the bottom or in slower sections of the river where the flies might have a chance to descend to the streambed. Tying a length of heavy wire on each side of the hook before tying the fly forces the curved-shank hook to flip over in the water.

In addition to using these patterns to imitate golden stoneflies, you can select materials in black or brown to match a variety of the largest stoneflies. Rather than the woven abdomen, you can tie a simple, dubbed abdomen. This is a very adaptable fly that meets a wide variety of fishing situations.

Spend some time on your fishing outings examining streamside rocks, vegetation, and even manmade structures, such as bridges and culverts. You'll often find the empty cases of stonefly nymphs still clinging to these objects; if you're lucky, you might even discover a real stonefly splitting out of its nymphal skin to turn into a winged adult. These events are almost as memorable as the fishing!

Woven Copper John

Hook: 2X-long wet-fly hook, sizes 10 to 6.
Thread: Black 6/0 (140 denier).
Tail: Brown goose or turkey biots.
Abdomen: Tan and green Ultra Wire.
Thorax: Peacock herl.
Legs: Mallard flank fibers.
Wing case: Pearl Flashabou or a similar material, coated with a drop of epoxy.

TURN THE PAGES OF THIS BOOK, AND YOU'LL FIND THE standard Copper John and some of its offspring. They have become some of the most popular, bestselling patterns in the world. Most knockoffs involve substituting colors of materials or adding rubber legs and tails of various lengths. Linda Hotchkiss, on the other hand, brings her extraordinary tying skills to bear and transforms the Copper John into almost an entirely new pattern. Sure, it still has the biot tails, peacock herl thorax, and epoxy back, but check out that abdomen. It's woven wire!

Many tiers make woven bodies using embroidery thread and the shuttle weave. (You'll find instructions for making woven bodies on many fly-tying websites.) Linda also makes thread-woven bodies, and her flies look outstanding. Occasionally, however, she weaves a fly body using Ultra Wire. This copper wire comes in a wide variety of anodized colors and several sizes, so it is ideal for weaving the fine bodies of flies. Although not as forgiving as soft embroidery thread, you will use the same weaving method to create a two-tone body. This is Linda's woven version of a Copper John, but you can substitute colors to weave the bodies of other patterns. Work slowly and you'll soon learn the technique.

Deep-diving Caddis

Hook: Curved-shank emerger hook, sizes 18 to 14.
Bead: Tungsten.
Thread: Size 8/0 (70 denier) in a color to match the natural insect.
Rib: Copper Krystal Flash.
Thorax: Peacock herl.
Wing: McFlylon.

MANY YEARS AGO, GARY LAFONTAINE POINTED OUT THE value of fishing a caddisfly pupa weighted with wraps of lead wire. Eventually, tiers started adding bead heads to their flies to make them sink and reach trout lying along the streambed. Unfortunately, few anglers were hip to the effectiveness of these patterns and the importance of the fishing method; most remained locked into watching for adult caddisflies and obviously rising trout.

LaFontaine's Deep Sparkle Pupa is also a little difficult to tie. Neatly brushing the polypropylene fibers forward over the body to create an even outer skin is challenging. It would be nice to have a simple caddisfly pupa for fishing deep. Dennis Charney's Deep-Diving Caddis is an answer to this problem.

A caddisfly has a "complete" lifecycle. It starts as a larva and then changes form into a pupa. The pupa then rises to the surface of the water to emerge into a winged adult. Insects with incomplete lifecycles, such as mayflies and stoneflies, do not have a pupa stage.

Hours before the expected hatch, the real caddisfly larvae are turning into pupae and swimming and tumbling along the streambed. This is the perfect time to fish the Deep-Diving Caddis. Cast slightly up- or across-stream and allow the fly to sink. Keep an eye peeled for striking fish. As the fly reaches the end of the drift, tighten the line and allow it to rise like an emerging caddisfly.

Rock Candy Caddis

Hook: Curved-shank caddis hook, sizes 18 to 14.
Head: Black bead.
Thread: Black 8/0 (70 denier).
Abdomen: Green braid.
Thorax: Arizona Synthetic Peacock Dubbing.
Back: Green Thin Skin.
Rib: Black Ultra Wire.

DO YOU PREFER TYING FLIES USING NATURAL OR SYN-thetic ingredients? A lot of tiers prefer using only natural feathers and furs, and some willingly blend both to design better fish-catching patterns. Some flies, such as Dennis Charney's Rock Candy Caddis, feature all synthetic materials.

The Rock Candy Caddis is a great pattern for fishing along the stre-ambed where real caddisfly larvae live. The black tungsten bead gives it ample weight so the fly descends quickly, and the back of the fly, made using a strip of Thin Skin (you may substitute with Scud Back or a similar mate-rial), is durable and withstands abrasion from rocks and gravel.

Imitations of green caddis larvae are very popular; you'll find them in the bins of almost any fly shop. But, you should also tie the Rock Candy Caddis in tan and brown. Some anglers swear that red is also a winning color for catching trout. John Barr, who created the famous Copper John, says his favorite color is red. Tie the Rock Candy Caddis with a red abdo-men, and use it as a dropper in a multi-fly rig paired with another, more realistic-looking pattern. It will be interesting to see how many fish strike the red fly.

Baltz's Caddis Pupa

Hook: Curved-shank emerger hook, sizes 14 to 8.
Bead: Metal bead in your choice of color.
Thread: Brown 8/0 (70 denier).
Abdomen: Hare's mask dubbing with marabou pulled over the top.
Rib: Copper wire.
Thorax: A bend of gray squirrel dubbing, scrap cul de canard, and Ice Dub.
Swimmers: Pheasant tail fiber tips.
Antennae: One strand of pearl Krystal Flash.
Hackle: Cul de canard.

TOM BALTZ IS AN ORVIS-ENDORSED GUIDE WHO LIVES IN Pennsylvania. Tom is a talented tier, and all of his patterns, such as Baltz's Caddis Pupa, are based on his years of fishing experience.

Baltz's Caddis Pupa is very buggy looking. Tom blends his own dubbing for tying the abdomen; the mixture even includes a few cul de canard fibers that he sweeps off the top of his tying bench. The CDC creates air bubbles in the body of the fly to mimic the gases generated under the skin of a real ascending caddisfly pupa. The back of the abdomen is marabou, which creates a two-tone body and gives the fly additional swimming movement.

Feel free to experiment with the color of the bead head. Select gold or brass to imitate a more natural color, or use a brightly painted bead to add a hot spot to the fly. A lot of tiers create the hot spot using a dash of bright dubbing in the body, but a colorful bead that stands out in the water and catches the eye of a fish works just as well. The jury is still out on the use of hot spots—whether or not they really work—but an increasing number of anglers insist they catch more fish using patterns that contain hot spots.

CHAPTER SEVEN

Flies for Fishing Still Waters

Maple Syrup

Hook: 4X-long nymph or streamer hook, sizes 18 to 12.
Thread: Red 8/0 (70 denier).
Tail: Yellow kip tail.

THE MAPLE SYRUP GETS MY VOTE FOR BEING THE SIMPLEST pattern in this book. Surprisingly, it is also one of the most effective for catching stillwater trout. This simple pattern was first tied and sold through Theriault Flies, in Stacyville, Maine.

What can I tell you about Alvin Theriault and Theriault Flies? First, if you blink, you'll miss Stacyville. This tiny town is in the middle of Maine, just east of Baxter State Park and home to some of the best stillwater trout fishing in the Northeast. Theriault Flies looks like a small farm because, besides running his fly shop, Alvin Theriault raises much of his own hackle, jungle cock, and assorted other birds and animals. Theriault Flies has one of the largest selections of fly-tying materials I have ever seen; if you like sorting through fly-tying materials, looking for exactly the ingredient you want, you could easily spend hours in Alvin's shop. And finally, Alvin is a rabid rock hound, and he sells all sorts of minerals and gems at his store. The collection of rocks on display is about as vast as the assortment of fly-tying materials.

Alvin describes the Maple Syrup as a "universal nymph" imitation. As silly as the fly looks, large numbers of anglers throughout New England tell stories of using this pattern (is it really a "pattern"?) to catch memorable numbers of fish.

Most anglers fish the Maple Syrup from about mid-June to the middle of July, roughly during the period when the *Hexagenia* mayflies hatch. Fish the fly deep and very slow like a swimming nymph.

Just to change things up, Alvin and many other tiers create variations on the classic Maple Syrup. You can easily change the colors of tail and body, or use marabou for the tail; this swimming tail definitely increases the action of the fly in the water.

Rapunzel

Hook: Tiemco TMC200R, sizes 14 to 10.
Bead head: Red metallic glass.
Thread: Size 8/0 (70 denier).
Tail: Grizzly marabou.
Abdomen: Midge Tubing or Micro Tubing.
Ribs: Ultra Wire and ostrich herl.
Legs: Speckled Centipede Legs.
Wing pads: Grizzly marabou.
Wing case: Natural bustard Thin Skin.
Thorax: UV Ice Dub.
Eyes: Clear, glass beads of melted monofilament.
Collar: Red UV Ice Dub.

VINCE WILCOX IS AN ACCOMPLISHED GUIDE, AUTHOR, AND fly designer. He eagerly uses the newest materials to create fresh fish-catching patterns. He also gives his flies fun names. The Rapunzel, which is a damselfly imitation, is a good example of his work.

Study the pattern recipe, and you'll see that I recommend colors for only a couple of materials. Vince ties the Rapunzel in olive and tan, so select tail, body, leg, and wing-pad materials to match. In many of my local trout ponds, some of the real damselfly nymphs are bright green, so I always carry a few imitations in chartreuse; these bright flies always catch fish.

Centipede Legs are extra-fine rubber legs. They come in a wide range of solid and speckled colors. If your local fly shop doesn't offer Centipede Legs, substitute with another brand of fine rubber legs.

The tail and wing pads of the Rapunzel are made using grizzly marabou. This soft ingredient gives the pattern an outstanding swimming action. Feathers called Chickabou, offered by Whiting Farms, are an even better choice. These small feathers, which come from chickens, have all the properties of marabou. They are ideal for tying small nymphs such as the Rapunzel. They come in a variety of solid and grizzly colors, including olive and tan.

Ultra Damsel Nymph

Hook: Short-shank nymph hook, size 16 or 14.
Thread: Size 8/0 (70 denier).
Abdomen: Shane Stalcup's Damsel Nymph Body.
Thorax: Tying thread.
Legs: Metallic sewing thread.
Wing case: Swiss straw, Scud Back, or a strip clipped from a plastic freezer bag.
Eyes: Melted monofilament or plastic dumbbell.

TWO THINGS STRIKE ME ABOUT DAMSELFLY IMITATIONS. First, few anglers carry these important patterns in their fly boxes, but real damselflies reside in still waters and most anglers fish rivers. Second, most damselfly patterns are entirely too fat. It's usually not that the tiers did poor work and made their flies too thick, but the designs specified using the wrong ingredients. Real damselflies have remarkably slender bodies, and so should your imitations.

Colorado's Shane Stalcup understood this, and his Ultra Damsel Nymph has a very realistic silhouette. Shane developed a product for tying the abdomen called Stalcup's Damsel Nymph Bodies, and even though he passed away several years ago, you'll still find this product in some fly shops. If you can't find Damsel Nymph Bodies, substitute a piece of Ultra Chenille with a sprig of marabou tied to one end.

Making a chenille abdomen is easy. Place a fine sewing needle in your vise. Start the thread on the slender tip of the needle. Tie the end of the Ultra Chenille to the top of the needle. Next, tie on a short marabou tail and place a drop of superglue on the thread wraps. Tighten the thread, and quickly slip the body from the needle. Clip the butt end of the chenille to length, and tie the abdomen to the hook. This do-it-yourself damselfly abdomen actually has better swimming action in the water.

Tie the svelte Ultra Damsel Nymph in olive, tan, and even bright green.

Crystal Midge

Hook: Curved-shank midge hook, sizes 24 to 16.
Head: Small, glass bead.
Thread: Size 8/0 (70 denier).
Body: Tying thread.
Rib: Extra-fine gold or silver wire.
Wing buds: Pearl Krystal Flash.
Thorax: Super Fine Dubbing.

ACCORDING TO THE FEDERATION OF FLY FISHERS WEBSITE, "There are thousands, perhaps hundreds of thousands, of midge (Chirono-mid) patterns." Well, I don't know if there are hundreds of thousands, but there are certainly a lot. And, there are a great many called the Crystal Midge.

Here's a very basic example of the Crystal Midge. This version is remark-ably easy to tie, so even a novice tier can easily fill several rows of a fly box with fish-catching midge imitations. And, the Crystal Midge is adaptable; select thread and dubbing in black, olive, gray, and red.

Midges are vitally important to consistent fly-fishing success. They hatch on most water through the year, and it is estimated that these diminutive insects make up more than 20 percent of the diets of most trout; on some waters, they make an even larger part of the fishes' diets.

Wapsi Fly offers a very large assortment of glass beads that are ideal for making patterns such as the Crystal Midge. These beads come in a rainbow of colors, from large to extra-small sizes. The clear beads are silver lined to mimic the air bubble of a rising midge or caddis pupa. You'll find these beads in most well-stocked fly shops. The short pieces of pearl Krystal Flash, which imitate expanding wing buds on the back of the fly, also attract the attention of feeding trout.

Hovering Dragonfly

Hook: 2X-long wet-fly hook, size 8.
Thread: Brown 6/0 (140 denier).
Abdomen: Mottled, brown or olive rabbit fur.
Thorax: Brown or dark-olive rabbit dubbing or your favorite shaggy nymph dubbing.
Wing case: Brown or olive Medallion Sheeting, brown turkey feather, or a similar material.
Legs: Brown or olive rubber Sili Legs or rubber legs.
Eyes: Brown or olive closed-cell foam.

I GOT THE IDEA FOR THE HOVERING DRAGONFLY NYMPH from Canadian fly-fishing guru Phil Rowley. Phil ties a similar nymph for fishing trout ponds and lakes, and he described the theory behind the pattern.

According to Phil, most Stillwater anglers mistakenly use weighed patterns when fishing deep along the bottom of ponds. As he correctly points out, these flies dive to the bottom and quickly snag weeds or even more solid objects.

"Rather than use a weighted fly," Phil said, "select a pattern that floats, but fish it with a fast-sinking line. The line will draw the fly close to the bottom, but the fly will hover above the weeds and snags. You'll spend a lot more time fishing, and less time cleaning debris off the hook."

This idea made perfect sense to me, so I set about creating a dragonfly imitation that has great swimming action but does not sink. The rabbit fur abdomen and rubber legs make the fly look alive with each strip of line, and the large, closed-cell foam eyes make the fly float just above the weed line. Fish the Hovering Dragonfly using a 5- or 6-weight, fast-sinking line and short leader. Allow the line to settle to the bottom, and retrieve the fly using short, irregular strips. Work very slowly—I often count to twenty before beginning my retrieve—and allow the fly to rest before strips.

The Hovering Dragonfly Nymph has become one of my most important, go-to flies when fishing trout ponds. I took the fly in the photo from my fly box.

Simple Damsel

Hook: 4X-long streamer hook, sizes 14 to 10.
Thread: Olive 6/0 (140 denier).
Tail: Brown hackle fibers.
Abdomen: Olive Stretch Tubing.
Thorax: Olive rabbit dubbing.
Wing case: Tan turkey tail.
Eyes: Extra-small dumbbell.

ALTHOUGH I'M SURE YOU'LL FIND A SIMILAR PATTERN IN many fly catalogs, I cooked up this damselfly nymph imitation without referring to another recipe. I needed a slightly weighted damselfly with a very slender body, and I wanted to tie it in smaller sizes to match the real damselfly nymphs living in my local trout ponds. I rummaged through my fly-tying materials and quickly created the Simple Damsel.

We're all familiar with lead dumbbells; however, most come in sizes better suited for tying Clouser Minnows and other streamers. But, did you know that Wapsi Fly offers an assortment of micro and extra-small dumbbells? These open a world of possibilities for fashioning patterns such as the Simple Damsel. They do a fine job of imitating the large eyes of a real damselfly nymph and add just enough weight that the fly will sink, not plunge to the bottom and quickly snag. Even though I tied the dumbbell to the bottom of the hook, I soon discovered that the fly would flip over while fishing. Slightly bend the front of the hook up, and the fly will ride in the correct position while fishing.

Tie the Simple Damsel to your leader using a loop knot. This allows the tippet to remain loose at the hook-eye and the fly bobs up and down with a slight jigging action while fishing. Use a gentle strip-and-pause retrieve when fishing the fly to accentuate the jigging action. Since the Simple Damsel is weighted, I use a floating line when fishing it in the shallows and switch to a slow-sinking or sinking-tip line when exploring deeper water.

###

SALTWATER
FLIES

SALTWATER FLIES

WHAT TYPE OF FISH DO YOU WANT TO CATCH: STRIPED BASS, bluefish, false albacore, bonefish, permit, snook, or tarpon? Perhaps you have another species of fish in mind: redfish, bonito, barracuda, snapper, or something else. Our oceans are chock-full of worthy targets, but you will need the right flies to attract them.

101 Favorite Saltwater Flies is a smorgasbord of great patterns designed to catch a wide variety of our favorite gamefish. In addition to the fly recipes, I include histories and offer insights about how to fish or tie them. The stories of these flies are as varied as the patterns themselves. Eat as much as you like, and then come back for more.

A great many anglers have played key roles in my development as a fly fisherman and tier. Without them, my life and fishing would be poorer. The following folks—in no particular order—have offered important contributions to this book, and I offer them my thanks. Tie or buy their flies, and you will catch fish.

CHAPTER EIGHT

Attractor Patterns:
Flies for Fishing
Anytime and Anywhere

Black Death

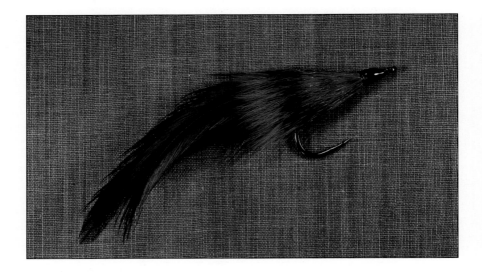

Hook: Tiemco TMC600 SP, sizes 2 to 4/0.
Thread: Red 3/0.
Tail: Black saddle hackles.
Collar: Gray squirrel tail hair dyed red.
Nose: Red tying thread.

THERE ARE A LOT OF TARPON PATTERNS CALLED BLACK Death. When writing this book, it was tough to choose which Black Death to include. Maybe, because there are several versions of this pattern, it really doesn't matter: when getting ready for your next tarpon-fishing adventure, just be sure to include a selection of dark-colored flies.

Hook selection is critical. Hooks for tarpon flies are made using heavy wire. These hooks are extremely strong to catch these fierce-fighting fish. A tarpon's mouth is also very hard, so these hooks are extremely sharp—sharper than many other hooks—so they sink home. The shanks are usually slightly short and the points are curved up, which also helps in hooking tarpon.

The pattern recipe recommends the Tiemco TMC600 SP for tying the Black Death. This hook is widely available, but you may substitute with any similar hook. Tie the Black Death and other tarpon flies in a range of sizes, although many guides prefer smaller flies for attracting these large fish.

In addition to tying the tail using saddle hackles, you may substitute with a black rabbit Zonker strip. This is easy to tie to the hook, and the soft fur flows in the water when retrieving the fly. Also, rather than using squirrel tail hair for the collar, substitute with red or black saddle hackle.

Play around with different materials and dark colors, and create your own version of the Black Death. Just be sure to release the tarpon alive!

Devil's Daughter

Hook: Tiemco TMC811S or Daiichi 2546, size 1 or 1/0.

Thread: Black Danville 210 denier.

Tail: Peacock herl and black ostrich plume.

Body: Black marabou plumes.

Head: Black deer body hair, spun on the hook and clipped to shape like a Muddler Minnow.

MOST EXPERIENCED TARPON ANGLERS SAY YOU MUST have patterns tied in a variety of basic colors: bright flies (white chartreuse, and yellow) for fishing on bright days and over light-colored flats, and at least one black pattern for dark days or those times when the fish show no interest in brighter flies. This approach makes a lot of sense, especially for newer tarpon fishermen filling their first box of flies: keep it simple and you'll increase your odds of success.

The very best tarpon anglers also recommend flies that "push" water. The gentle disturbance created by a fly moving through the water on the retrieve mimics the vibrations of a feeling baitfish. Tarpon and other game-fish detect these vibrations through their lateral lines which helps them home in on the fly. The head on the Devil's Daughter, which is deer hair spun and clipped to resemble the head of a Muddler Minnow, does a fine job of pushing water. And the fly's black color is ideal for anchoring the dark end of your fly box.

Although the original Devil's Daughter is tied in black, you can use the basic design to create tarpon flies in a variety of other colors. Retain the deer-hair head, but tie the fly in any color you wish using hackles. A head of natural-colored deer hair and white feathers for the wing would be especially effective.

White Noise

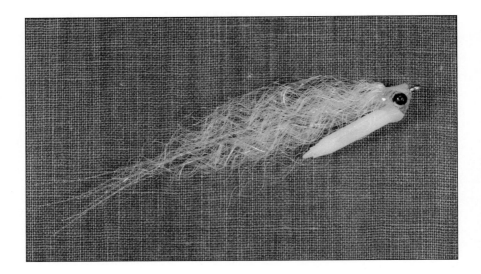

Hook: Tiemco TMC811S or Daiichi 2546, size 1 or 2.
Thread: Clear monofilament.
Body: Steve Farrar's SF Flash Blend (white) and pearl UV Krystal Flash.
Eyes: Large black plastic dumbbell.
Head: Five-minute epoxy or light-cured acrylic.
Rattle: Glow-in-the-dark plastic worm rattle.

ACCORDING TO FLY-DESIGNER DREW CHICONE, HE CAME up with idea for the White Noise while fishing the beaches of Captiva. All the bait he was encountering appears semi-translucent, and he wanted a pattern to match. Steve Farrar's SF Flash Blend, with a few sprigs of UV Krystal Flash, comprise the wispy now-you-see-it, now-you-don't body of the fly. The White Noise is not an exact imitation of any particular form of bait; it might resemble many things predator fish will eat.

In addition to designing a very sparse fly, Drew wanted his new pattern to make a little noise to attract fish. He had not tied many flies containing rattles because most were glass; Drew says that glass rattles look too fragile, and they are too hard to tie to a hook. Drew uses a plastic worm rattle in the White Noise, which is far more durable and easy to secure to the fly. Do rattles really work on fishing flies? Dr. David Ross, of Woods Hole Oceanographic Institution and a fly-fishing fanatic, insists rattles improve many flies and help catch fish. He tells stories of seeing fish turn and travel great distances to locate patterns containing rattles.

Tie and fish the White Noise and judge for yourself. Or, add rattles to some of your favorite patterns and see if they catch more fish. I'll enjoy hearing the results of your experiments.

Asphyxiator

Hook: Daiichi 2546, size 4 or 2.
Thread: Black 6/0.
Tail: Four grizzly hackles and two strands of root beer Krystal Flash.
Body: Two grizzly hackles.
Eyes: Medium copper bead chain.

ARE YOU NEW TO TYING FLIES? DO YOU WANT A SIMPLE pattern for learning the basics of starting the thread and securing basic materials to the hook? The Asphyxiator is the fly for you.

Check out the list of tying materials: a hook, thread, hackles, flash material, and bead-chain eyes. That's it! For about $20 you can get enough ingredients to fill a fly box full of fish-catching flies. And, you can gradually make this pattern in other colors to meet a wide range of fishing situations.

I always recommend that new tiers start with three or four patterns that catch fish in their local waters. Become an expert in tying those flies and gain confidence that your handiwork will really catch fish. Add new patterns slowly and you will reduce the amount of money you spend on your new hobby. You will also discover that you can use many of the materials you have to tie other flies.

In this case, the Daiichi 2546 is an ordinary hook suitable for tying dozens of different flies. A spool of black thread is one of the most generic materials and is called for in hundreds of pattern recipes. Grizzly hackles are as common to fly tying as chickens are to barnyards. Krystal Flash and bead-chain eyes are also popular ingredients.

Drew Chicone's Asphyxiator is a great first fly.

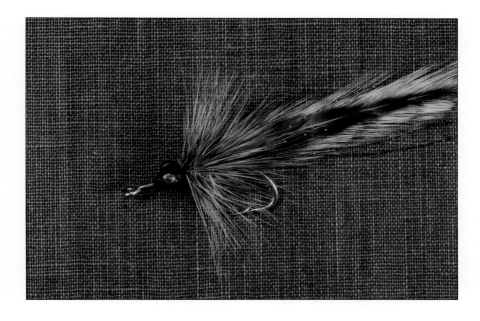

Disco Shrimp

Hook: Mustad 34011 or a similar long-shank saltwater hook, size 1 or 2.
Thread: Brown Danville 210 denier.
Head: Red fox tail hair.
Antennae: Peacock Krystal Flash.
Eyes: Melted monofilament.
Legs: Tan rubber legs.
Body: Golden brown Ice Dub.
Back: Tan 2-millimeter-thick closed-cell foam.
Rattle: Plastic worm rattle.
Tail: Two 4-millimeter gold sequins.

MOST ANGLERS THINK THAT SHRIMP IMITATIONS ARE always subsurface patterns, but nothing is further from the case. I have caught baby tarpon in the canals of the Florida Keys using topwater shrimp imitations. This is especially fun sport in the evening when the tarpon are feeding on real shrimp under street lights and porch lamps. Cast your fly in the vicinity of feeding fish, let it rest for a few moments, and then impart a slow, chugging retrieve. It might take several casts, but a tarpon will eventually take your fly.

Of course, topwater patterns are used for catching a great many species of fish. Drew Chicone designed his Disco Shrimp for catching mangrove snapper, but it will also catch striped bass and more.

The Disco Shrimp has two features that create fish-enticing noise. First, before tying the fly, slip two 4-millimeter gold sequins on the hook and behind the eye. When drawn through the water, the sequins act like a tiny popping head. Second, a plastic worm rattle is tied to the end of the hook shank and shrouded under the fox fur. When you shake the Disco Shrimp in your hand, you can feel the rattle jingling. Both of these great features get the attention of the fish.

Lefty's Deceiver

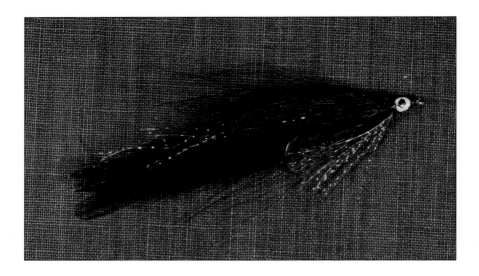

Hook: Regular saltwater hook, sizes 8 to 2/0.
Thread: Size 3/0.
Tail: Saddle hackles with strands of your favorite flash material.
Body: Flat silver tinsel.
Back: Bucktail.
Belly: Bucktail.
Eyes: Painted or adhesive eyes coated with epoxy.

FLY-FISHING LEGEND LEFTY KREH DESIGNED HIS LEFTY'S
Deceiver many years ago. Thousands of anglers use this great pattern to
catch a wide variety of fish. If you tie your own flies, you must put Lefty's
Deceiver on your list of patterns.

Tie Lefty's Deceiver in a range of sizes and colors. The most popular
color combinations are blue/white, olive/white, and chartreuse/white; an
all-white Deceiver is also a favored fly. Some anglers also carry a few black
Deceivers for fishing on cloudy days; the theory is that a dark pattern presents a better silhouette for the fish to spot the fly.

Adding a few strands of Krystal Flash or Flashabou gives the Deceiver a
little fish-attracting twinkle. And when tying the tail, try using saddle hackles that have somewhat stiff quills; this will help prevent the feathers from
twisting around the bend of the hook when casting.

If you wish to add eyes to your Deceiver, tie the fly using size 3/0 thread;
this will allow you to quickly wrap a larger head as a base for the eyes. You
can make the eyes using enamel paint, or use small adhesive eyes. Coat the
eyes with thick head cement or epoxy.

Bendback

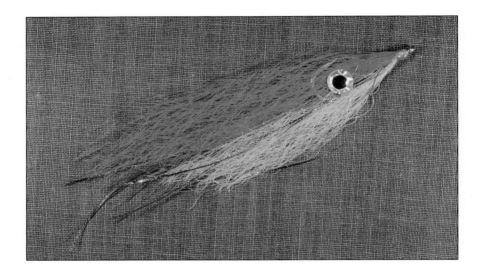

Hook: Long-shank saltwater hook, sizes 4 to 2/0.
Thread: Size 3/0.
Body: Ultra Wire, tinsel, or Mylar tubing.
Wing: Bucktail, FisHair, or your choice of wing material.
Flash material: Flashabou, Krystal Flash, or your choice of flash material.
Eyes: Enamel paint or holographic eyes glued to the sides of the head.

GO ONLINE AND SEARCH FOR THE BENDBACK AND YOU'LL be blown away by the wide variety of flies tied using this format. When it was first created, the Bendback was very simple: a tinsel body, bucktail wing, and thread head. Today, inventive tiers convert many of their favorite patterns into Bendbacks.

The term "bendback" refers to the shape of the hook, not the materials used to tie the fly. The hook is bent up slightly about one-third of an inch from the eye. Place the altered hook in the vise with the point on top and tie the pattern. The altered shape of the hook and the full wing encourage the fly to fish with the point on top so it does not snag on rocks and weeds.

Once upon a time, Mustad manufactured hooks for tying Bendbacks, but they have been discontinued. You can easily bend a stainless steel hook into the proper shape using small pliers, and experiment with hooks of various degrees of bend. Another option, overlooked by many fly tiers, is hooks designed for rigging plastic worms when fishing for freshwater bass. I tie Bendbacks, and simply bend my hooks to shape.

Whether you fish marl flats for redfish or rocky outcroppings for striped bass and bluefish, use Bendbacks to prevent snagging the bottom and to keep fishing.

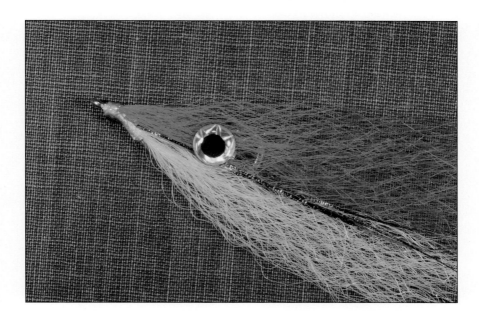

Flashtail Clouser Minnow

Hook: Targus 9413 or TFS 5444 60-degree bent-shank jig hook, size 2/0.

Thread: White Danville Fly Master Plus and red Fly Masters Plus.

Eyes: Spirit River Real Eyes Plus, 7/32-inch, nickel/yellow.

Flashtail: Silver and pearl Flashabou.

Tail: White bucktail and white Slinky Flash.

Side flash: Silver and pearl Flashabou.

Belly: White bucktail and white Slinky Flash.

Wing: White bucktail, white Slinky Flash, chartreuse Slinky Flash, and chartreuse bucktail.

Topping: Light blue Krystal Flash.

BOB CLOUSER'S FAMOUS CLOUSER MINNOW—THE ORIGINAL version or the Flashtail Clouser Minnow—has to be included on many top-10 lists of saltwater patterns. Like many great flies, the Clouser Minnow offers a base for experimenting and making innovative modifications. Striper-fishing guru Dan Blanton's Flashtail Whistler, an outgrowth of the original Whistler, is a wonderful example. In fact, after tying his Flashtail Whistler, he quickly recommended adding flashtails to the Clouser Minnow, Lefty's Deceiver, and many other flies. The synthetic materials brightened these patterns and, under the right conditions, made them more effective.

The weighted Flashtail Clouser Minnow cuts through heavy currents to reach fish holding in eddies and seams. You can modify the weight of the fly when selecting dumbbell eyes and materials. The Flashtail Clouser Minnow, with the dumbbell placed near the hook eye, bobs up and down in the water like a jig. Tying the fly to your leader using a loop knot will accentuate this jigging action.

Flashtail Whistler

Hook: Gamakatsu 29111-25 or an equivalent, sizes 1/0 to 4/0.
Thread: Clear medium monofilament or chartreuse Danville Flat Waxed Nylon.
Eyes: Extra-large silver bead chain.
Weight: Size .030-inch lead or nontoxic wire.
Flashtail and side flash: Pearl Flashabou.
Tail: White, chartreuse, and misty blue H2O SF Flash Blend.
Wing: White H2O SF Flash Blend.
Topping: Light blue Krystal Flash.
Collar: Medium red Vernille.
Hackle: White medium saddle or large neck hackles.

DAN BLANTON TIED THE WHISTLER IN THE 1960S TO IMITATE a bucktail jig, the most effective striped bass lure ever created. Dan's first Whistlers were pretty dull, tied using only bucktail and feathers. But, in the early 1970s, Dan added Mylar tinsel and eventually Flashabou to the tail of Whistler, and the pattern quickly became a fish-catching sensation.

"Flashtails on flies are like the tail of a comet or the flaming exhaust of a rocket heading into orbit on a black night," Dan once wrote.

In addition to the Flashtail, Dan added synthetic body materials and a 60-degree jig hook. All these synthetic materials are easy to use, and once you find a winning color combination, you can always find the exact same materials in the fly shop. And, a Flashtail Whistler is a very durable pattern.

A Flashtail Whistler pushes water, making it especially effective for attracting fish in stained conditions. Tie it to imitate the color of local prey or in brighter hues as an attractor pattern; it's hard to avoid adding chartreuse to the Flashtail Whistler. You can also tie Dan's pattern with more translucent synthetic materials for fishing in the clearer water conditions common in the Southeast.

Purple Tide Slave

Hook: Gamakatsu SC-15, size 1/0.
Thread: Purple 3/0.
Weight: Large tungsten dumbbell painted purple.
Mouth parts: Fluorescent fire orange or root beer Krystal Flash.
Eyes: Extra-large EP Crab/Shrimp Eyes.
Legs: Purple/pumpkin Fly Enhancer Legs.
Body: Sand EP Foxy Bush and tan arctic fox fur.
Extras: Clear Cure Goo Hydro and Sally Hansen Miracle Gel Nail Polish—Too Haute 520.

A GREAT FISH-CATCHING FLY IS A BLEND OF SEVERAL important elements. First, the pattern must reach the correct depth in the water column; too high or too low, and fish might miss seeing it or they might be locked into feeding on bait at a different depth. Size is also an important consideration; typically, a fly can be a size or two smaller than the real bait, but fish often pass on a fly that is too large. Color is some-times critical, although I have played with the idea of tying all my flies in chartreuse; I suspect I wouldn't catch fewer fish, and there are times I might actually catch more. And last, but hardly least, a good fly creates a natural swimming or moving action in the water when retrieved. The Tide Slave, which is tied using several soft flowing materials, has terrific swimming action when moving through the water.

This slightly larger Tide Slave, dressed on a size 1/0 hook, is a good choice when fishing for permit. The dumbbell eyes will help the fly sink quickly to the right depth before the fish turn and swim in a new direction. Scale the Tide Slave down to size 4 or 2, and substitute with bead–chain eyes, and you'll have a first-rate bonefish fly.

Green Deceiver

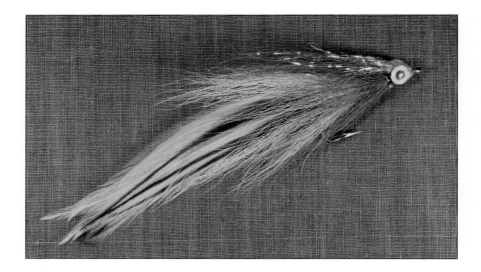

Hook: Regular saltwater hook, size 2/0 or 4/0.
Thread: Clear monofilament.
Tail: White and chartreuse saddle hackles.
Body: White, chartreuse, and olive bucktail.
Back: Green thin Flashabou or a similar material.
Eyes: Medium pearl 3-D eyes.

THIS FLY, TIED BY JERE HALDEMANN, WON THE SALTWATER category in the fly-tying contest held at the annual 2014 International Fly Tying Symposium.

Every November, tiers gather outside New York City in Somerset, New Jersey, to share their latest flies and newest tying techniques. A fly-tying contest is one of the features of the Symposium. Participants to the contest do not have to be present to win, so flies arrive from around the world. The judges are many of the tiers in attendance, which has included Bob Popovics, Bob Clouser, Jay "Fishy" Fullum, Gary Borger, and many other famous anglers. These esteemed judges selected Haldemann's Green Deceiver as the winner.

In addition to being a first-rate example of a Deceiver, Haldemann's Green Deceiver points to the importance of blending colors. Sure, there are plenty of solid-color flies—white, chartreuse, black, and more—and they all catch fish. But, nothing in nature is a solid color. Whether for camouflage or perhaps to attract a mate, most fish, birds, and other forms of wildlife are many colors. This Green Deceiver is a wonderful blend of colors that give it the general appearance of a real baitfish.

Think about blending colors when tying flies. Select contrasting shades of feathers and furs and your flies will look more lifelike.

Tabory's Snake Fly

Hook: Varivas 990S or a similar hook, size 2/0 or 3/0.
Thread: White 3/0.
Tail: White, pink and olive ostrich herl, and pearl Flashabou.
Head: White deer hair.
Eyes: Doll eyes or a weighted dumbbell.

LOU TABORY ROCKED THE FLY-FISHING WORLD IN 1992 when he published his book *Inshore Fly Fishing*. Although anglers had trekked the coasts for years in search of striped bass, bluefish, and other favorite gamefish, Lou laid all the secrets bare: tackle selection, rigging, fishing techniques, and flies. Thousands of fly fishermen discovered a new way to enjoy their sport. As a result of this interest, tackle manufacturers introduced new rods, reels, and lines, and fly tiers started making new patterns. Because of this profound impact, one angler from the New Jersey Shore said that Lou Tabory was saltwater fly-fishing's version of Theodore Gordon.

Tabory introduced this pattern, called the Snake Fly, in *Inshore Fly Fishing*. Fish this pattern near the surface using a floating line, with a sinking-tip, or a full sinking line to reach deeper into the water column. The version of the Snake Fly we see here is tied using metal dumbbell eyes to add weight and swim deep, but you can also glue lightweight 3-D or small doll eyes to the top of the clipped deer-hair head.

The broad head will push water and help the fish find the fly. In addition to white, tie Tabory's Snake Fly in any of your favorite fish-catching colors. And, rather than constructing the tail using fragile ostrich herl, substitute with bucktail.

Tarpon Toad

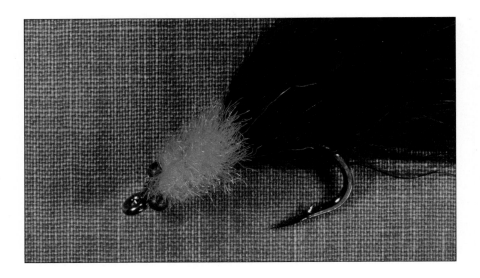

Hook: Regular saltwater hook, size 2/0.
Thread: Black 3/0.
Tail: Black marabou.
Head: Red rug yarn.
Eyes: Black plastic dumbbell.

THE TARPON TOAD, SOMETIMES CALLED SIMPLY "THE TOAD," is based on Del Brown's famous permit fly called the Merkin. Del tied pieces of stiff rug yarn perpendicular to the hook shank to create the oval body of a crab. This pattern has become a universal hit, and other tiers have created new patterns using this design.

Gary Merriman created the Tarpon Toad in the 1990s using Brown's idea for making the body of his fly. Gary's goal when designing the Tarpon Toad was to create a pattern that would remain suspended higher in the water column and have a lot of natural swimming action. Although the original Tarpon Toad was tied using light-colored yellow materials, you can make this pattern in any colors you wish. Here we see a black–and–red version of the fly which is perfect for when you want to fish with a dark-colored fly.

Two versions of the Tarpon Toad have evolved over the years. The original had a tail tied using a rabbit Zonker strip; this style of pattern is still very popular. The second, which we see here, omits the Zonker strip. The fluffy marabou tail still imparts a lot of swimming action, and there is no long rabbit strip to foul around the hook while casting.

Cyclops

Hook: Regular saltwater, size 1/0.
Thread: White 3/0.
Tail: White and blue Big Fly Fiber, and red, white, and blue calftail or a substitute.
Eye: Adhesive eye.

MATT RAMSEY, WHO DESIGNS FLIES FOR UMPQUA FEATHER Merchants, created this cool topwater pattern called Cyclops. The Cyclops is a slider and is perfect for casting to striped bass when they are feeding on baitfish near the surface of the water. It is also simple to make and perfect for new tiers looking for their first topwater fly.

Big Fly Fiber is a long crinkled hair material suitable for making very large flies. It comes in a rainbow of colors, so you can tie Cyclops to suit your mode as well as the mode of the fish. Because of its crinkled nature, you can tie a full-bodied fly using only a small bunch of material.

Matt and his fishing partner, Scott Nelson, own an outfitting business called Two Dudes Flyfishing, in Eugene, Oregon. Matt says he created the Cyclops for catching taimen in Mongolia. Taimen are the world's largest salmonid. The Cyclops was a hit for catching those strong fish, but the Cyclops had obvious application for saltwater fly fishing.

The head of the fly is folded closed-cell foam. The tail of the Cyclops sinks slightly into the surface film, but the foam head remains above the surface. Place a single eye on the bottom of the head so that it faces down, making the fly simulate a wounded baitfish lying on the surface. Coat the bottom of the head with head cement to seal the eye in place.

Rattle Rouser

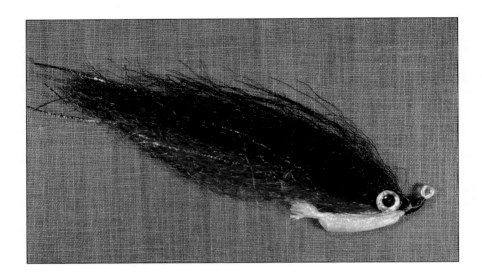

Hook: Eagle Claw 413, sizes 2 to 3/0.
Thread: Black 3/0.
Body: Pearl Mylar tubing.
Rattle: Large glass rattle.
Wing: Big Fly Fiber, Super Hair, or your favorite synthetic hair material, and strands of Flashabou or a substitute.
Eyes: Large silver 3-D eyes.

ACCORDING TO MY RESEARCH, EXPERT FLY DESIGNER Kirk Dietrich, of Louisiana, created the Rattle Rouser. It is a fine searching pattern although you can tie it in colors to match most of our favorite large baitfish: mackerel, bunker, herring, and more. Substitute colors of materials and use waterproof pens to add barring and other markings to imitate all these species of prey.

The Eagle Claw 413 is an economical jig hook suitable for use in salt water. This heavy-wire hook comes with Eagle Claw's Seaguard finish, which protects the hook and prevents it from corroding. The shank is bent at a 60-degree angle near the hook eye. This hook works better than a jig hook bent at a 90-degree angle for a streamer such as the Rattle Rouser. The fly swims through the water more naturally yet the hook point still remains on top.

The glass rattle, inserted in the Mylar tubing, appears as a belly on the fly and gets the fishes' attention. Many anglers argue that a fly containing a rattle catches more fish. Tie a few Rattle Rousers and see if you catch more fish.

The sealed glass rattle adds buoyancy to the belly of the fly. Although the shape of the jig hook forces the fly to ride with the hook point on top, the rattle encourages the fly to flip over. Slip a couple of BBs in the Mylar tubing before adding the rattle. This small amount of ballast keeps the Rattle Rouser tracking true through the water.

Buzzi's Painted Poppers

Hook: 4X- or 6X-longer saltwater hook in your choice of sizes.
Body: Pre-formed foam popper. Wrap the hook shank with thread, and
then glue the body in place using epoxy. Paint the body using the Copic
Airbrush System.
Tail: Feathers, fur, or your favorite tail materials.
Eyes: Paint or adhesive.

POPPERS ARE SOME OF OUR FAVORITE TOPWATER FLIES.
Poppers are commonly used for catching striped bass, bluefish, and other
aggressive meat-eating fish, but some anglers use smaller poppers for catching redfish and even sea trout. The key to catching reds and "specks" with
a popper is not to spook the fish, so retrieve the fly gently, creating only a
very light chucking sound.

All fly shops carry a selection of poppers, or you can make your own.
Typically, however, homemade poppers look a little boring; they usually
have rough bodies and are solid colors. Popper-making guru Brad Buzzi
creates poppers complete with painted scales and other patterns that you
commonly find only on manufactured lures. While the fish don't care about
the finished appearance of a popper, he is a master at crafting poppers that
appeal to anglers.

Brad paints the bodies of his flies using the Copic Airbrush System,
which you can find in almost any well-stocked crafts store, online, and in
a few fly shops. The Copic airbrush uses permanent-marker ink, which
comes in dozens of colors. If you paint a large number of poppers, you can
purchase marker refills suitable for coloring dozens of flies; after the initial
investment for the airbrush, you can paint flies for just a few cents apiece.

Brad first sprays the base colors on the body (working from light to
dark), and then allows the ink to dry. Next, he wraps nylon screen or netting on the body as a mask and paints the popper with a contrasting color.
Removing the netting reveals wonderful scales. Finally, Brad adds eyes, seals
the body with thirty-minute epoxy, and ties the tail. The results are outstanding, and this is something you can do—really!

Clouser Minnow

Hook: Long-shank saltwater hook, sizes 8 to 2/0.
Weight: Dumbbell or bead chain.
Thread: Your choice of color, size 3/0.
Body: Flat silver or pearl tinsel.
Wing: Bucktail or your favorite fine-fibered synthetic hair, your choice of colors.

THE CLOUSER MINNOW HAS BEEN ONE OF OUR MOST popular streamers for many years. Born on Pennsylvania's Susquehanna River for catching smallmouth bass, it quickly migrated to the salt and became a favorite pattern for catching striped bass, bluefish, sea trout, and a wide variety of other species.

A lot of anglers overlook the Clouser Minnow as a worthy fly for catching wary flats fish such as bonefish, permit, and redfish. I always carry Clouser Minnows tied on size 8 hooks with small bead-chain eyes and chartreuse craft-fur wings; more than one shallow-water guide has plucked this pattern out of my fly box and said, "Try this first."

Several years ago, while visiting Florida to attend a wedding, I took off for an afternoon to fish Indian River Lagoon with Captain John Kumiski. We caught several ladyfish and crevalle jacks, and near the end of the day, John motored us across the lagoon to a flats where he thought we'd have a shot at redfish. Sure enough, within just a few minutes, we spotted three reds pushing water and heading our way. I cast one of those lightweight flies well ahead of the fish and let it sink. Finally, as the redfish moved within three feet of my fly, I tightened the line and gently lifted it from the sandy bottom. The slight movement triggered the fish to attack: they burst forward and one snatched the fly. I repeated this tactic several more times that day and caught half a dozen powerful redfish.

Apte Tarpon Fly

Hook: Long-shank saltewater hook, sizes 6 to 1/0.
Thread: Orange 3/0.
Tail: Orange and yellow saddle hackles.
Collar: Orange saddle hackle.
Body: Orange tying thread.

THE LEGENDARY STU APTE, ONE OF OUR GREATEST TARPON
fly anglers, once wrote: "A typical tarpon fishing scenario might have
you standing on a casting platform for hours, holding your rod with
one hand, the fly in the fingers of your other hand, and waiting for that one
opportunity. All of the sudden the guide excitedly whispers, 'There she is
. . . 11 o'clock . . . sixty feet. Make the cast! Drop it right in front of her face.
Now! NOW!'"

No one knows tarpon fishing better than Stu. He has spent untold thousands of hours pursuing trophy tarpon, and he has caught hundreds of these
fish. In fact, Stu has landed more tarpon than most avid saltwater anglers
see in a lifetime.

The Apte Tarpon Fly is a simple concoction: hook, thread, and hackles.
Some anglers say that the pattern's characteristic long snout simulates a
needlefish, and the long, feathered tail creates excellent swimming action.
One of the keys of the Apte Tarpon fly is the heavy hackle collar tied at the
end of the hook shank. The thick collar "pushes" water when the pattern is
stripped through the water, creating a disturbance that helps a tarpon locate
the fly.

The classic Apte Tarpon Fly, which was featured on a US postage stamp,
is tied in orange and yellow. Many knowledgeable anglers choose this version on sunny days and when fishing over bright flats. Use this pattern as a
model, but change colors to create a fly box full of fish-catching patterns for
meeting any fishing condition.

Remember that fishing for trophy tarpon is not about casting; instead,
you will spend a great deal of time searching the water looking for a big
fish to slide within casting range. You will want a fly you can depend on.
The Apte Tarpon Fly is a time-honored pattern that you will want in your
fishing kit for your next trip to the flats.

Caloosahatchee Cannibal

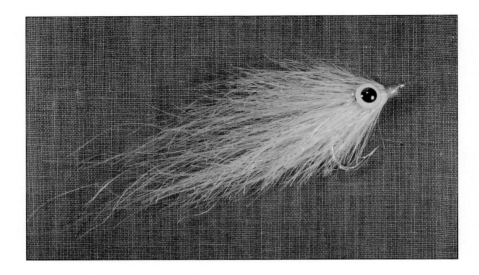

Hook: Gamakatsu SC-15, size 2/0.
Thread: Clear monofilament.
Belly: White saltwater yak hair and pearl Wing N' Flash.
Back: White, tan, and yellow saltwater yak hair.
Eyes: 8-millimeter clear doll eyes.

THE CALOOSAHATCHEE RIVER IS ON THE GULF COAST IN southwest Florida. The mouth of the river, near Fort Myers, Cape Coral, and Sanibel Island, has long been a prime fishing destination. In *The Book of the Tarpon*, which was written in the early part of the twentieth century, early angling authority A. W. Dimock describes fishing the Caloosahatchee River. *The Book of the Tarpon* is considered the first volume devoted to this magnificent game fish.

Although the river has changed since Dimock fished there, it is still considered a prime tarpon destination; some anglers consider it the most consistent producer of tarpon in Lee County, Florida. In addition to tarpon, the area's mangroves hold snook. Tie Drew Chicone's Caloosahatchee Cannibal, and a variety of similar flies, and you'll surely enjoy some fine fishing. And be sure to pack some small crab imitations and other small patterns for catching redfish and sea trout.

There are plenty of fine guides in the area, and you'll easily find lodging in Fort Myers or Cape Coral. If you prefer roughing it, check out Caloosahatchee Regional Park, which is operated by Lee County Parks & Recreation. The park offers inexpensive camping, and you're just a short drive from good fishing.

The water in the Caloosahatchee River is somewhat stained. The tall Caloosahatchee Cannibal, which is a general baitfish imitation, pushes water so hungry fish can easily locate the fly.

Captiva Cannibal

Hook: Gamakatsu SC-15, size 2/0.
Thread: Monofilament.
Belly: White saltwater yak hair and pearl Wing N' Flash.
Back: White, gray, tan, and turquoise saltwater yak hair, and silver Wing N' Flash.
Eyes: 8-millimeter clear doll eyes.

NOTHING EVER STAYS THE SAME, AND THIS IS ESPECIALLY true along the storm-swept Florida Coast. Strong winds, hurricanes, and tidal surges are continually changing the coastline. For example, Captiva Island was part of neighboring Sanibel Island to the southeast. In 1926, a hurricane's storm surge created a new channel, separating Captiva from Sanibel. And North Captiva Island was severed from Captiva during a hurricane in 1921, creating Redfish Pass. (Hmm, wonder how it got its name?) Captiva is a barrier island to Pine Island, which was once surely part of the mainland.

All of these islands contain flats, mangroves, and backchannels, the kinds of places that hold fish. Hire a guide and his boat if you are new to the area; there are plenty of expert anglers who can show you the best fishing. Or, if you like to explore and want to plan your own trip, take or rent a kayak to access many miles of fine fishing.

The Captiva Cannibal is the cousin to the Caloosahatchee Cannibal. Make both patterns using the same tying methods, just alter the colors of the materials used in constructing the backs and bellies. Drew Chicone says he ties the Captiva Cannibal for fishing the turquois-colored water surrounding the island. This is a great fishing destination; you could spend a week there and never get bored.

Crease Fly

Hook: Long-shank saltwater hook, sizes 4 to 2/0.

Thread: Your choice of color, size A.

Tail: Bucktail and Krystal Flash, your choice of colors.

Body: Closed-cell foam, your choice of color.

Eyes: Gold or silver adhesive eyes.

CAPTAIN JOE BLADOS, OF GREENPORT, NEW YORK, CREATED the innovative Crease Fly. Captain Blados designed the Crease Fly to catch the striped bass, bluefish, and other species that visit Long Island every summer. The pattern is a lightweight, easy-to-cast alternative to a popper. The narrow profile slices through the air, yet the fly, with its cupped face makes a lot of commotion on the surface of the water when retrieving the fly.

The Crease Fly is fun and easy to make. First tie the tail using bucktail in your choice of colors. Include a few sprigs of Krystal Flash to add a twinkle to the tail when the fly is resting on the water. The butt end of the tail should extend along the entire hook shank to create a solid base for gluing on the foam body.

The body of the Crease Fly is thin closed-cell foam folded and glued to the hook using superglue. Cut the foam to shape using heavy hobby scissors, not fine fly-tying scissors. Check out the photo of the Crease Fly; use that as a guide when shaping the foam for your flies. A company called River Roads Creations offers a set of cutters, similar to cookie cutters, designed to punch out the bodies of foam Crease Flies.

After gluing the body of the Crease Fly to the hook, you may add eyes and color the foam. Coating the finished fly with epoxy dramatically increases the durability of the finished pattern, and you can use one fly to catch dozens of fish.

Blonde

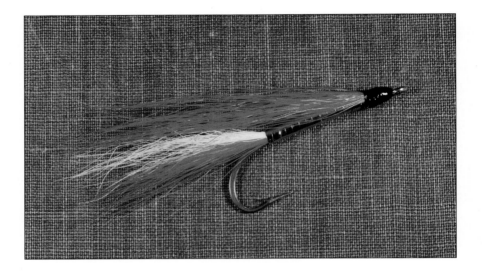

Hook: Regular saltwater hook, sizes 8 to 2/0.
Thread: Black 6/0.
Tail: Bucktail.
Body: Flat, round, or braided tinsel.
Wing: Bucktail.
Note: Select bucktail in the colors of your choice.

THE BLONDE IS A TRUE FLY-FISHING CLASSIC. GENERALLY credited to famed angler and author Joe Brooks, Colonel Joseph Bates, a serious student of the history of flies and fly fishing, says both Brooks and Homer Rhode Jr., created the Blonde. Of course, the Blonde is such an incredibly simple fly that I am sure many tiers, working independently, made the same type of basic pattern; what's hard about tying a bucktail wing and tail to a hook?

In 1963, Brooks wrote an article for *Outdoor Life* about a fishing trip he took to Argentina. He said, "This was my first trip to Argentina, back in 1955. Packing my tackle at home I kept thinking about the 10, 12, 14 and even 20-pound brown trout that Jorge Donovan had told me were in the Argentine rivers. Remembering that old theory that a big trout likes a big mouthful, I had reached into my salt-water tackle box and picked out a handful of 'blonde' flies—big, white bucktails that I used for striped bass."

The Blonde is still a great pattern for catching striped bass, but it is also a terrific choice for bluefish and other toothy species that shed flies; tying a Blonde takes only a couple of minutes and the materials are inexpensive, so you'll shed no tears if the fish destroy a couple of flies.

The name of the fly comes from the fact that the Blonde was originally tied in white, cream, and pale yellow, but you may use any colors you like— red, olive, black, tan, and more. The Blonde is a particularly fine fly for new tiers; it requires only the most basic skills to make.

Homer Rhode Tarpon Fly

Hook: Regular-length saltwater hook, sizes 1/0 to 3/0.
Thread: Black 3/0.
Wing: Grizzly, white, and yellow saddle hackles, or in the colors of your choice.
Collar: White and yellow saddle hackles, or in the colors of your choice.

WITH THE EVOLUTION OF NEW TACKLE, FISHING FOR tarpon grew in popularity. For some anglers, it is their passion; they spend almost all their time on the water searching for these mighty fish. Fiberglass and then graphite rods, and the development of nylon and fluorocarbon leaders, made it possible to hook and hold large tarpon. Even before these remarkable pieces of tackle were available, anglers competed to see who could land the biggest tarpon.

The Miami Beach Rod and Reel Club started the Metropolitan Miami Fishing Tournament in 1935. The purpose of this fly-fishing event was to encourage tourism and fishing in South Florida. In 1940, Howard Bonbright set the tournament record for tarpon at 36.5 pounds, but in 1952, H. K. Atkins set a new tournament record with a tarpon weighing 51.8 pounds. Although they were a long way from catching 100-pound-plus freight-train tarpon, the hunt was on for trophy fish.

Homer Rhode was an early champion of catching tarpon on flies. He was a ranger in Everglades National Park, and was catching bonefish and permit on flies in the 1930s. This fly is considered the forerunner of the Seaducer series of patterns.

Tie the hackle collar of the Homer Rhode Tarpon Fly full so it "pushes" water when stripped on the retrieve. Many experienced anglers swear that this sets off subtle vibrations through the water that help the fish locate the fly. Also notice that this pattern is tied in the classic tarpon–fly format with a small bare space behind the eye for tying the fly to the leader.

Joe Brooks Tarpon Fly

Hook: Your favorite brand of regular-length saltwater hook, sizes 1/0 to 3/0.

Thread: Red 3/0.

Wing: White saddle hackles.

Collar: Red marabou.

SOME KNOWLEDGEABLE ANGLERS CONSIDER JOE BROOKS the father of modern fly fishing. You've never head of him? Well, Joe died in 1972 while on a fishing trip to the Yellowstone Country, and so he has become overlooked by many younger anglers. Today, most anglers would mention Lefty Kreh as our most significant fly fisherman, but even the great Lefty wrote, "Joe Brooks had the biggest influence on me; he got me into writing and got me into fly fishing. He got me interested in salt water fishing."

Brooks was a worldwide ambassador for all forms of angling, and trekked across the globe in search of good fishing. He was an author and tackle innovator. He also designed very simple yet effective flies. For example, the Blonde, a simple pattern we are including in this book, is a fly even novice tiers can quickly make. The Joe Brooks Tarpon Fly is another simple pattern you will want to add to your fishing kit.

The Joe Brooks Tarpon Fly helped shape what we think of as the classic-fly form. The long tail hackles are tied splayed near the end of the hook shank, and the thread nose occupies the middle one-third of the shank; there is a bare space behind the eye for tying the fly to the leader using a turle knot. Tie the collar using a small marabou feather rather than hackle. The hackle is full enough to "push" water on the calm tarpon flats and gives the fly a pulsating, lifelike swimming action.

Billy Pate Homassasa Tarpon Fly

Hook: Your favorite brand of regular-length, heavy-wire saltwater hook, sizes 2/0 and 3/0.
Thread: Size 3/0.
Wing: Saddle hackles in your choice of colors.
Collar: Bucktail in your choice of colors.
Eyes: Medium chrome dumbbell.
Note: Here's another pattern for fishing very deep.

BILLY PATE WAS ONE OF THE LEADERS IN THE EVOLUTION of fly fishing for tarpon. In 1982, he set a world record by boating a fish weighing 188 pounds using a 16-pound-test tippet. He caught that fish in Homassasa, Florida, and for almost twenty years, anglers gathered in those storied waters to try to break his record. In addition to this impressive record, Pate was also the first angler to catch all four species of marlin—black, blue, white, and striped—using a fly rod. These feats, and more, made him a big-game fly-fishing legend.

Pate, who passed away in 2011 at the age of eighty, was a much beloved figure in the fly-fishing world. He was inducted into the Fishing Hall of Fame at the International Gamefish Association, and was a member of the Everglades Protection Association, Trout Unlimited, the Bonefish & Tarpon Trust, the Don Hawley Foundation, the Miami Beach Rod and Reel Club, and the Islamorada Fishing Club. Billy spent many years working in the carpet business, and eventually he and Captain George Hommell founded a terrific business called World Wide Sportsman, in Islamorada, Florida. Billy and George eventually sold the business to Pro Bass Shops, but you can still stop at World Wide Sportsman when passing through Islamorada.

His Homassasa Tarpon Fly is tied using a medium chrome dumbbell. The dumbbell, perched on the top of the hook shank, adds a small amount of weight to the fly which makes it ideal for casting to fish lying in deeper water.

Gurgler

Hook: Long-shank saltwater hook, sizes 2 to 2/0.
Thread: Size 3/0.
Tail: Bucktail or your favorite long hair and strands of Krystal Flash, Flashabou, or another brand of flash material.
Body: Krystal Chenille.
Body hackle: Saddle hackle.
Back: Closed-cell foam.

THE GURGLER MAY BE THE BEST-KNOWN PATTERN
designed by the late Jack Gartside.

Jack was an entertaining figure at almost all of the East Coast fly-fishing
shows. He was also a very talented pattern designer. His specialty was creating fish-catching flies using a minimum number of ingredients. The Gurgler is a great example of his ingenuity.

The Gurgler is one of the most popular floating saltwater flies ever
devised. It is very easy to tie, and although the body is foam, it is surprisingly durable. A sharp-toothed bluefish might destroy a Gurgler, but you
can catch a couple dozen striped bass using the same fly. In fact, I have several Gurglers in my fly box all sporting tags of monofilament on the hook
eyes; I used these flies, and they are all in good enough condition to use
again in the future.

Tie the Gurgler in a variety of sizes and colors. A yellow or orange Gurgler is easy to see on the surface of the water when the fly is at rest.

Sometimes a popper makes too much noise, especially when fishing on
the flats or in shallow water. A Gurgler, however, makes a more subtle noise.
The gentle gurgling sound attracts rather than repels fish. Tie or purchase
a few Gurglers, and they will quickly become an important part of your
fishing kit.

FishHead

Hook: Mustad 34007, 3407DT, 3366, or Daiichi 2546, sizes 4 to 2/0.
Thread: White and red, size 3/0.
Tail: Grizzly saltwater neck hackle with pearl Krystal Flash.
Hackle collar: Grizzly.
Body: ½-inch-diameter pearl Corsair, EZ Body tubing, or Flexo tubing.

JACK GARTSIDE WAS A TERRIFIC FLY DESIGNER. HIS PATTERNS were usually very simple; using only a couple of materials, Jack could create a fly that would catch fish. Check out his other fly called the Gurgler in this book. Even a novice tier can fill a box full of his original patterns and be confident that he would have effective flies for his next fishing trip.

Mike Hogue, the proprietor of Badger Creek Fly Tying, an online fly-tying catalog, recently reminded me of Gartside's unique brand of creativity. Mike sent three flies Jack developed called the FishHead. Jack made the head of the original FishHead using a tough, flexible tubing he called Corsair. Today, most fly shops carry a product called EZ Body tubing, which is very similar to the original Corsair; these products are interchangeable.

To make the head of the fly, simply tie the end of a piece of EZ Body tubing behind the hook eye and facing forward; the tubing completely encircles the eye. Tie off and clip the thread. Next, push the tubing back toward the rear of the hook to form the head. Restart the thread on the tubing behind the hook eye. Pull the thread tight to form a bullet-shaped head, clip the excess tubing around the eye, and wrap the thread head.

Corsair is a bulletproof type of tubing. The FishHead is suitable for using wherever you find small baitfish. Change the colors of the materials to match the baitfish in your local waters, and be sure to tie a few FishHeads in black and bright attractor color schemes.

Coyote

Hook: Tiemco TMC811S, size 1.
Thread: Clear monofilament. **Eyes:** Meadium Real Eyes with adhesive eyes on the sides.
Body: Flat pearl braided tinsel.
Monofilament spike: 40-pound-test monofilament.
Tail: Rabbit Zonker strip.
Wing: Bucktail.
Flash: Pearl Krystal Flash.
Spinner blade: Size #00 gold or nickel Colorado blade, a size #12 barrel swivel, and size #0 split ring.

A FLY-FISHING PAL CREATED THIS UNUSUAL PATTERN called the Coyote. A small spinner blade, tied to the underside of the hook, is the outstanding feature of this pattern.

I know some fly fishers might look askance at the Coyote because of the spinner blade, but then patterns tied using synthetic materials were once not considered proper "flies." It didn't take long, however, before anglers saw the value in Surf Candies and this whole host of new fly designs. Today these patterns are the staples of many fly boxes; in the world of saltwater fly fishing, using synthetic materials might even be more popular than natural ingredients.

There might not be a great difference between using a spinner blade and a rattle when tying a fly. These components are not traditional materials, yet both are designed to make noise and grab the attention of the fish. So why use one and not the other?

Casting the Coyote is easy. Even though it has a spinner blade, the blade rarely tangles in the leader.

The Coyote is a fine striped bass and bluefish fly, and it also catches its share of snook. It's an unusual pattern, but fun to tie and fish.

Half and Half

Hook: Mustad 34007, sizes 2 to 2/0.
Thread: Danville Flymaster Plus.
Eyes: Lead or chrome dumbbell.
Tail: Saddle hackles and Flashabou.
Collar: Bucktail.
Belly and back: Bucktail.

THE HALF AND HALF IS A BLEND OF TWO OF OUR BEST-known patterns: the Lefty's Deceiver and Clouser Minnow.

Look closely and you'll see features of the two flies. The hackle tail and bucktail belly and back are inspired by the Deceiver; the dumbbell eyes, tied on top of the shank so the hook flips over when fishing, are taken from the Clouser Minnow.

Even a novice tier can craft a fish-catching Half and Half. All fly shops carry the ingredients, and they are easy to tie to the hook. Let's start with the tail.

The length of the hackle tail is about one and one-half times the overall length of the hook. Strip the fluffy fibers from the base of the feathers until they are the correct length. Add a few strands of Flashabou or another brand of flash material on both sides of the hackle tail.

Tie the collar around the base of the tail. Do not use the bucktail fibers from the base of the tail. These are coarse and will flair like deer body hair. Clip the hair from the top two-thirds of the deer tail.

Tie the dumbbell eyes on top of the hook shank, but leave ample room to tie on the belly and back, and to wrap a neat thread head.

Tie the Half and Half in a range of colors. Red and white are classic colors for flies and lures, but an all-white, black, or chartreuse Half and Half also catches fish. You can also use these same materials to tie simple Deceivers and Clouser Minnows.

Tarpon Toy

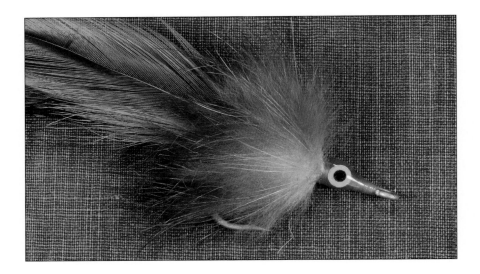

Hook: Tiemco TMC811S or your favorite saltwater hook, size 3/0.
Thread: Brown Monocord for tying the tail, and switch to orange 3/0 for wrapping the nose of the fly.
Tail: Red squirrel tail hair, gold Flashabou, and furnace hackles.
Collar: Natural gray rabbit strip.
Eyes: Small yellow adhesive eyes.

THE TARPON TOY LOOKS GREAT WHEN STRIPPED THROUGH
the water. The rabbit fur collar comes alive and gives the fly a lifelike swimming action.

There are two types of rabbit strips; the material you purchase should
match the application for the flies you are tying. The most common are
Zonker strips. These are cut with the fur flowing the same direction as the
leather strips. They are perfect for making the tails on flies.

The second are crosscut rabbit strips. This material is cut across the hide
of the rabbit so the fur flows perpendicular to the direction of the strips.
Select crosscut rabbit strips for wrapping around the hook, such as tying
the collar of the Tarpon Toy.

The Tarpon Toy is one of Captain Lenny Moffo's patterns. Captain
Moffo is a topnotch guide working the waters of the Florida Keys. I met
Lenny many years ago while tying flies at the Miami Boat Show. Lenny
came up from the Keys for the day, and it was great learning more about
fishing the Keys from such an accomplished angler. As you can see, he is also
an expert fly tier. His patterns go through hundreds of hours of testing and
tweaking; if Captain Moffo says it's a good pattern, it is probably something
you should add to your personal fly box.

Snag-Free Delight

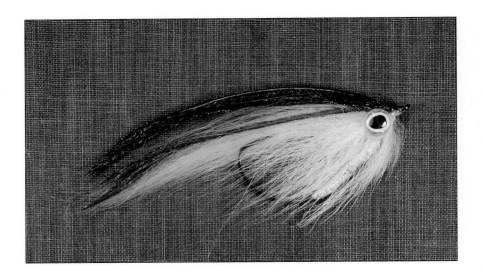

Hook: Plastic worm hook, sizes 2 to 3/0.
Thread: Clear monofilament.
Body: Pearl Mylar tubing.
Belly: Pink SF Flash Blend.
Back: White, yellow, and chartreuse SF Flash Blend.
Topping: Peacock herl.
Eyes: Large 3-D eyes.

CAPTAIN CHRIS NEWSOME SPECIALIZES IN FISHING VIRGINIA'S Chesapeake Bay. If you haven't visited this area, you should: it is rich in gamefish and fly-fishing opportunities.

Captain Newsome fishes the entire Hampton Roads area including the waters surrounding the Chesapeake Bay Tunnel Bridge. If you hit it right, the water flowing under the bridge can contain hundreds of striped bass, and you can actually become weary from catching them. I once fished this area at about 3 o'clock in the morning. Bass were boiling on the surface of the out-going tide, and we hooked a fish on almost every cast. Amazing!

In addition to being an expert angler, Captain Newsome is an inventive fly designer. In this case, when tying his Snag-Free Delight, he uses a hook designed for fishing conventional plastic worms. The hook is bent behind the eye, which encourages the fly to ride with the point on top. Chris first wraps lead wire on the shank to ensure that the pattern rides in the correct position. You can fish the Snag-Free Delight around pilings and near the bottom with little fear of hooking nothing but the fish. Plastic-worm hooks also have large gaps that aid in hooking fish.

This Snag-Free Delight is tied using only synthetic materials, but Captain Newsome makes larger versions using a blend of hackles and synthetic hairs for the wings. Tie the Snag-Free Delight in sizes and colors to match real baitfish, and make a few in attractor colors such as chartreuse, orange, and black.

Inside Counts

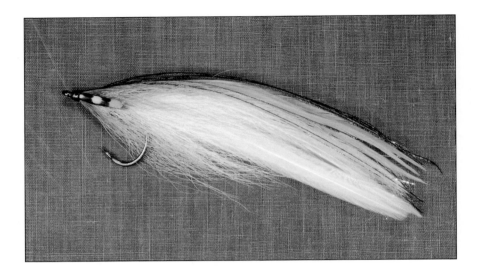

Hook: Tiemco TMC811S or your favorite saltwater hook, size 3/0.
Thread: Black 3/0.
Weight: Plastic-worm cone weight.
Belly: Chartreuse and olive bucktail.
Flanks: Pink and white bucktail.
Wing: White and light olive hackles, and pearl Flashabou.
Back: Chartreuse and olive bucktail.
Topping: Peacock herl.
Cheeks: Jungle cock.

WHEN I OPENED CAPTAIN CHRIS NEWSOME'S PACKAGE AND examined his flies, I thought that Inside Counts was an odd name for a pattern. The "inside" of what? *It's probably someplace where he fishes,* I thought. He is a top guide fishing Virginia's Chesapeake Bay, so I assumed this was a fly he used up inside the Bay.

I was wrong.

The Inside Counts is one of the most beautiful patterns in this book. The jungle cock cheeks and peacock herl topping gives it a classic look. But, the blend of bucktail and saddle hackles give it a very fishy appearance; when retrieved through the water, the colors flow together and make the fly look like a baitfish.

But, it is what's inside the fly that counts.

Captain Newsome slips a small plastic-worm cone weight onto the hook before tying the fly. This adds heft to the pattern and acts as a spreader; any materials tied on behind the hook eye splay around the cone. Chris ties on the hackles and pink bucktail behind the cone, and he places the belly and back in front of the cone. That's a great idea!

I experimented with some hooks and lead cones. Although the lead is soft, getting the cone into position is not easy. You may have to widen the hole in the cones using a drill, and gripping it with pliers will help. But, the extra effort pays off; this is an ingenious idea that you can use to tie interesting weighted flies.

Stinger Deep Minnow

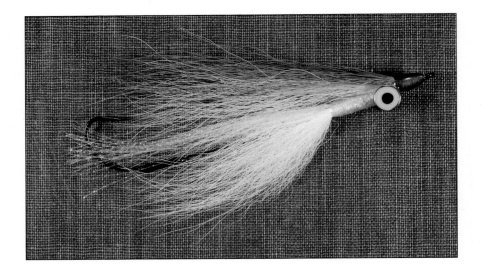

Hooks: Two regular saltwater hooks, size 2.
Thread: Olive 3/0.
Eyes: Medium chrome dumbbell.
Connecting wire: 50-pound-test steel leader.
Tail: White calftail or another fine-fibered hair, and strands of pearl Krystal Flash or a similar material.
Body: Pearl braided tinsel.
Wing: Pink and olive bucktail.

HERE IS A GREAT TAKE ON THE VENERABLE CLOUSER DEEP Minnow.

The Clouser Minnow is one of the bestselling patterns of all time. It is also one of the first patterns taught in beginning fly-tying classes. Why? Because it catches fish!

But what if the fish have sharp teeth? Bluefish, for example, are tough on flies. Not only do they destroy patterns, their teeth easily slice through monofilament and fluorocarbon leaders. In the flash of an eye, you can go from a solid hookup to a limp line. This is very frustrating.

The Stinger Deep Minnow solves both of these problems. A stinger hook, linked to the main body hook using a piece of stout wire leader, keeps the pattern well forward when hooking a fish. This protects both the fly and leader from the teeth of the fish. It's a simple solution to these common problems, and you can use this design on most flies.

The added advantage is that you can use a standard leader, rather than a stiff wire bite tippet, when targeting bluefish.

Use a loop knot when tying any type of Clouser Minnow to your leader. The loop knot remains slightly open, not cinched tight against the hook eye, so the pattern moves freely at the end of the leader. This allows the Clouser Minnow and similarly weighted flies to bob up and down when retrieved through the water, giving the fly an added realistic swimming action.

Dinah-Moe Drum

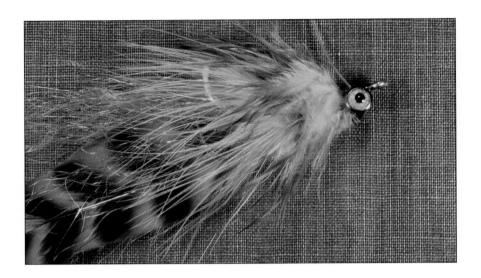

Hook: Regular saltwater hook, size 3/0.
Thread: Olive 3/0.
Eyes: Large chrome dumbbell with adhesive eyes.
Tail: Grizzly hackles dyed golden olive.
Collar: Copper Angel Hair, golden-yellow marabou, and grizzly marabou dyed gold.
Weed guard: 20-pound-test stiff monofilament.

S.S. FLIES IS A UNIQUE FLY-TYING OUTFIT BASED IN MY HOME state of Maine. Every year the guys at S.S. Flies pump out more than 20,000 flies—all tied in their establishment—for guides and fly shops around the world. That's an amazing output!

In addition to making many standard patterns, they also design custom flies to meet the demands of the most accomplished saltwater guides and anglers. Their custom pattern called the Dinah-Moe Drum is a good example of their creativity.

According to Peter Smith, the head man at S.S. Flies, "For the longest time we knew we needed a big, heavy redfish fly. The pattern called Willy the Pimp is big and effective but isn't terribly heavy, and our Clousers are heavy but not really big. Finally, we came up with this fly called the Dinah-Moe Drum. It's four inches long and heavy enough to get down to the fish quickly."

Some anglers search for trophy-size redfish. They require large patterns to catch these big fish. Dinah-Moe Drum is a good answer to this problem.

This is the golden-olive Dinah-Moe Drum, but S.S. Flies also ties it in chartreuse and natural-colored materials. The Angel Hair and marabou give the fly excellent swimming action in the water. This fly would also be a top candidate for catching striped bass and many other species of our favorite gamefish.

Boehm's Gurgler

Hook: Long-shank saltwater hook, size 2/0.
Thread: Tan 3/0.
Tail: Tan rabbit Zonker strip and tan craft fur.
Body: Pearl Krystal Flash.
Collar: A large tuft of tan rabbit fur.
Back: Tan closed-cell foam.

ACCORDING TO PETER SMITH OF S. S. FLIES, "WE DEVELOPED this Gurgler years ago for Capt. Alex Boehm. He had just signed on as a full-time private guide for an angler in Key West, a man who had the means to employ a captain on his personal staff. One of Alex's first big trips was to Ascension Bay and he needed a baby tarpon fly. This was before we had the ability to send photos back and forth, so we talked about a few patterns and I started tying samples and sending them back and forth; it took a while. We ended up with a Gurgler-style fly with a rabbit fur tail and front collar. Alex wanted a fly that would keep pulsing after being stripped, and fish in or just under the surface."

Yes, tarpon do take surface flies; this is how I have caught many baby tarpon. It's a fun game, especially when fishing canals under street and porch lights. You see a swirl and hear a watery smack several feet beyond the end of your line, and you set the hook. Sometimes the line goes tight and you feel a sharp thump, the sure sign that you are into a fish.

Tie this pattern for catching tarpon, but it will attract any other species of fish that will suck in floating flies.

CHAPTER NINE

Match the Hatch Saltwater Style:
Flies That Imitate Common Baitfish

King's Hoo Fly (Anchovy)

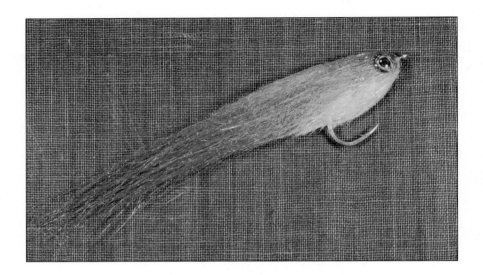

Hook: Gamakatsu SL12S, size 2.
Thread: Fine Uni–Mono.
Tail: Tan craft fur.
Body and head: Dark tan and yellow over silver minnow belly and pink Senyo's Laser Dub, coated and shaped with Liquid Fusion.
Eyes: Fish-Skull Living Eyes.

JONNY KING STARTED TYING SALTWATER FLIES IN 1990. HE
has fly fished throughout much of the world and has caught almost every
species of inshore saltwater fish. Jonny especially enjoys fishing for striped
bass and bluefish on Cape Cod Bay and New York Harbor. When he's not
fishing, you might find Jonny playing jazz at one of Manhattan's music
hotspots.

Jonny taught himself to tie as a young teenager reading Poul Jorgenson's
instructional books, and has tied virtually every kind of pattern: tiny dry
flies, bass bugs, steelhead patterns, Northeast striper flies, tuna flies, and flats
patterns for bonefish, tarpon, permit, and snook. He has come a very long
way since reading Poul's books, and now creates his flies using a blend of
natural and synthetic ingredients. This anchovy version of his Hoo Fly is a
little unusual in that he tied it using only durable synthetic materials.

Senyo's Laser Dub is a product of Hareline Dubbin. Hareline Dubbin
teamed with pattern designer Greg Senyo to create this useful blend of Ice
Dub and acrylic fibers. You'll find Senyo's Laser Dub in many well-stocked
fly shops.

Liquid Fusion, which is used to form the head of the fly, is a clear ure-
thane adhesive that is nontoxic and has very little order. Look for Liquid
Fusion in your local craft store.

King's Kinky Muddler (Sand Eel)

Hook: Gamakatsu SL12S, size 2/0.
Thread: Uni-Mono.
Tail: Light purple bucktail under pairs of olive and rusty brown saddle hackles tied tented so they create an inverted V.
Body and head: Brown over white Slinky Fiber or Slinky Fiber Flash Blend.
Eyes: Fish-Skull Living Eyes.

HERE IS JONNY KING'S INTERPRETATION OF A SAND EEL, and it's a real winner! This pattern is easy to make and it will fill an important slot in your fly box.

We typically think of finding sand eels on Northeast fishing flats, but they are far more widespread. You will find sand eels along the coasts of Europe from Spain to Scotland, and in the Mediterranean.

The term "sand eel" is used to describe a large number of species of long, narrow fish; they really aren't eels. They prefer habitat with soft, sandy bottoms. Sand eels burrow into the bottom in order to escape predators, including many species of our favorite gamefish.

Most sand eel imitations are tied from three to about six inches long. Select soft materials that give your flies a flowing, swimming action when stripped through the water. And, although there is a temptation to fish these patterns slowly, real sand eels can move quickly through the water when frightened. Use an erratic retrieve when fishing a sand eel imitation, giving your fly a natural darting action.

Fish-Skull Living Eyes, which Jonny King uses on this pattern, is a product of Flymen Fishing Company. These eyes are very realistic looking and make the head of the fly really "pop" to attract the attention of fish.

King's Kinky Muddler (Atlantic Herring)

Hook: Owner 5320 Spinner bait hook, size 5/0.

Thread: Fine Uni-Mono.

Tail: White bucktail under pairs of pink, pale green and blue hackles tied tented so they create an inverted V.

Body: Two collars of light blue bucktail, and a collar of pink and blue marabou wrapped on the hook.

Head: Blue over white Slinky Fiber or Slinky Fiber Flash Blend, V-tied and trimmed, with pink cheeks.

Eyes: Fish-Skull Living Eyes.

FLY DESIGNER JONNY KING TIES HIS SERIES OF KINKY MUD-
dler patterns using half natural and half synthetic materials. The tails are
tented saddle hackles, and the heads are Kinky Fiber Flash Blend clipped
and trimmed like deer hair. A Kinky Muddler has a dense head that looks
opaque like the head of a baitfish, and the sparse tail flutters like the tail of a
real fish. King says, "The purpose of tenting the saddles is to create a fuller,
rounder body profile and to maximize movement."

Here we see Jonny's imitation of an Atlantic herring. Use this pattern
wherever herring play an important part of the forage base for gamefish.

Slinky Fiber is sometimes packaged under the name Slinky Fibre; they
are the same materials. Slinky Fiber is a product of an innovative company
called H2O. Slinky Fiber is a kinky, fine synthetic fiber that is great for
tying bulky flies without having to pile on a bunch of material, or you can
use only a pinch of material to tie a slender pattern. Slinky Fiber comes in
twenty colors and is very easy to use. Change colors of materials to make
imitations of mackerel, mullet, and generic amber-looking baitfish. If your
local fly shop doesn't stock Slinky Fiber, you may substitute with FisHair or
a similar synthetic material.

Farrar's Peanut Bunker MV Baitfish

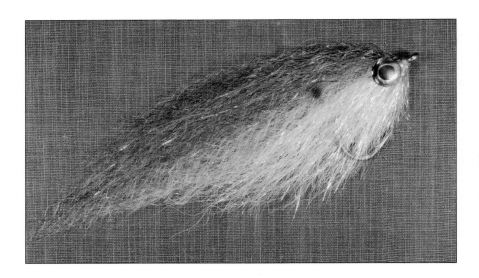

Hook: Mustad C68SZ, size 5/0.
Thread: Danville Clear Monofilament.
Wing: Bronzeback and peacock Slinky Fiber Flash Blend, over olive and bronzeback, over yellow.
Underbelly: Off-white Slinky Fiber Flash Blend.
Throat: Electric pink Angel Hair.
Eyes: Epoxy 3-D.
Adhesive: Plasti Dip.

IF YOU SPEND ANY TIME FLY FISHING ON THE EAST COAST, you will hear the term "peanut bunker." A bunker, sometimes called a pogie or mossbunker, is a menhaden. It is one of the most common and important baitfish on the coast. Once ranging from Nova Scotia to Florida, their range has been diminished, but not their importance to high-quality fishing. In fact, the health of striped bass and bluefish populations is often directly related to the health of the menhaden population. A peanut bunker is a small, juvenile menhaden. (Curiously, I have never heard anyone refer to a "peanut pogie," which actually sounds a little poetic.)

Anyway, late summer and into the fall, striped bass will key into juvenile menhaden. These small baitfish are typically two to three inches long, and you should use a pattern of matching size. There are dozens of imitations of peanut bunker, and Steve Farrar's Peanut Bunker MV Baitfish is one of the best. It is just the right size and shape, has the perfect amount of flash, and those eyes convince predator fish that it is something good to eat. Even though this is a small pattern, few striped bass and bluefish will escape the large size 5/0 hook.

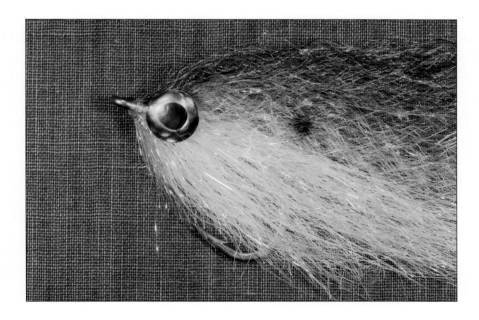

Farrar's Anchovy MV Baitfish

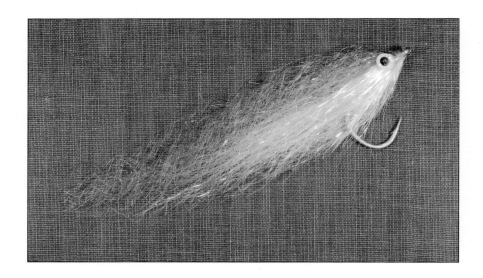

Hook: Varivas 990S, size 1/0.
Thread: Clear monofilament.
Wing: Brown, olive, and sea blue over anchovy Slinky Fiber Flash Blend.
Underbelly: White UV Slinky Fiber Flash Blend.
Flash: Pearl/green and pearl/blue Angel Hair.
Eyes: Epoxy 3-D.
Adhesive: Plasti Dip.

I DID SOME RESEARCH ABOUT ANCHOVIES, AND DISCOVERED some interested facts on the website of the National Oceanic and Atmospheric Administration. When you consider these facts, there is little wonder that anchovies are an important source of food for our West Coast fisheries.

There are more than twenty species of anchovies in the family Engraulidae. The northern anchovy, *Engraulis mordax*, is commercially harvested off the West Coast, mainly as bait for catching other fish although it is sometimes processed as fishmeal. Once upon a time, when the Pacific sardine fishery collapsed, anchovies were caught and sold for human consumption. Although the terms sardine and anchovy are sometimes used interchangeably, make no mistake: they are not the same fish. Also, according to the NOAA website, anchovies along the Pacific Coast are not being overfished, which is a true marvel considering the long list of depleted fish stocks.

An anchovy grows five to eight inches in length, so you should tie imitations in similar sizes. Even though anchovies are found in the Pacific Ocean and parts of Europe, Farrar's Anchovy MV Baitfish is a pattern that has wide application. Use this fly wherever small baitfish are on the gamefish menu. It would be particularly effective for matching many forms of similar-sized bait along the East Coast of the United States.

5-Minute Finger Mullet

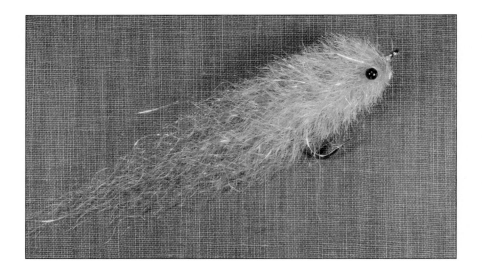

Hook: Daiichi 2546, size 2 or 1.
Thread: Monofilament.
Wing: Steve Farrar's Flash Blend—shrimp, gray, and mullet brown.
Eyes: Large black EP Crab/Shrimp Eyes.
Head: Steve Farrar's Flash Blend—dubbing brush gray and mullet brown.

LET'S TALK ABOUT THE MULLET, NOT THE GOOFY HAIR style but the fish.

Mullet are very widespread around the world and so are an important source of food for many of our favorite gamefish. A mullet has two dorsal fins, a small mouth, and no distinguishable lateral line. Mullet are sometimes called jumping or happy mullet because they occasionally leap out of the water and skip along the surface. Mullet will also gather in large schools.

Mullet are generally small, and real finger mullets are very popular with bait fishermen. Fly imitations of mullet are excellent for catching striped bass and bluefish along the New Jersey Coast and nearby waters. Mullets are also common in Florida, so have a few imitations in your fly box when fishing in the Sunshine State.

Drew Chicone uses a Steve Farrar Dubbing Brush for fashioning the head of his 5-Minute Finger Mullet. A dubbing brush is a piece of thin doubled wire similar to an extra-large piece of chenille. The dubbing brush can contain many types of fur as well as natural and synthetic hair. In this case, the brush contains Steve Farrar's Flash Blend.

After making the long fur wing of the fly, tie the end of the dubbing brush to the hook at the base of the wing. Wrap the brush up the hook shank; brush back the fibers after each wrap to prevent trapping the fur. Next, tie and cut off the remaining piece of brush (save it for tying another fly), and clip the head to shape. Dubbing brushes are easy and quick to use, and you will be satisfied with the results.

GT Pinfish

Hook: Daiichi 2546, sizes 4 and 2.
Thread: Clear monofilament.
Tail: Tan craft fur and lavender DNA Holo-Fusion.
Belly: White saltwater yak hair and blue/pearl Angel Hair.
Back: Tan saltwater yak hair and gold Angel Hair.
Eyes: 8-millimeter gold Orvis Jurassic Eyes.
Gills: Red saltwater yak hair.

A PINFISH IS A SMALL BAITFISH THAT GROWS TO LITTLE more than four inches long. Pinfish exist from the Mexican Gulf Coast and Bermuda along the Atlantic Coast of the United States all the way to Massachusetts. Although adult pinfish prefer deeper waters, you'll encounter immature pinfish around mangroves, pilings, and jetties. As a result, tie smaller versions of this pattern to closely match the local bait. Sea trout, red drum, and lady fish are especially fond of pinfish.

Yak hair is a particularly good fly-tying material. The fibers are long and soft, and have a great flowing action when drawn through the water. It is ideal for tying the bodies on baitfish imitations. If your local fly shop doesn't stock yak hair, you can usually substitute with craft fur.

Yak hair actually comes from yaks, which are ox-like animals native to the Himalayas and Tibet. Curiously, large quantities of yak were imported for the manufacture of wigs and hair extensions, but it was discovered that many people are allergic to the fibers when worn for prolonged periods of time. Fortunately, yak hair is still being imported so we can use it to tie fish-catching flies. Use it as the main component in a body or add some craft fur or bucktail. Also include a few strands of Krystal Flash to add sparkle to your fly.

Kintz's Major Herring

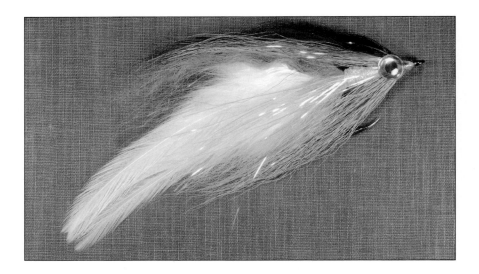

Hook: Regular saltwater hook, size 3/0.
Thread: White 3/0.
Tail: White saddle hackles with bright blue Polar Fiber on top and gray Polar Fiber on the bottom. Pearl Flashabou on the sides.
Body: Mylar braid.
Flanks: Pearl Flashabou.
Underwing: Gray bucktail.
Wing: Blue and black Polar Fiber, and pearl Flashabou.
Belly: Gray bucktail.
Eyes: Gold 3D eyes.

THOMAS KINTZ CREATED THIS PATTERN HE CALLS THE
Major Herring for Umpqua Feather Merchants. It's a terrific option for
when striped bass, bluefish, and other gamefish are feeding on herring.

The trouble with tying a tall, full-bodied fly such as the Major Herring is
creating a fly that loses its profile when fishing. On an ill-conceived pattern,
the soft feathers and furs collapse around the hook when the fly is drawn
through the water. A simple solution is to tie a few strands of bucktail to the
top of the fly as an underwing, and then place other material—in this case
Polar Fiber—on top. The bucktail holds the wing up, maintaining the tall
silhouette of a real herring.

I have fished for striped bass that were busting in schools of herring. When
they are keying into this bait, the fish easily mistake a well-made fly for the
real bait. I typically fish a pattern such as Kintz's Major Herring using a line
with a sinking tip. Since the fish are feeding aggressively, they are not leader
shy; a 15-pound-test tippet will not dissuade the bass from striking. Since you
are using a sinking line, the leader only needs to be four to five feet in length.

Big Eye Baitfish Mackerel

Hook: Regular saltwater hook, size 1.
Thread: Black 2/0.
Tail: White saddle hackle and green grizzly saddle hackle.
Back: Pearl, green, and black crinkled Flashabou or a similar material, and black bucktail.
Belly: White bucktail.
Throat: Red pearl Krystal Flash.
Cheeks: Green holographic sheet material.
Eyes: Silver adhesive eyes.

PAGE ROGERS HAS HAD A LASTING IMPACT ON SALTWATER fly fishing. She has spent many seasons designing patterns and sharing what she knows with fellow tiers. Although she is well into retirement years, I saw Page at a recent fly-fishing show. She looked fit and still ready to tangle with a strong striped bass. Check the bins at your local fly shop, and you will find her patterns the Slim Jim, Rogers Sand Eel, and this Big Eye Baitfish Mackerel.

Mackerel are a common baitfish, and there are many patterns designed to match them. The challenge is to re-create the marble-like green turquoise and pearl color of the back of the fish. Page uses a blend of the feathers—white and green grizzly—and flash material to imitate the back and sides of a mackerel.

The foil cheeks give the head of the fly a solid appearance, and of course a place to position the adhesive eyes. Coat the eyes with a drop of adhesive to lock them to the foil.

Use the Big Eye Baitfish Mackerel along the Atlantic Coast wherever you might encounter schools of mackerel. They are a favorite prey of striped bass and bluefish. Page uses this design to tie the Big Eye Herring, and also flies in the basic fish-catching colors black, blue, and chartreuse. Simply select materials in your favorite colors.

Cowen's Albie Anchovy

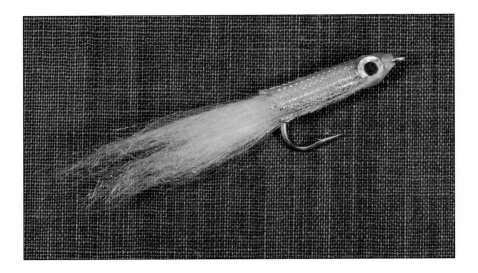

Hook: Tiemco 811S, size 4.
Thread: Fine Danville Clear Monofilament.
Wing: Shrimp Polar Fibre.
Underbelly: Shrimp Polar Fibre.
Belly sac: Silver Gliss N Glow.
Body: Medium natural EZ Body.
Eyes: Silver prismatic adhesive eyes.
Adhesive: Clear Cure Goo or a similar light-activated adhesive.

HENRY COWEN IS A MASTER FLY DESIGNER. AFTER SPENDING most of his life in the Northeast chasing striped bass and bluefish, he now lives in North Carolina and plies his flies in those waters. He is also an authority at catching freshwater striped bass.

Many of the flies in this book are tied using Tuffleye, Clear Cure Goo, or one of the other light-activated adhesive products; you'll see those materials listed in the pattern recipes. These adhesives are taking the place of epoxy on many tying benches. These acrylic products are cured using a blue or ultraviolet light; because of safety concerns, the distributors recommend using a blue light.

Acrylic adhesives come in convenient syringes. Unlike epoxy, they require no mixing, they don't cure until you apply the blue light, and there is no waste. To cure the adhesive, apply the material to the fly, and then shine the light; the adhesive fully cures in twenty to thirty seconds.

There is a small initial investment when working with light-cured acrylics, primarily for the flashlight blue light; all the distributors sell kits containing lights and adhesives. After purchasing the light and using the adhesive in the kit, you'll only need to purchase additional syringes of adhesive to tie more flies. The convenience of using this extremely durable material, and the fact that there is no waste, makes it a very strong competitor to epoxy.

Cowen's Sand Eel

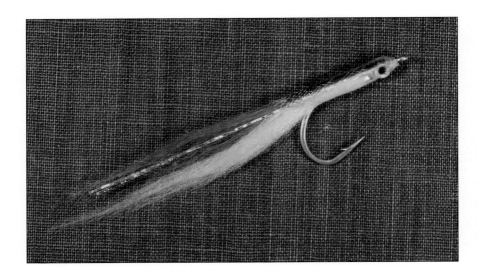

Hook: Gamakatsu SC15, size 1/0.
Thread: Danville Clear Monofilament.
Wing: Olive and white Polar Fibre.
Lateral line: Narrow holographic tinsel.
Body: Small natural EZ Body.
Eyes: Silver prismatic adhesive eyes.
Head: Clear Cure Goo.

LET ME TELL YOU A TRUE STORY ABOUT THE IMPORTANCE
of sand eels to good fishing.

Many years ago, my family was visiting West Dennis Beach at the mouth
of the Bass River on Cape Cod. Due to tide conditions, fishing was best
early in the morning and early evening. This schedule allowed ample time
during the day to tour the Cape with the family.

One hot afternoon, we stopped at Dennis Beach for a swim. It was low
tide and the sun was bright in a cloudless sky. Fishing seemed out of the
question, but then a funny thing happened.

Boats started gathering at the edge of the sand flats; the water was little more than a couple of feet deep. The occupants of the boats had rakes
with long handles, and they began raking the sand. A couple of automobiles
pulled into the parking lot, and the occupants got out and headed into the
shallow water with rakes and buckets, and also started raking the sand. They
were all collecting sand eels. It wasn't long before swarms of gulls gathered
and started feeding on the eels. It was a sight to see!

Some time passed and another automobile pulled into the parking lot.
Two fellows got out of the car and strung up fly rods. They watched the
bait collectors and birds for a few minutes, and then waded into the middle
of the action. Both anglers made single casts and were fast into fish. Despite
the low water and blazing sun—typically very poor fishing conditions—the
eels attracted a large school of striped bass. I immediately retrieved my rod
from our car, waded into the skinny water on the flats, and was quickly into
a bass. It was a fine day of terrific fishing that I will never forget.

Mayan Cichlid

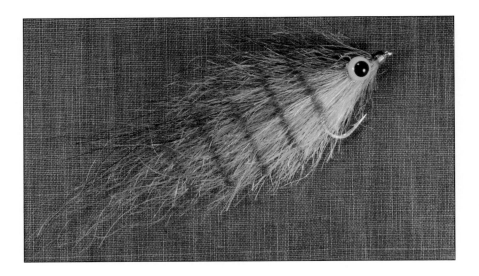

Hook: Gamakatsu SC–15, size 2/0.

Thread: Monofilament.

Belly: A blend of white and tan saltwater yak hair, and a blend of white and orange saltwater yak hair.

Back: A blend of olive, chartreuse, and tan saltwater yak hair, and a blend of olive and brown saltwater yak hair.

Throat: Orange saltwater yak hair.

Eyes: 8-millimeter orange or yellow doll eyes.

CICHLIDS ARE PART OF THE FAMILY OF FISH CALLED CICHLIDAE. This family contains more than 1,600 species, and more are still being discovered. Typically found in fresh water, some species do live in near-shore brackish water and are available as food to some of our favorite gamefish. Some cichlids display a rainbow of colors and are quite beautiful; they have long been popular among aquarium hobbyists.

The Mayan cichlid is a native to South America, and is now found in the waters surrounding South Florida. Most biologists agree that Mayan cichlids, which are considered an invasive species in the Northern Hemisphere, were introduced to Florida by people discarding unwanted fish from their aquariums and perhaps fish farm escapees. Today you'll find these fish in South Florida's brackish creeks and canals. They are a good source of food for tarpon and snook.

This pattern calls for a large number of colors of yak hair. While this is fine tying material, your local fly shop might not have all of these colors. The goal is to create a fly with a tall, narrow profile; kinky-fibered yak hair creates bulk on the hook without using too much material. Ordinary craft fur is a poor substitute because the fibers will collapse around the hook when the fly becomes wet and you'll lose the necessary profile. If you must substitute with another ingredient, try synthetic FisHair or a similar kinky material.

ALF Stir Fry

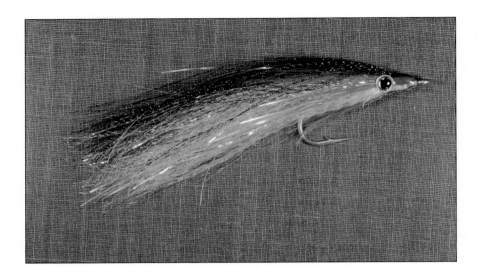

Hook: Long-shank saltwater hook, size 3/0.
Thread: Clear monofilament.
Belly: White Ultra Hair.
Flanks: Chartreuse or yellow Ultra Hair and pearl Flashabou.
Back: Peacock Krystal Flash and green Flashabou.
Side of head: Red Super Hair.
Under the head: Copper narrow Flashabou.

KATE AND BILL HOWE ARE TWO PROFESSIONAL FLY FISHERS and pattern designers from California. They have created many terrific off-shore patterns tied on monster double-hook rigs to smaller patterns such as the ALF Stir Fry.

According to Trey Combs, in his book *Bluewater Fly Fishing*, ALF is an acronym for "Any Little Fellow." The ALF Stir Fry is the Howes' imitation of an anchovy, but you can use the design to mimic many of the baitfish in your local waters. Change colors of materials to match these baits.

This is a commercially tied version of the ALF Stir Fry. Although it is a fine looking fly, in *Bluewater Fly Fishing* the Howes give detailed instructions on how they blend colors of materials to create convincing looking bait-fish imitations. They also blend Super Hair, Ultra Hair, and an ingredient called Ocean Hair when tying the wing, taking advantage of the properties offered by all of these materials. Check your local well-stocked fly shop for these materials, and ask the clerk about substitutes. Many synthetic ingredi-ents are packaged under different trade names, and you will discover other materials for tying similar flies.

Many tiers prefer using synthetic materials because they make it easy to reproduce successful flies. The quality and colors of natural ingredients can vary widely, so it is sometimes difficult to purchase more materials to tie those winning patterns. With synthetic materials, the quality and colors are almost always identical, so you can easily restock your bench and keep tying.

Skok's Mushmouth

Hook: Owner AKI 2/0 or other short shank–hook, size 2.
Thread: Monofilament.
Tail: White Super Hair and gold Flashabou.
Belly: Pearl Wing 'N Flash.
Back: Peacock Light Brite.

DAVID SKOK IS A LEADING OUTDOORS PHOTOGRAPHER based in Boston. Although he lives in the Northeast, David travels the world in search of good fishing and photographs. You'll find his great photos in most of the leading fly-fishing magazines, and it has been featured in several beautiful books.

David is also an inventive fly designer. His Mushmouth series of baitfish patterns are some of his most famous flies. They are tied using entirely synthetic materials so they are very easy to reproduce.

After starting the thread on the hook, tie the first bunch of Super Hair or your favorite fine-fibered synthetic hair material; craft fur, however, won't work for the Mushmouth. Study the picture of the fly and look for something to match. Coat the material right behind the hook with Softex or a similar clear, fast-drying finish. This stiffens the fibers and helps the fly maintain its shape when fishing. Continue adding small bunches of material to form the belly and back of the fly.

To complete the Mushmouth, pinch the front of the fly between your fingers to flatten the head. Place an eye on each side of the head. Coat the head and eyes with a generous drop of Softex.

The Mushmouth is a flashy fly that stands out in a large school of baitfish. It is also extremely durable. Select colors of materials to tie Mushmouths to match many of the baitfish in your favorite water.

Surf Candies

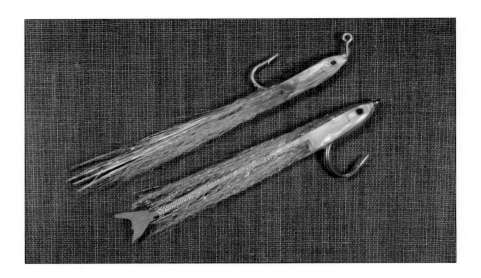

Hook: Regular saltwater hook, sizes 6 to 2.
Thread: Clear monofilament.
Tail: Ultra Hair or bucktail, and thin Flashabou or Krystal Flash.
Body: Silver or pearl tinsel.
Head: Epoxy or light–activated acrylic.

THIRTY YEARS AGO, THERE WAS A FLY SHOP IN KNOXVILLE, Tennessee, called The Creel. One Saturday while visiting the shop, four or five fellows were crowded around the tying table, making a new type of fly. It was something featured in the latest issue of what was then called *American Angler & Fly Tyer* magazine. They were having fun making the pattern, but debated whether it was really a fly; the synthetic fiber tail and epoxy head broke all conventions about what a fly should look like. There was no question, however, that the fly certainly looked fishy.

I didn't know it at the time, but I was looking at Surf Candies, the revolutionary flies developed by Bob Popovics.

More than two decades later, while interviewing Bob about the history of Surf Candies, he explained that he developed his idea in the 1970s. He needed flies that toothy bluefish couldn't destroy. The first Surf Candies were nothing more than bucktail streamers with epoxy heads. Eventually, Bob made the tails using FisHair and similar synthetic fibers, and he added eyes to his flies. Using these materials, he designed Surf Candies in colors and sizes to imitate spearing, small sand eels, and a wide variety of the baitfish he found in his home waters along the New Jersey shore.

Here we see the most recent generation of Surf Candies. The heads are flanked with small pieces of foil called Fleye Foils, and rather than using epoxy, Bob coated the heads with a light-activated acrylic called Tuffleye.

The Surf Candy is a very adaptable pattern. Add a small metal cone to the nose before tying the fly to create the Deep Candy. If you fish tropical waters, use the Surf Candy design to tie an imitation of a needlefish that no barracuda can destroy. The Surf Candy is bulletproof.

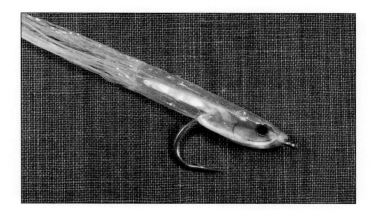

Thunder Creek Bunker

Hook: Long-shank saltwater hook, size 1.
Thread: White 6/0.
Body: Gray and olive bucktail for the back, pale yellow bucktail for the belly, and a few strands of silver Krystal Flash.
Gills: Red enamel paint.
Eyes: White and black enamel paint.

IN THE EARLY 1970S, NEW YORK'S KEITH FULSHER PUBLISHED *Tying and Fishing the Thunder Creek Series*. In this small book, he described how to make a family of patterns he calls Thunder Creek streamers. In essence, Keith applied the idea of matching the hatch to making imitations of freshwater baitfish. His Thunder Creek flies match the shape, sizes, and colors of black-nosed dace, perch, immature trout, and more. His flies look fit and trim in the vise, and in the water they become sleek and streamlined. Until this point, most tiers made baitfish imitations using saddle hackles, marabou, or bucktail for the wings of flies; Keith used bucktail to make the heads as well as the bodies of his Thunder Creeks. (Keith's idea was not entirely new. Decades before, Carrie Stevens also made reverse-bucktail flies, but these were overshadowed by her famous feather-wing streamers such as the Gray Ghost.)

In 2006, I collaborated with Keith to write a new edition of his book, this time titled *Thunder Creek Flies: Tying and Fishing the Classic Baitfish Imitations*. In addition to featuring an expanded list of freshwater streamers, Keith included a series of wonderful imitations of saltwater baitfish. He used the same tying methods, but selected larger stainless steel hooks and bucktail in colors to match saltwater forage. These lightweight flies are easy to tie and cast, and assume the shape of baitfish when stripped through the water.

Here we see Keith's rendition of a baby bunker. This fly will become one of your favorite patterns if you fish for striped bass.

Thunder Creek Tinker Mackerel

Hook: Long–shank saltwater hook, size 1.
Thread: White 6/0.
Wing: Grizzly saddle hackle dyed light olive.
Body: Gray and dark blue bucktail for the back, white bucktail for the belly, and a few strands of silver Krystal Flash.
Gills: Red enamel paint.
Eyes: White and black enamel paint.

SMALL MACKEREL, OFTEN CALLED TINKER MACKEREL, ARE favorite forage for striped bass and bluefish. You'll want some type of tinker mackerel imitation in your fly box, and Keith Fulsher's Thunder Creek Tinker Mackerel is a great candidate.

Selecting the right materials when tying a Thunder Creek pattern is critical. The pegboard in the tying section of your local fly shop will be filled with packaged bucktails, but not all will work for making a nice Thunder Creek. Sort through the tails and reject those with crinkled or wavy hair; this hair will not make a sleek, streamlined fly. Look for tails that have long, straight hair in the desired colors.

When tying the fly, clip the hair from about the top two-thirds of the bucktail. The hair in the bottom one-third of the tail is thicker and behaves more like deer body hair when tying; tighten the thread, and this hair will flair.

Most tiers use entirely too much hair when tying Thunder Creeks. Tie a spare fly, and you will be happy with the results. And use only a few sprigs of Krystal Flash to add just a dash of flash to the fly.

Tie the bucktail to the top and bottom of the hook pointing forward over the eye. Fold the hair back and pinch the head of the fly. Make two or three firm thread wraps to form the body of the fly. Release the thread and check your work. If you are pleased with the appearance of the fly, you can whip-finish and clip the thread; if you think you can do better, unwrap the thread and try again.

Keith coats the heads of his flies with epoxy. Select thirty-minute epoxy so you can coat the heads of several flies at a time.

The Thunder Creek Tinker Mackerel has a wing of grizzly saddle hackles dyed light olive. This imitates the colored barring of a real mackerel.

Hines's Walking Cinder Worm

Hook: Regular saltwater hook, size 2.
Thread: Black 3/0.
Body: Red and brown chenille or Crystal Chenille, and red closed–cell foam.

REAL CINDER WORMS, WHICH RANGE ALONG THE ENTIRE
East Coast, generally measure one to four inches long. They have black
heads and pinkish red to brownish bodies. Cinder worms spend most of
their lives burrowing in the mud bottoms of bays and estuaries until the
time is right to emerge and spawn. At these times they swarm to the surface
and mate. They are easy feed for gamefish and generate some of the most
exciting fly fishing of the season for striped bass, tarpon, and more. Successful anglers have patterns that match real cinder worms; they enjoy saltwater
fly-fishing's version of match the hatch.

The cinder worm emergence may begin in mid-April and last until the
middle of June. Water temperatures are one of the keys: in the Northeast,
ideal water temperatures range from the mid-50s to the mid-60s. Each emergence begins in the evening near the time of the full moon and increases to
a maximum intensity during successive nights.

Cinder worm imitations are generally simple flies. Hines's Walking Cinder Worm, featuring a head and tail of buoyant closed-cell foam, floats on
or right under the surface of the water. Cast the fly out, and use a very slow
retrieve. The bright moon will illuminate the water, so keep your eye peeled
for a large swirl in the water, a sure sign that a fish has taken your fly.

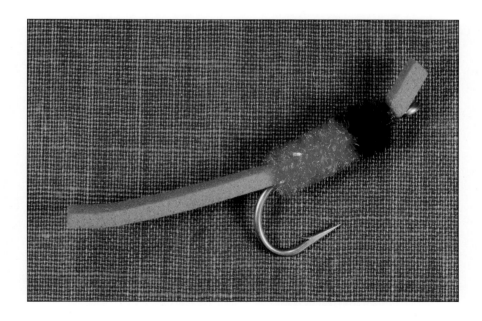

Hines's Simple Cinder Worm

Hook: Regular saltwater hook, size 2.
Thread: Black 3/0.
Tail: Red marabou.
Body: Red and brown chenille or Crystal Chenille.

BOB HINES IS A CAPTAIN WITH WIDE FLY-FISHING EXPERI-
ence. Although he specializes in showing clients the best fishing along
the coast of Rhode Island, he has traveled far and wide in search of good
angling. Bob is also a professional casting instructor and fly designer. Hines's
Simple Cinder Worm is a good example of his creativity.

The cinder worm hatch occurs over muddy bottoms from April through
June. Early in the evening during the full moon, the worms leave the pro-
tective shelter of the bottom and begin swimming to the surface to spawn.
The local gamefish gather for the feast, and this is a good time to use a
weighted cinder worm imitation.

Hines's Simple Cinder Worm, which is little more than two inches long,
has a small amount of lead wire wrapped on the hook shank. Cast this sinking into the swarming worms and let it sink. Retrieve the fly slowly toward
you so it starts to rise, and hold on tight for the strike.

Anglers from the Northeast to the Florida Keys plan fishing trips around
the cinder worm hatch. Even trophy tarpon feast on this easy meal and provide memorable fly-fishing action. If you'd like to try your hand at catching
a tarpon during the cinder worm emergence, contact a guide specializing
in fly fishing in the Keys. Tie Hines's Simple Cinder Worm, and his Walking Cinder Worm, pack a 12-weight rod, and get ready for some of the best
fishing of your life!

Shark Chum Fly

Hook: Regular saltwater hook, size 3/0.
Thread: Black or red 3/0.
Body: Dark or purple Zonker rabbit strip.

IS THE FISHING SLOW BUT YOU WANT TO FEEL A TUG AT THE end of your line? Would you like to feel a really strong tug; would that get your interest? Then perhaps you should spend a day fishing for sharks.

Although not widely practiced, shark fishing is great fun. It is practiced on both the East and West Coasts, so there are plenty of opportunities to catch these fascinating creatures.

I suspect most anglers haven't fished for sharks because a seaworthy boat is required. In some areas, you only have to motor a few hundred yards to reach sharks; in other locations, such as my home state of Maine, you have to travel up to twenty miles from shore, well over the horizon and out of sight of land. If you own or have access to a good boat, you can easily fish for sharks.

Using chum is the key to attracting sharks. After traveling to a likely destination, turn off the motor and allow the boat to drift. Drop a bag full of chum, which you can obtain at most saltwater bait shops, into the water. The boat will continue drifting and the oily chum slick will spread, attracting any nearby shark.

Use a very stout rod, wire leader, and fly designed to look like a chunk of chum. Chuck Furimsky's Shark Chum Fly, which is simply a rabbit Zonker strip wrapped on the hook shank, is a good example. A wad of feathers lashed to the hook will also work.

When a shark approaches, cast the fly right on its nose. The shark, excited by all the fishy aroma in the water, will grab the fly. Hang on tight: depending upon the species, a shark can weigh from fifty to a couple hundred pounds. They are strong fighters and will give a fine tussle.

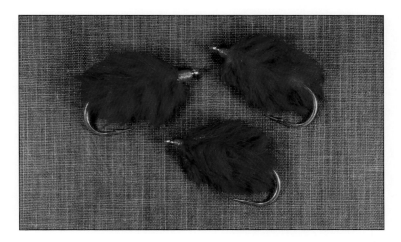

Art's Shrimp

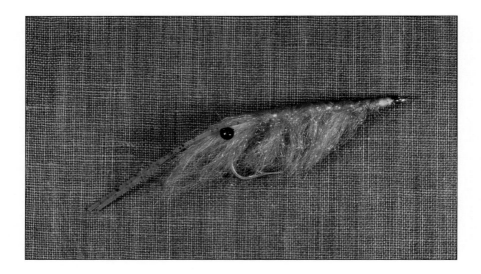

Hook: Long-shank saltwater hook, sizes 8 to 1/0.
Thread: Size 3/0, color to match the body of the fly.
Antennae: Rubber legs to match the color of the body.
Head: A small pinch of dubbing.
Eyes: Melted monofilament.
Body: Shaggy dubbing—tan, pink, or orange. Standard SLF Dubbing is a good choice, but you may select your favorite brand of dubbing.
Back: Thin Skin in a color to match the color of the body.
Rib: 20-pound-test monofilament.

THIS FLY IS NEAR AND DEAR TO MY HEART, AND IT DEFI-
nitely catches fish. I am happy to include it in this book about favorite
saltwater patterns.

Art Scheck was once the editor of *Fly Tyer* magazine. He offered me my
first job in publishing and taught me the ropes of how to be a magazine
editor. He was a very talented author and editor, and also one hell of a fly
designer.

Art created this fly close to twenty years ago. It had no name at the
time—I don't know if Art ever named any of the patterns he designed—so
I call it Art's Shrimp. It has been a part of my fishing kit all these years. It is
great for catching striped bass, and tied in smaller sizes, it is a good candidate
for catching bonefish and redfish. When fishing in Corpus Christi, it was a
top pattern for catching sea trout.

Art's Shrimp is a good candidate for new tiers. The key material is shaggy
dubbing, which you can find in any fly shop. Standard SLF Dubbing is a
good choice, but any similar material will work. You can use a strip of Thin
Skin for tying the shell back, or you may clip a strip from a clear plastic
freezer bag.

Although a lot of shrimp imitations are tied in orange, live shrimp are
usually light tan; shrimp turn orange when cooked. Tie Art's Shrimp in a
similar color to match real shrimp.

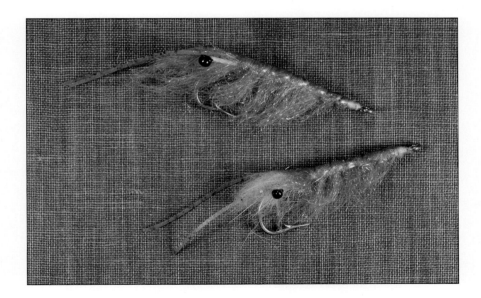

RM Shortfin Squid

Head

Thread: White 3/0.

Tentacles and mouth parts: Saddle hackles, Krystal Flash, marabou, and Sili Legs or rubber legs.

Head: Large EZ Body tubing.

Eyes: Extra-large 3D eyes.

Body

Hook: Long-shank saltwater hook, size 4/0.

Thread: Clear monofilament.

Underbody: Chenille, Crystal Chenille, or Cactus Chenille.

Body: Extra-large EZ Body tubing.

Fins: Krystal Flash and marabou.

RICH MURPHY IS A STUDENT OF STRIPED BASS AND HOW to catch them on flies. His book, *Fly Fishing for Striped Bass*, might be the last word on the subject; it is well researched and thorough. Only a master angler could write such a book.

Rich's flies are also well thought out. Here we see his RM Shortfin Squid. Well, actually, Rich didn't tie this fly—I did. I have several in my fly box because they are great for catching striped bass, bluefish, and anything else that feeds on squid.

Real squid are an important part of the diets of many gamefish. There are actually several species of shortfin squids, including the northern shortfin squid. This variety ranges from the Florida Straights to Newfoundland. It is migratory, so you may very well encounter schools of squid and feeding fish.

Tie the head of the RM Shortfin Squid on a heavy needle, such as your bodkin, placed in your tying vise. Tie on the tentacles and mouth parts. Next, remove the bodkin from the vise. Slip a piece of EZ Body tubing over the handle. Tie down the end of the tubing on the base of the head materials. Tie off and clip the thread. Push the tubing back onto the head ingredients. Glue eyes onto the sides of the head. Now you're ready to make the body of the fly.

Place a hook in the vise. Tie on the completed head. Slip a piece of larger tubing over the hook eye. Wrap the chenille underbody, and push the tubing back over the chenille; the completed squid body is actually two layers of tubing, which makes the fly bulletproof. Add the marabou fins and complete the fly.

Tie the RM Shortfin Squid in off-white and tan.

Space Needle

Hook: Regular saltwater hook, size 2.
Thread: Pink 3/0.
Body: Pink chenille tied on Flymen Fishing Company Articulated Fish-Spines.
Tail: Pink marabou.
Eyes: Large 3-D eyes.

THE SPACE NEEDLE IS A COOL IMITATION OF A NEEDLEFISH. This common tropical baitfish lives in shallow marine habitats and is a favorite prey for gamefish such as barracuda. The problem, of course, is preventing sharp-toothed barracuda from slicing the leader and getting away with our flies. Captain Chris Newsome's Space Needle is a fine solution.

Tie the snout of the Space Needle on a long-shank hook with the bend and point removed. Tie the body on a series of interlocking shanks, such as Articulated Fish-Spines. These heavy-duty shanks come in several lengths. Use as many shanks as you wish to create a fly of any length. The Space Needle is tied using a series of short shanks, which makes the fly undulate like a snake. Perhaps the pattern should have been called Space Snake!

A real needlefish has a long snout, which is replicated by wrapping thread on the front hook shank. Coat the head area and the snout of the fly with epoxy. Glue an eye onto each side of the head.

When fishing, the rear hook is several inches from the forward hook eye and the leader. This keeps the mouth of the barracuda well back from the leader. Only an enormous fish—one with the mouth the size of an alligator's—could cut the leader. Chances are you wouldn't want to land that barracuda, anyway!

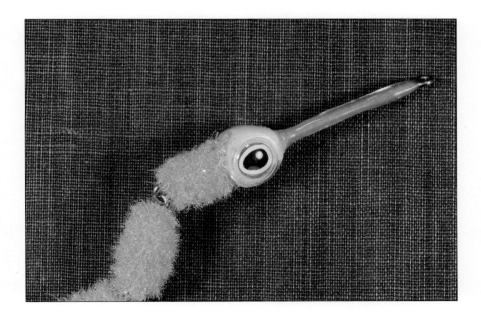

Masked Minnow

Hook: Regular saltwater hook, sizes 4 to 1.
Thread: White 3/0.
Head: Flymen Fishing Company Fish-Mask.
Wing: White and olive bucktail, and pearl Flashabou.
Belly: Pearl Ice Dub.
Eyes: 3D eyes, size to match the Fish-Mask.

ONE OF THE PLEASURES IN WRITING A BOOK SUCH AS THIS
is learning about all the new materials being used to design better flies. Sure,
I'm including the usual—and expected—Clouser Minnows and Deceivers. Those are favorite patterns and are staples in many fly boxes. But once
you've tied or bought enough of those flies, you'll want to know about
what is new and fresh.

The Masked Minnow is certainly a new design. At first glance it doesn't
seem new, but the lightweight plastic Fish-Mask creating the head gives the
pattern a realistic silhouette, and it is easy to make.

Fish-Masks are a product of the Flymen Fishing Company. They slip on
the hooks, giving finished baitfish patterns a realistic look. They are also the
ideal place to hang eyes, a key trigger for feeding gamefish. Fish-Masks won
the best-in-show award for a new fly-tying product at the International Fly
Tackle Dealer show in 2013.

Although Flymen Fishing Company sells these light-colored Masked
Minnows, you can tie this pattern in your choice of realistic and attractor
colors using your choice of natural or synthetic furs and hairs. Simply tie the
fly in the normal manner, add a thick drop of cement on the front of the
fly, and then slip the Fish-Mask into place. Add the eyes and your pattern is
ready for fishing. How simple is that?

Flatfish

Hook: Saltwater jig hook, size 2/0 or 3/0.
Weight: Lead wire.
Body: Leather.
Fins: Grizzly hackle.
Eyes: Medium 3D eyes.

CHUCK FURIMSKY'S FLATFISH IS ONE OF THE MOST UNU-
sual patterns in this little collection of flies. Even though it looks a little
whacky, it really does catch fish!

Chuck spent many years working in the leather goods business. While
he specialized in selling clothing, he developed a line of fly-tying products
called Bug Skin. It comes in a wide range of colors and textures, and has
many applications for designing new patterns.

The Flatfish is an imitation of a baby flounder. A flounder, which lies flat
on the ocean in the mud and ambushes its prey, is a fascinating creature. At
hatching, a flounder has an eye situated on both sides of its head. As the fish
grows from the larval to the juvenile stage of development, one eye migrates
to the other side of the head. An adult flounder has both eyes situated on
the same side of the head. When at rest, the fish lies on its side with both
eyes looking up.

Striped bass feed on flounder, and the Flatfish fly is a good imitation.
Making the Flatfish requires no thread. First, wrap lead wire on the hook
shank to weight the fly and get it to sink quickly to the bottom; the jig hook
will keep the Flatfish turned in the correct position when fishing. Next, cut
two pieces of Bug Skin in the shape of a flounder.

Cement the bottom piece of leather to the top of the hook using superglue. Glue a grizzly hackle along each side of the body; the feather stem is
on the edges of the leather. Poke a hole in the top half of the body using a
bodkin. Thread the hook through the leather, and glue the top half of the
body in place.

CHAPTER TEN

Flats Flies:
Patterns for Fishing Skinny Water

Winston Moore's Permit Crab

Hook: Mustad 34007, size 2 or 1.

Thread: Chartreuse 3/0.

Weight: 1/40 ounce or 1/30 ounce nickel-plated dumbbell. The size of dumbbell should match the hook size and depth of water you plan to fish.

Claws and antennae: Furnace brown hackle tips flanked with white marabou, then two strands of Krystal Flash, all equal to one and one-half times the length of the hook shank.

Body: Cream, brown, or tan tufts of wool, clipped from the hide and rolled into bunches.

Legs: White round rubber legs barred with a permanent marker. Tie the legs between the bunches of wool while making the body.

EVEN THOUGH HE HAS CAUGHT WELL MORE THAN 100 permit Winston Moore is one of our sport's unsung permit-fishing masters, and his simple-looking permit fly is the sleeper crab pattern of all time.

After tying sheep's wool to the hook shank, Winston flattens the material into a thin carapace using contact cement to create a body that lands and sinks well. The cement gives the wool a stiff profile that is slightly porous so, with a heavy dumbbell placed at the leading edge of the fly, it slices through the water at an angle and gets down in front of fish a lot faster than other Merkin-style yarn crabs.

Winston shapes the body by pressing contact cement into the wool in stages. And because it takes the cement a while to dry, he continues pressing it into shape while it is hardening; he moistens his fingers in a bowl of water before touching the wool to prevent the glue from sticking to them. Winston ties the fly in cream, brown, and tan.

McFly Crab

Hook: Gamakatsu SC-15, size 1/0.
Thread: Tan 6/0.
Weight: .025 non-lead wire.
Legs and claws: Tan micro Ultra Chenille.
Eyes: Large EP Crab/Shrimp Eyes.
Body: Tan and brown McFly Foam.
Extras: Clear Cure Goo Hydro and tan or off-white fabric paint.

IS IT FAIR TO CALL A FLY "CUTE"? IF IT IS, THEN THE McFLY Crab is very cute. And it's also a fine fishing fly.

Making the McFly Crab requires part tying and part construction techniques. First, wrap a small amount of wire around the hook shank. Next, tie on the legs and claws using short pieces of Ultra Chenille. Lightly melt the tips of the chenille using a cigarette lighter so the material does not unravel when fishing. Now you're ready to craft the body of the fly.

McFly Foam is typically used for making egg patterns and the heads on Wool-Head Sculpins. McFly Foam isn't actually foam, but a type of yarn. It comes in a rainbow of colors so you can use it to tie dozens of different patterns. On the McFly Crab, tie the yarn to the hook and clip the shell body to shape. Glue the eyes to the bottom of the body using light-cured acrylic or epoxy. Color the adhesive using off-white or light tan fabric paint.

Even with a few wraps of lead wire on the hook shank, the McFly Crab is lightweight and lands softly. It is the ideal pattern for fishing to wary bonefish in shallow water. It is also a good choice for casting to redfish and other species of fish that eat crabs.

Hochner's Defiant Crab

Hook: Regular saltwater hook, sizes 6 to 2.
Thread: Chartreuse 3/0.
Weight: Medium lead dumbbell.
Head: Calftail hair and pearl Krystal Flash.
Claws: Badger hackle.
Eyes: Beads of epoxy on monofilament, or small beads glued to the ends of monofilament.
Body: Stiff rug yarn or a similar material.
Legs: Sili Legs.

WOW, WHAT A PATTERN! AT FIRST GLANCE, HOCHNER'S Defiant Crab seems unusual. Most crab imitations are flat, but the body on this pattern is semicircular. Why?

When resting on the bottom, the dumbbell eyes force the nose of the fly down, and the head and claws raise up into a fighting, defiant position. Give the fly gentle strips, and the nose cocks up and the head dips, making the Defiant Crab look as though it is fleeing. Lex Hochner, from Texas, hit upon a great idea when designing this unique pattern.

The Defiant Crab is a fine pattern for catching permit and redfish. Many anglers would consider it a tad heavy and large for bonefish, but you can tie it in smaller sizes and experiment with bonefish.

Lex says most flats anglers fish their flies too slowly for permit. Rather than making short strips, he prefers stripping the line from the bottom guide to the reel seat. In addition to being the best correct length, this method will keep you in firm contact with the fly. Too many anglers don't even know permit have eaten their flies and they miss fish.

Here we see the tan Defiant Crab, which is fine for fishing over sand flats. Be sure to make this fly in olive and brown to fish over other colors of flats.

Miheve's Flats Fly

Hook: Regular saltwater hook, sizes 8 to 2.
Thread: Tan 6/0.
Eyes: Small silver bead chain.
Tail: Tan calftail hair and pearl Krystal Flash.
Body: Tan D Rib.
Body hackle: Tan saddle hackle.
Weed guard: Stiff 20-pound-test monofilament.

A PATTERN DESIGNER NAMED GREG MIHEVE CREATED THIS nifty little bonefish fly. And although Miheve's Flats Fly was designed as a bonefish pattern, it is also a good choice for casting to skittish permit and redfish.

Over the years I have become particularly fond of sparse flies such as Miheve's Flats Fly. Like many tiers creating their first bonefish flies, my patterns were too dense and had too much material. As a result, they hit the water too hard and spooked fish. I started looking in the fly boxes of far more experienced bonefish anglers and noticed my flies were too bushy— almost clunky.

Miheve's Flats Fly is very sparse and appears as just a wisp of fleeing bait when stripped through the water. Given the splayed calftail hair tail, I suspect the fish mistake it for a small shrimp or some other crustacean inhabiting the flats.

When researching Miheve's Flats Fly, I tripped onto a website called DIY Bonefishing. It's a fine resource of anglers eager to plan their own bonefishing trip. This website lists Miheve's Flats Fly as one of its favorite patterns for the do-it-yourself angler. I would also say that it is a good fly for new tiers looking for a simple, fish-catching pattern. The key is to tie it sparse. Use too much material and you'll create one of those overdressed flies that brought me so much disappointment.

Detonator Crab

Hook: Gamakatsu SC15 or similar saltwater hook, size 2/0.

Thread: Blue Danville Flat Waxed Nylon 210.

Eyes: Black extra-large EP Crab/Shrimp Eyes.

Mouth parts and head: Tan Krystal Flash, tan grizzly marabou, and olive Polar Chenille.

Claws: Light brown rabbit Zonker strip.

Body: Mutton snapper EP Fiber 3-D, and olive and tan marabou.

Legs: Pumpkin Fly Enhancer Legs.

Adhesive: Clear Cure Goo Hydro and tack-free Flex.

More stuff: Red, orange, and blue permanent marker.

DREW CHICONE IS ONE OF THE NEW YOUNG GUNS OF FLY tying and fishing. He is a promising fly pattern designer, good writer, and fine photographer. His enthusiasm is contagious, and he is very eager to share what he knows about flies, materials, and fishing. With guys like Drew working at the vise, fly tying has a very bright future.

Drew conceived of the Detonator Crab while fishing for tarpon in the Florida Keys. As he tells the story, "A tennis ball–sized crab caught my attention as it passed the boat in the water beneath my feet. My focus was immediately drawn to the vibrant shades of blues and reds that outlined its legs and claws. Two tarpon approached the boat, and I saw the first fish gracefully gulp the crab from the surface."

While many tiers go to great lengths to design crab imitations featuring stiff shells, Drew created a fly that emphasizes an irresistible swimming action in the water. The claws of the Detonator Crab are rabbit Zonker strips stiffened with Clear Cure Goo or a similar light-cured adhesive, but the rest of the pattern is tied using soft materials: marabou, EP Fibers, and rubber legs.

In addition to tarpon, cast the Detonator Crab to bonefish, redfish, striped bass, and any other species of gamefish that feed on crabs.

Mosquito Lagoon Special

Hook: Mustad 3407, size 6.
Thread: Brown 3/0.
Eyes: Small lead dumbbell.
Wing: Red squirrel tail hair and long strands of copper or gold Krystal Flash.
Head: Deer hair natural.

ORLANDO IS ONE OF NORTH AMERICA'S FAVORITE vacation destinations. Within an hour is some of the best saltwater fishing in the United States. This area is home to Captain John Kumiski.

Captain Kumiski designed the Mosquito Lagoon Special. Mosquito Lagoon is rich in opportunities to fish for tarpon, redfish, lady fish, crevalle jack, and more.

Mosquito Lagoon is one of the least developed regions on the east coast of Florida. A large part of the area is protected in the Mosquito Lagoon Aquatic Preserve. When visiting, keep your eye peeled for the resident population of Atlantic bottlenose dolphins.

In addition to using a boat, Captain Kumiski takes more adventuresome anglers fishing using kayaks. These small craft are ideal for accessing narrow backwaters and exploring areas that see few anglers. It's also a great way to get close to the local crocodiles. In addition to kayaking the backwaters surrounding Mosquito Lagoon, Captain Kumiski kayaks the Everglades in search of good fishing.

Captain Kumiski prefers using natural materials when designing many of his patterns. The Mosquito Lagoon Special, which features squirrel tail and deer hair, is typical of his flies. It is a fine pattern for catching redfish and other species that feed on the flats. This is also a good pattern for novice tiers because all fly shops carry inexpensive materials. The deer hair makes the fly suspend in the water so it is easily visible to the fish.

EZ Slider

Hook: Regular saltwater hook, size 6.
Thread: Black 6/0.
Eyes: Small lead dumbbell.
Tail: Tan Polar Fiber, craft fur, or your favorite synthetic hair.
Body: Brown Crystal Chenille.
Body hackle: Grizzly.

CAPTAIN JOHN KUMISKI CREATES STRAIGHTFORWARD fishing flies: basic materials, basic designs—excellent results. The EZ Slider is one of his typical patterns.

You'll find all the materials you need to tie the EZ Slider at your local fly shop. Although this is the tan version of this pattern, you can tie it in white, chartreuse, or any other color. The tan EZ Slider, however, is perfect for fishing sand flats for bonefish, redfish, and sea trout. You could fill half a fly box with this simple pattern in an evening and be ready to take the saltwater flats by storm.

Note the barring on the synthetic tail. Few things in nature are one solid color. Almost all natural baits exhibit a variety of colors, often masking them from predators. Captain Kumiski adds bars to the tail of the EZ Slider using a permanent marker. This is a common technique that makes the fly look somewhat like a small baitfish when retrieved through the water. Use markers to add bars and spots to many flies tied with synthetic wings and tails.

The EZ Slider is a fairly lightweight pattern. Although it is tied with a small dumbbell, it lands gently and rarely spooks fish. Let the fly sink to the sand and allow the fish to approach. When the fish get within a couple of feet of the pattern, tighten your line and raise the fly off the bottom as though it is a piece of fleeing bait. The fish will bust forward and inhale it.

Cathy's Fleeing Crab

Hook: Mustad 34007, sizes 4 to 1.
Thread: Chartreuse 3/0.
Weight: Metal dumbbell—small for hook size 4, medium for size 2, or large for size 1.
Tail: White over orange marabou.
Body: Tan Sea Fibers or EP Fibers.
Legs and wing: Fire-tip clear/orange Sili Legs.

CATHY AND BARRY BECK ARE TWO OF OUR BEST-KNOWN fly fishers. They are superb photographers, great teachers, and just fine people. I met them close to thirty years ago at a fly-fishing show in Carlyle, Pennsylvania, when they owned a fly shop, and I still see them from time to time.

Not many people know that the Becks are also talented fly designers. Although they spend a good deal of time fishing for trout on the Keystone State's limestone streams, they also lead groups of anglers around the world in search of good saltwater angling.

This imitation is called Cathy's Fleeing Crab. It is an excellent flats pattern for catching bonefish and permit. The Fleeing Crab sinks quickly, and its long silicone legs come alive as it drops through the water column. Its bicolor marabou tail helps the Fleeing Crab attract fish even when the fly is stationary.

The Fleeing Crab is considered a good choice for catching a grand slam where permit and bonefish share the flats. In addition to tan, tie Cathy's Fleeing Crab in olive and brown to match dark-colored flats.

If you ever see the Becks, be sure to stop and say hello. You'll be glad you met these nice people.

Dick's Phantom Permit Crab

Hook: Gamakatsu SL-12 or Mustad 34007, size 2 or 1.

Thread: Orange 3/0.

Weight: Plain dumbbell—small (1/30 ounce) for hook size 2, or large (1/20 ounce) for size 1.

Flash (optional): Two short strands orange Krystal Flash.

Egg sac: Orange rabbit hair.

Eyes: Melted monofilament.

Legs: Two short tan/black or white/black grizzly-barred round rubber legs.

Body: Fluorescent orange and tan blended dubbing, combed toward the hook bend and flattened.

Carapace: Steve Farrar's Flash Blend (mullet brown and off-white) tied at hook eye, brushed flat, and trimmed to shape.

DICK BROWN IS A LEADING SALTWATER ANGLER. HE TRAVELS
the world in search of good fishing, and he uses his experiences to design
better flies. Fortunately for us, he describes his patterns and how to fish them
in magazine articles and two highly respected books.

This is his Phantom Permit Crab. Dick says he designed this fly with an
"angular, streamlined profile" so that it drops quickly through the water column "faster than just about any crab pattern I've used." Dick also says that
the soft fiber carapace lands on the water more quietly than conventional
round- and oval-shaped crab imitations.

Dick really poured it on when he created his Phantom Permit Crab. The
pattern includes monofilament stalks for extended eyes, soft rabbit hair for
mouthparts, rubber legs, and orange rabbit hair for an egg sac.

After tying the body, Dick says you can use a fine-toothed comb to
smooth out and align the Flash Blend fibers, and then press a small amount
of head cement or GOOP into the fibers to flatten and fix them into the
fan-shaped carapace.

The Kwan

Hook: Tiemco 800s or Mustad 34007, sizes 2 to 1/0.

Thread: Brown 3/0.

Weight: Lead dumbbell sized to suit the desired sink rate.

Tail: Tan Fly Fur or Polar Fibre barred with a brown permanent marker.

Tail support: Stiff deer hair fibers tied on at the bottom and top of the hook bend to keep the tail from fouling.

Body: Alternating brown and tan rug or acrylic yarn.

PATRICK DORSEY IS AN EXPERT AT FISHING THE FLATS, AND
he fishes in permit tournaments in the Florida Keys. He created the Kwan, a
universally popular pattern, and says it is one of his best patterns for catching
permit. The Kwan is also an ideal fly for catching a grand slam of a permit,
bonefish, and tarpon.

Tying the Kwan is fairly straightforward. Use stiff yarn—rug yarn is a
favorite material—for making the body of the fly. Tie strands of yarn—
single or alternating colors—to the hook shank using figure-eight wraps.
Clip the body to shape, and add a bead of cement on the thread wraps to
lock the yarn to the hook.

The tail is Fly Fur, Polar Fibre, or even just craft fur. Don't overdress
the tail; keep it sparse and willowy so it swims and waves with the slightest
twitch of the line. Most tiers add bars to the tail using permanent marker.

Flats fly-fishing authority Dick Brown tied this version of the Kwan for
catching permit. If you are targeting bonefish, you should scale the pattern
down and tie it on hook sizes 8 and 4.

Palometa Crab

Hook: Mustad 34007, sizes 4 to 1.

Thread: Chartreuse 3/0.

Weight: Metal dumbbell—small (1/40 ounce) for hook size 4, medium (1/30 ounce) for size 2, or large (1/20 ounce) for size 1.

Tail and claws: Chartreuse marabou flanked by a pair of grizzly hackle tips.

Body: Strands of tan EP Fibers. Sprinkle very short, finely cut pieces of EP Fibers on top of the finished carapace (brushed with head cement) for added realism.

Legs and wing: Black and white barred round rubber legs.

THIS MODIFIED DERIVATIVE OF THE MERKIN AND RAG Head is a favorite of the Punta Allen and Ascension Bay areas; it has evolved with some tweaking by the local guides in this great permit fishery. Its strongly barred legs and chartreuse tail create essential triggering elements that give it a well-deserved reputation for delivering the goods on the toughest days. Gluing shorts strands of EP Fibers onto the carapace with a bit of head cement has a hardening effect similar to the contact cement used on Moore's Permit Crab, giving the Palometa Crab a sleeker profile and faster sink rate.

Bastard Permit Crab

Hook: Mustad 34007, size 2 or 1.
Thread: Fluorescent pink 3/0.
Weight: Dumbbell—medium (1/30 ounce) for hook size 2, or large (1/20 ounce) for size 1.
Tail: Clump of pale tan or cream marabou.
Body: Tan EP Fibers.
Legs and wing: Sand/orange flake Sili Legs.

AARON ADAMS'S BASTARD CRAB IS ONE OF MY FAVORITE bonefish patterns, and when tied in larger sizes and properly weighted, it has also become a major permit fly. Its long, staggered Sili Legs trail the fly when stripped, and like Cathy Beck's Fleeing Crab, they flutter on the drop. Tie this fly in tan, cream, or olive. The semitransparent legs give this pattern subtler animation than many other crab flies. The tail should be full rather than sparse, extending beyond the bend a distance equal to slightly more than the length of the hook shank.

To build the body, roll a bunch of EP Fibers between your fingers so they form a strand equal to the diameter of a piece of yarn. Cut the strands into short pieces about 1 inch long. Tie the short strands to the hook using figure-eight wraps. Tie the legs on the hook-point side of the body, straddling the shank and angling back toward the hook point.

Avalon Permit Fly

Hook: Tiemco 811S or Mustad 34007, size 2.
Thread: Tan 3/0.
Eyes: Silver or gold 1/8-inch dumbbell.
Keel: 20-pound-test hard nylon monofilament and four 7/64-inch-diameter silver or stainless-steel beads.
Mouth: Arctic fox tail dyed orange, 3/8-inch long.
Antennae: Black Krystal Flash, about 2 ¾-inches long.
Legs: Two strands of medium orange/black grizzly barred rubber legs.
Shellback: Two strands of pearl flat Diamond Braid.
Body: Tan marabou, wrapped on the hook and trimmed.
Claws: Two light tan Zonker strips tied delta-wing style.
Head: Fluorescent orange thread (210-denier).

CREATED AT CUBA'S AVALON FLY FISHING CENTER, THIS novel design captures the profile of a large shrimp and employs a keel-weighted device so it lands and remains right side up. The unique monofilament-strung beads that serve as weights also make tiny clicking sounds to attract fish.

With its rear-facing profile, the Avalon Permit Fly presents several enticing triggers to fish including long legs, antennae, and mouthparts, but perhaps the most inviting trigger is its pair of wavy rabbit-fur claws. Not only is the appearance of the fly a radical departure from other permit flies, its track record is remarkable: it has taken more than 450 permit since it was introduced in 2009!

You can add this method of stringing beads to a great many permit and larger bonefish patterns. It is a unique approach and points to the willingness of saltwater fly tiers to innovate and break any established ideas about what makes a proper fly.

Bone Appetite

Hook: Regular saltwater hook, size 6 or 4.
Thread: Orange 3/0.
Tail: Pearl Krystal Flash.
Body: Orange tying thread and pearl Krystal Flash.
Wing: Tan rabbit fur and silver-speckled clear Sili Legs.
Eyes: Small silver dumbbell.

THE BONE APPETITE IS A TERRIFIC PATTERN FOR NOVICE
tiers. Any fly shop worthy of its name will have all the ingredients, and
learning to make it is easy. Getting the hang of the proportions is the only
snag; beginning tiers tend to overdress their flies.

First, tie on the dumbbell eyes on top of the hook shank and well back
from the hook eye; this forces the fly to flip over in the water so it doesn't
snag the bottom. Use about eight strands of Krystal Flash for the tail of the
Bone Appetite. Do not clip the long extra portion of the Krystal Flash; save
this for wrapping over the thread body. Make a level thread body, and then
wrap the Krystal Flash. The small tuft of rabbit fur and Sili Legs give the
Bone Appetite good swimming action.

Don't let the name of the Bone Appetite fool you. Use this fly to catch
bonefish, but it is also a killer permit pattern. It would also be one of my
first choices when casting to redfish. Actually, the Bone Appetite will catch
any flats fish that feed on small shrimp and crustaceans.

For a little variety, switch thread colors to tie other versions of the Bone
Appetite. You might also select other colors of rabbit fur and Sili Legs. Tie
the Bone Appetite in olive, light olive, and tan. And, you can substitute with
lighter small bead-chain eyes to create a selection of flies for fishing especially skinny water.

Bonefish Slider

Hook: Mustad 34007, sizes 8 to 2.
Thread: Flat Wax Nylon.
Eyes: Small lead dumbbell.
Tail: Craft fur.
Collar: Saddle hackle.
Head: Deer body hair.

THE BONEFISH SLIDER WAS CREATED BY TIM BORSKI. TIM grew up in Stevens Point, Wisconsin, spending time ice fishing. When in his twenties he moved to Miami, and eventually to the Florida Keys. Today, Tim makes his home in Islamorada.

Although Tim has created several terrific patterns over the years, he is probably better known as a fine artist. Tim works in oils and acrylics. His subjects are mostly the fish and wildlife he sees in the Keys, but other paintings depict striped bass, Mongolian trout, taimen, marlin, and birds not commonly seen in Florida. One of his greatest honors was to be included in an article for *Men's Journal* magazine. This article had nothing to do with fishing; it was about unusual characters living in the Keys.

In the recipe for the Bonefish Slider, I elected not to include colors for the various materials. A regular Bonefish Slider is tied in tan, but you can also make it in chartreuse, black, olive, or any other color. Although it was originally used to catch bonefish, it is also fine for catching redfish and sea trout.

The Bonefish Slider is easy to tie, but don't over-tie it with too much material; the best Slider is sparse and wispy. Add bars on the tail using a brown or black permanent marker. The tail makes the fly look alive when stripped through the water.

Merkin Crab

Hook: Regular saltwater hook, size 6 to 1/0.
Thread: Chartreuse 3/0.
Eyes: Small lead dumbbell.
Tail: Barred ginger hackles and pearl Flashabou.
Body: Light tan rug yarn.
Legs: Rubber legs.

PERMIT ARE EXTREMELY DIFFICULT TO CATCH; SOME anglers spend many thousands of dollars and hundreds of hours pursuing this top-notch gamefish. The Merkin Crab, designed by angler Del Merkin, is one of the most famous flies for catching wary permit.

The small dumbbell eyes encourage the hook to flip over so the fly fishes with the point on top so the Merkin does not snag on the bottom. The long rubber legs give the Merkin excellent action and suggest a fleeing crab.

Make the body of the Merkin using rug yarn; common cotton and other soft-fibered yarns are not suitable for this fly. Rug yarn is stiff so the fly holds its shape. Tie strands of yarn to the hook, and clip the body to shape. I have given the recipe for a tan-colored crab, but many anglers tie olive Merkins for fishing on marl and weedy flats. I have also seen Merkins tied using alternating colors of rug yarn, such as tan and light brown; perhaps the slight barring gives these flies a more realistic appearance.

Does the original Merkin look like a crab? Not to me, but beauty is in the eye of the beholder. To permit and bonefish, the round flat profile and swimming legs is enough to convince them that the Merkin is something good to eat.

Here is my version of the Merkin. I selected alternating colors of tan and brown rug yarn for the body, and brown rubber legs. I have caught many fish using this color combination. Remember: pattern recipes are just suggestions. Just like when following a cooking recipe, you can change ingredients to please your own taste.

Bob's Mantis Shrimp

Hook: Mustad 34007, sizes 6 to 1.

Thread: Tan 3/0.

Weight: Lead dumbbell, small (1/40 ounce) or medium (1/30 ounce).

Antennae: Two strands of black Krystal Flash.

Eyes: 80-pound-test melted monofilament painted with black finger-nail polish.

Rostrum/head (tail of fly): Tan craft fur.

Mouthparts: A tuft of tan rabbit fur cut from the hide and equal to one-third the length of the rostrum.

Body: Tan dubbing.

Legs: Sili Legs.

IT'S IMPOSSIBLE TO PIGEONHOLE BOB VEVERKA. HE WROTE one of the best books about how to tie Spey flies, the beautiful patterns originated on Scotland's River Spey. Before that he wrote a terrific book titled *Innovative Saltwater Flies*. Along the way, his patterns—salmon, saltwater, and trout—have appeared in articles and books written by other authors.

This is Bob's imitation of a Mantis shrimp. You can tie this pattern in a smaller size 6 for catching bonefish, or sizes 2 and 1 for permit. Bob's Mantis is especially popular in the Bahamas.

Mantis shrimp are curious creatures. They are members of the order Stomatopoda. Mantis sometimes reach 12 inches in length, but of course we do not tie flies to imitate these large shrimp. They are common on tropical and subtropical flats, but we only recently began understanding them because they spend most of their lives hiding in burrows and holes. When smaller Mantis shrimp do appear, however, bonefish and permit eagerly feed on them. Mantis shrimp have strong claws that they use to spear, stun, and dismember their prey.

Bob's Mantis has a lot of built-in movement. Almost any pattern tied using rabbit fur will catch fish, and Bob uses this soft material for the head and mouth. The body is dubbing, which is also soft and creates a lifelike fly. And finally, the rubber legs make the pattern look alive when stripped through the water.

Rocket Man Mantis

Hook: Mustad 34007, sizes 4 to 1.

Thread: Chartreuse 3/0.

Weight: Nickel-plated lead barbell, select a size to achieve the desired sink rate; typically 1/40 or 1/30 ounce.

Eyes: Two strands 80-pound-test melted monofilament painted with orange or black fingernail polish.

Antennae: Two strands black Krystal Flash.

Rostrum/mouthparts: Chartreuse rabbit hair cut from the hide.

Egg sac and underbody: Orange sparkle yarn.

Legs and claws: Two pairs of splayed Sili Legs, fire tipped orange/clear or your choice of color.

Body: Watery olive Wapsi SLF Saltwater Dubbing, spun in a dubbing loop.

Wing/carapace: Olive Polar Fibre or craft fur, then two strands pearl Krystal Flash.

THE ROCKET MAN IS PATTERNED AFTER SAMPLES OF THE scurrying rock mantises that inhabit coral and rubble bottoms. It includes seven visual triggers—eyes, antennae, working mandible, forelegs, egg sac, inner glow, and pulsating thorax—to entice permit. Most of these stimulators come alive after the drop even when the fly is stationary, a definite plus with these picky fish. When you fish the Rocket Man Mantis, be sure to let these tantalizers do their thing. You can tie a bright version of this pattern with chartreuse thread, a dull version with olive thread, and a spawning version with an orange egg sac.

Gotcha

Hook: Regular saltwater hook, sizes 8 to 2.
Thread: Tan or pink 6/0.
Eyes: Small stainless-steel bead chain or extra-small lead dumbbell.
Tail: Pearl Mylar tubing.
Body: Pearl Body Braid.
Wing: Craft fur and a couple of strands of Krystal Flash.

THE GOTCHA IS ONE OF THE BEST-PRODUCING BONEFISH
flies ever created. It is easy to tie, lands softly, and rides with the hook point
on top so it doesn't snag grass.

The Gotcha is an ideal selection when you want a small fly with a little
flash. The tail is Mylar tubing picked out and frayed. Tie the butt end of the
tubing the entire length of the body to create a level underbody. Pearl Body
Braid is commonly used for making the body of the Gotcha, but this material also comes in a variety of dyed colors; tan and or light brown matches a
real shrimp. Once you master the basics of making this pattern, you might
want to add narrow barring to the wing using a brown or black permanent
marker.

Craft fur, used for the wing, is very soft and has a realistic swimming
action in the water. You'll find this material in a wide variety of colors;
white, pink, and orange are popular, but light olive and tan are also good
choices.

Most Gotchas are tied with small stainless-steel bead-chain eyes to create flies that land gently and do not spook the fish. But, for fishing deeper
water, you can tie Gotchas using extra-small lead dumbbells. And for fishing
extremely shallow water, you might want to carry a few Gotchas with no
eyes at all!

In addition to bonefish, the Gotcha is a fine redfish, permit, and speckled
trout pattern. The Gotcha has wide application, so you will want to carry a
few of these flies in your fishing kit.

Crazy Charlie

Hook: Regular saltwater hook, sizes 8 to 4.
Thread: Size 6/0, color to complement the wing.
Body: Silver, gold, or pearl tinsel, and clear medium D-Rib.
Eyes: Small bead chain.
Wing: White, tan, pink, or chartreuse calftail.

THE CRAZY CHARLIE IS CONSIDERED A CLASSIC BONEFISH pattern. Many anglers cut their teeth fishing the flats using the Crazy Charlie, and it is one of the first patterns tiers make when they fill a box full of flies for their first flats-fishing trip. In addition to bonefish, the Crazy Charlie is a fine fly when fishing for redfish and even permit. And it's fairly lightweight, so you can use this pattern and scale down the size of your tackle if you are casting to smaller fish or if the wind drops.

The Crazy Charlie fits into the category of patterns called "attractors." An attractor fly matches nothing specific in nature, but its size, color, and general action convince the fish that it is something good to eat.

Seasoned guides say that your flies should match the color of the flats you plan to fish, and this is easily accomplished with the Crazy Charlie. Change the color of the wing to match the flats you will visit. Favorite colors for Crazy Charlies are white and tan for fishing over light-colored, sandy bottoms, and light olive and olive for marl flats.

Some calftails have curly hair, but I prefer tails with slightly straighter hair. Also, don't overdress the wing on the Crazy Charlie; a small bunch of hair is ample to make a nice fly.

Bonefish Bitters

Hook: Regular saltwater hook, sizes 8 and 6.
Thread: Tan or olive 6/0.
Head: Small bead chain coated with epoxy or fabric paint.
Legs: Tan or olive rubber or Sili Legs.
Wing: Pearl Krystal Flash and deer or elk hair.

EVER SINCE CRAIG MATHEWS DEVELOPED THE BONEFISH Bitters for fishing Belize's Turneffe Island, it has become one of the most popular flats flies in the world. It's very easy to tie, and catches fish even when it's at rest; the bonefish see this stylized crab sitting on the sand or coral, and they snatch it.

I discovered this pattern when preparing for my first trip to Turneffe Island. The lodge, Turneffe Flats, included it on the list of recommended patterns for catching bonefish. It looked simple to tie and could be made in a variety of colors, so I made a dozen or more in olive and tan. The "Bitters," as the locals call it, is very lightweight and perfect for casting with a lighter rod; Belize bonefish run on the small side, and you can scale back the size of your tackle if the wind is calm.

A lot of anglers dream of fishing Turneffe Island, and I will give you another tip: Carry plenty of flies. Many of the best flats are sharp coral that can slice through a leader, and you will lose fish and flies. But, there are herds of bonefish, and they are easy to catch.

Sometimes this pattern is called Pops Bonefish Bitters, in honor of Winston "Pops" Cabral, one of the favorite guides at Turneffe Flats. I spent a week fishing with "Pops," and he recommended a very simple technique: when a school of bonefish approaches, cast the fly several feet in front of the fish and let it settle to the bottom. Next, wait for the school to pass over the fly and the line to tighten, a sure sign that a fish has picked up your fly.

Merkwan Permit Fly

Hook: Mustad 34007, sizes 6 to 2.
Thread: Fluorescent pink 3/0.
Eyes: Lead dumbbell sized to suit the desired sink rate; typically 1/40 or 1/30 ounce.
Tail: Tan craft fur barred with a black permanent marker.
Body: Brown and tan EP Fibers.

THE BONEFISH & TARPON TRUST'S AARON ADAMS CREATED the Merkwan. It is named for its marriage of two of our best permit flies, the Merkin and the Kwan. The Merkwan gives us a subtle alternative to leggy crab-style flies by substituting a barred craft-fur tail for the usual trailing swimming legs. This is among the easiest and quickest of permit patterns to tie.

Roll EP Fibers between your fingers so they look like a strand of yarn. Tie on strands of rolled fibers perpendicular to the hook shank, just as you would when making a standard Merkin. Clip the body to shape and complete the fly.

The Bonefish & Tarpon Trust, based in Key Largo, Florida, is a leading organization researching and protecting our marine environment. The BTT deserves all of our support.

Turneffe Crab

Hook: Tiemco TMC811S, size 8 or 6.
Thread: Tan 6/0.
Eyes: Small lead dumbbell.
Body: Furry Foam.
Legs: Rubber legs.
Back: Deer hair.

THE TURNEFFE CRAB IS SOMETIMES CALLED THE BELIZE Crab.

Every year, hundreds—probably thousands—of anglers visit Belize to enjoy this small Central American country's fine fishing. Belize borders the Caribbean and offers opportunities to catch snook, tarpon, permit, and bonefish.

Belize is at the top of the list of fishing destinations for many new saltwater fly fishermen. Although most of the bonefish are not large—travel to the Bahamas or the Florida Keys if you must have big bonefish—you will encounter large schools of bonefish in Belize. It would be a tough trip if you spent a few days on the flats around Turneffe Island, off the coast of Belize, and did not catch a few bonefish.

The schools of bonefish are so large that most guides advise you to cast your fly several feet ahead of the roving fish, let the school move over your fly, and wait until a bonefish simply plucks it up. The greatest challenge is preventing the fish from tangling your line around one of the many large coral heads; these sharp features easily cut through a monofilament leader. It's heartbreaking to hook a nice fish and suddenly feel the line go limp.

The Turneffe Crab is simple to tie. It is a fine, basic crab imitation that will catch fish in many parts of the world. Tie the fly in tan and olive to match the colors of the flats and crabs whereever you fish.

UV2 Shrimp

Hook: Regular saltwater hook, sizes 8 to 4.
Thread: Tan 3/0.
Weight: Small chrome dumbbell.
Tail: Tan craft fur and pearl Krystal Flash.
Eyes: Melted monofilament.
Mouth: A small tuft of tan UV2 Scud and Shrimp Dubbing.
Body: Tan UV2 Scud and Shrimp Dubbing.
Legs: Clear Sili Legs.

THE UV2 SHRIMP IS A SIMPLE IMITATION OF A REAL SHRIMP that has a lot to recommend it.

First, the UV2 Shrimp is very easy to make. First tie the dumbbell to the top of the hank so the hook flips over when fishing and the fly is less likely to snag the bottom. Tie on the tail and mouth, and then spin a pinch of dubbing on the thread. Tie on the legs while wrapping the dubbing up the hook shank. The key is to make the fly sparse; the UV2 Shrimp should appear slightly transparent in the water like a real shrimp.

UV2 Scud and Shrimp Dubbing is a product of a fly-tying materials company called Spirit River. According to Spirit River, fish have the ability to see colors in the ultraviolet wavelength that we cannot see, and fish more easily see flies tied using materials processed with their exclusive ultraviolet light treatment. Does this really work?

I have heard from many anglers who insist that they are catching more fish using flies with UV2 ingredients: feathers, furs, dubbing, and more. In one report, anglers used the same patterns on the same water to catch striped bass; the only difference was that some flies were tied using UV2 materials, and others were made using non-treated ingredients. The UV2 flies definitely caught more bass.

Salt Creature

Hook: Regular saltwater hook, size 4.
Thread: Tan 6/0.
Tail: Tan Sili Legs or rubber legs.
Body: Tan Crystal Chenille or Cactus Chenille.
Head: Small Flymen Fishing Company Baitfish Head.

THE FLYMEN FISHING COMPANY IS A LEADING INNOVATIVE fly-tying materials outfit based in North Carolina. Martin Bawden, the head honcho at the Flymen Fishing Company, is also coming up with fresh materials and patterns. His booth at the fly-fishing shows is always full of tiers eager to learn what is new, and how they can make better fish-catching flies.

The Salt Creature is one of Martin's patterns. It is designed for catching bonefish and redfish, but it also attracts sea trout and permit. Is it an imitation of a shrimp? Who knows! What matters is that the fish think it is something good to eat.

The Baitfish Head, a product of Flymen Fishing Company, is the key feature of this fly. The head adds weight and eyes to the fly. (Okay, with those eyes, the Salt Creature probably doesn't imitate a shrimp.) First, tie on the monofilament weed guard. Slip the Baitfish Head onto the hook and into position, and then tie the tail and body.

This is a lightweight Salt Creature suitable for casting to bonefish and redfish in especially skinny water. Tie the Salt Creature using a medium-size Baitfish Head for making a fly for catching permit and other species in slightly deeper water. This heavier fly will sink more quickly, and the slight splash from the extra weight should not spook the fish.

Ghost

Hook: Regular saltwater hook, size 6.

Thread: Clear monofilament.

Tail: Tan rabbit fur fibers plucked from hide and two strands pink shrimp Krystal Flash.

Eyes: Melted monofilament.

Body: Tan and pink Enrico Puglisi's Shrimp Dub or SLF Saltwater Dubbing.

THIS IS ONE OF DICK BROWN'S FAVORITE PATTERNS FOR catching bonefish. Dick is a leading authority on catching these elusive fish, and has written and lectured about the subject for many years. His book, *Fly Fishing for Bonefish*, is mandatory reading for anyone interested in this subject. Whether you are planning your first trip to the flats, or have chased bonefish for many seasons, you will learn something from this outstanding volume.

The Ghost is a lightweight, wispy pattern. It lands very gently so it will not spook fish, and the rabbit fur tail gives the fly excellent swimming action in the water. Whether dropping through the water or on the retrieve, the Ghost looks alive.

The Ghost is also economical and easy to make. You'll find the ingredients at almost any fly shop. If your local shop doesn't stock the recommended dubbings, you may substitute with another brand of fine-fibered saltwater dubbing. Tying the fly sparse is the key; do not overdress the Ghost. The goal is to create a shadowy fly that suggests life. The fish will think the fly is a shrimp or some other form of crustacean living on the flat. Dick says it is one of his favorite patterns for catching tailing bonefish, and that it works especially well for skittish fish. He recommends fishing the Ghost using short strips.

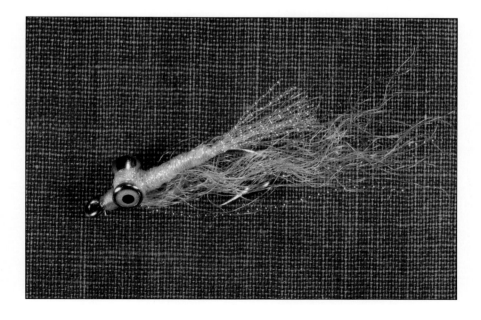

Reverend Laing

Hook: Regular saltwater hook, sizes 8 to 4.
Thread: White 6/0.
Eyes: Small dumbbell.
Tail: Pearl Midge Flash or Krystal Flash.
Body: Pearl braided tinsel.
Wing: Natural Kinky Fibre and root beer Midge Flash or Krystal Flash.

THE REVEREND LAING IS ANOTHER BONEFISH PATTERN recommended by fly-fishing authority Dick Brown. It is a collaboration of David Skok and Jaime Boyle. I've introduced David elsewhere in this book, so let me tell you about Jaime.

Captain Jaime Boyle offers fly and light-tackle fishing trips on the waters surrounding Martha's Vineyard. He specializes in catching striped bass, blue-fish, false albacore, bonito, and bluefin tuna. Depending upon the targeted species, he might use a smaller boat to fish in-shore, or step up to a larger craft to fish off-shore. He has been guiding clients for more than twenty years and is expert at finding and catching fish.

When he is not guiding, he might take a trip in search of different and more exotic fish. Change is good, right?

Jaime and David have traveled far and wide in search of good fishing. They also develop new patterns to match the conditions they find. The Reverend Laing is one of their flies. Although it contains nothing new or unusual, it is a fine fish catcher. Dress it sparse, and retrieve with short, gentle strips. Bonefish, redfish, and other inhabitants of the flats will mistake it for a fleeing form of prey and strike. Change the colors of materials—tan and light olive are obvious choices—to match the color of any flat you encounter. The Reverend Laing is an adaptable pattern, and I know it will find a place in your fishing kit.

The Other Crab

Hook: Long-shank saltwater hook, size 6.
Thread: Tan 6/0.
Eyes: Melted monofilament.
Body: Tan grizzly hackle coated with Softex.
Legs and claws: Tan grizzly hackles.

OVER THE YEARS, CAPTAIN TOM MCQUADE HAS SENT samples of his unique and innovative patterns. A native of the mainland, Captain McQuade moved to the Virgin Islands many years ago. He tests and improves his patterns on the waters of his adopted land, but they catch fish around the world.

The Other Crab is a fun little fly. He calls it The Other Crab to distinguish it from his first crab imitation, but he has tied many variations of crabs, so this example could be the second, third, or fourth iteration. But who's counting?

Almost the entire pattern is tied using tan grizzly feather. First, wrap one or two feathers on the hook. Tie off and snip the thread. Clip the fibers from the front, top, and bottom of the fly; the bottom of the fly is actually the top of the hook shank. Next, coat the top of the remaining fibers with Softex or a similar fly-tying adhesive. Pinch the body to bind the fibers together. Allow the adhesive to dry, and cut the edges into the shape of the crab body. Apply a second coat of adhesive, and place the legs and claws in the glue. After the adhesive dries, you may add markings using a waterproof pen. Even without additional markings, The Other Crab is a fine imitation of a tan crab.

Many crabs are weighted to drop to the bottom, but The Other Crab suspends in the water column. Use a slow retrieve to imitate a fleeing crab. This lightweight fly creates little disturbance when it lands and rarely spooks the fish.

Critter Crab

Hook: Regular saltwater hook, size 6.
Thread: White or tan 3/0.
Weight: Small lead dumbbell.
Eyes: Melted monofilament.
Head: Orange Crystal Flash.
Feelers: Tan saddle hackle.
Body: Tan rug yarn.
Weed guard: 25-pound-test stiff monofilament.

THE CRITTER CRAB IS A GREAT OLD PATTERN. IT'S BEEN around for many fishing seasons, and it is still popular. Sure, there are other flies that look more realistic, but this simple concoction of hackle, chenille, and yarn contains everything required for making a fish-catching crab imitation.

The small dumbbell adds just enough weight so the fly drops to the bottom, yet it makes only a very slight splash with touching the water. Tie on the monofilament eyes and chenille head, and then wrap the saddle hackle in front of the head. Brush the hackle fibers toward the rear of the fly, and add a few thread wraps to hold the fibers in place.

The body is tan or gold rug yarn tied perpendicular to the hook shank. This pattern requires only five pieces of yarn. Add the monofilament weed guard, and tie off and snip the thread. I place a thin bead of cement on the thread wraps in the center of the body to weld the yarn to the hook.

Clip the yarn body into the oval shape of a real crab. You can add the Critter Crab to your fly box, or color the back using a light brown or olive permanent marker. Color the fly to match the crabs you are likely to encounter, or tie Critter Crabs in a variety of colors to match any fishing situation. This fly is easy to make so you can quickly create a variety of crab imitations.

Imitator Shrimp

Hook: Regular saltwater hook, size 2.
Thread: Olive 3/0.
Head: A tuft of tan rabbit fur.
Antennae: Pearl Krystal Flash.
Claws: Tan grizzly hackle.
Eyes: Melted monofilament or a plastic dumbbell.
Body: Tying thread.
Rib: Pearl Krystal Flash.
Rattle: A small glass rattle.
Weed guard: 25-pound-test stiff monofilament.

IT'S COMMON TO ADD RATTLES TO LARGER BAITFISH imitations, but rattles do have other applications. In this case, adding a small rattle increases the power of the Imitator Shrimp to attract fish.

The Imitator Shrimp is a fine lightweight, semitransparent pattern that, on its own, does a good job of imitating a real shrimp. Cast the fly, allow it a moment to sink, and then begin a slow stripping retrieve. The small rattle makes just enough noise to help the fish locate the fly.

The Imitator Shrimp is a good choice when fishing for sea trout and redfish, but it will also catch bonefish. It will certainly catch other varieties of shrimp-eating gamefish.

After tying the body and completing the fly, tie off and snip the thread. Glue the rattle to the top of the hook shank using epoxy or a drop of super-glue. Add another drop of cement on the thread body, in front of the rattle, and between the monofilament eyes.

The Imitator Shrimp is a durable pattern, and it is lightweight enough to use on skinny-water flats. Tie this pattern using olive, pink, or tan thread. Changing the color of the thread does have a profound effect on the appearance of the finished fly. You can also use a larger hook and rattle to make bigger versions of the Imitator Shrimp for catching species such as snook and striped bass.

The Thing

Hook: Regular saltwater hook, sizes 8 to 4.
Thread: Clear monofilament.
Head: White calftail hair.
Antennae: Black Krystal Flash.
Feelers: Grizzly Sili Legs.
Eyes: Plastic dumbbell.
Body: Grizzly saddle hackle.
Weed guard: 25-pound-test monofilament.

CAPTAIN TOM MCQUADE'S PATTERN CALLED THE THING has been a top producer in my fly box for many years. This unique little fly looks like nothing in particular, or perhaps it looks like many things. Tom says it is designed to imitate many of the crustaceans living on the flats, and he must be right; I have used The Thing to catch redfish, bonefish, sea trout, and more.

The Thing requires only a couple of common ingredients: calftail, Krystal Flash, rubber legs, and grizzly hackle. Although I have given colors of materials in the pattern recipe, you can easily substitute with other colors. You can also substitute with other materials. For example, use a small tuft of rabbit fur instead of calftail hair for the head of the fly. The Krystal Flash antennae are not mandatory. And rather than a plastic dumbbell for the eyes, use two pieces of melted monofilament.

The Thing is very lightweight and ideal for casting with lighter tackle. An eight-weight outfit is usually recommended when fishing for bonefish, but when the fish are smaller, or in the evening when the winds drop and you no longer need the casting power of a stouter rod, drop down to a six-weight rod. The smaller rod is a lot of fun to use, especially after casting heavier tackle all day. And catching smaller fish—bonefish, redfish, and more—on the six weight is more enjoyable. Too many anglers think they should always use the same rod, but just like when catching other species of fish, match your tackle to the prevailing conditions.

Goat Belly Shrimp

Hook: Regular saltwater hook, size 4.
Thread: Red 6/0.
Weight: Small chrome dumbbell.
Antennae: Two strands of black Krystal Flash.
Feelers: Black speckled Sili Legs.
Eyes: Melted monofilament.
Egg sac: Orange badger tail fur.
Gills: Natural yellow goat dubbing or Superfine Dubbing.
Wing: Natural badger tail fur.

THE GOAT BELLY SHRIMP IS ANOTHER GREAT S.S. FLIES pattern. This fly contains all the attributes of a first-class shrimp imitation for fishing the flats. Whether you are targeting bonefish, redfish, sea trout, or another species, the Goat Belly Shrimp should be part of your fly selection.

Some tiers go to great lengths to create realistic shrimp imitations, but many of their patterns lack life; they look good in the vise, but seem more static than alive in the water. A better shrimp imitation has a good swimming action; even though the pattern only slightly resembles a shrimp, the materials pulsate when the fly is stripped through the water when retrieved. The fish see this lifelike movement, think it's something good to eat, and strike. If you're casting to a pod of fish, two or three might shift into high gear and burst forward to snatch the fly. Sometimes the action can be quite explosive, especially when casting to marauding redfish. The materials used in the Goat Belly Shrimp flow naturally when retrieving the fly.

A first-rate shrimp imitation should also be heavy enough to drop through the water to the proper depth—from just inches to perhaps two feet—yet not be so heavy that it hits with a loud splash. The fly should land with only a gentle plop. The small chrome dumbbell on the Goat Belly Shrimp is ample to accomplish the task without alarming the fish.

Flying Monkey

Hook: Regular saltwater hook, size 2.
Thread: Tan 3/0.
Head: Deer hair tips.
Eyes: Melted monofilament.
Antennae: Long, thin tan grizzly hackles.
Body: Deer hair.
Weight: Large lead dumbbell.

THIS IS AN UNUSUAL PATTERN, BUT IT HAS A SPECIFIC purpose.

Alan Caolo is a talented fly-pattern designer from Rhode Island. He is also a lecturer, photographer, and author. Alan has written two books that should be in your fly-fishing library. The first is *Fly Fisherman's Guide to Atlantic Baitfish & Other Food Sources*. Read this book if you wish to learn more about what striped bass, bluefish, bonito, and other favorite gamefish are eating. Use this information to create matching imitations.

Alan's other book is titled *Sight-fishing for Striped Bass*. This is a more advanced form of fly fishing. Too many anglers spend their time casting to fish they can't see, hoping their lines go tight with the weight of striking fish. But, much like stalking bonefish and permit flats, you can also stalk and cast to specific striped bass. This requires more hunting and less casting. You're playing the role of predator. And the rewards are more exhilarating.

This pattern, called the Flying Monkey, is the type of fly you will want for sight fishing to striped bass. These fish come onto the flats at high tide in the Northeast. They are looking for small baitfish, sand eels, and especially crabs. The fish will be moving—sometimes at a steady pace—so you will want your fly to drop down the water column quickly. The Flying Monkey has a large dumbbell for weight, but the splash of this pattern rarely spooks the fish; striped bass are not as skittish as bonefish. As the fish approaches, tighten the line and retrieve the fly. The bass will mistake it for a fleeing crab and attack.

Badger Tarpon Fly

Hook: Gamakatsu SC15 or your favorite brand of tarpon hook, size 2/0.
Thread: Chartreuse 3/0.
Eyes: Melted monofilament.
Tail: Chartreuse grizzly hackles.
Collar: Badger fur.

THE BADGER IS A CUSTOM PATTERN OF S.S. FLIES, A LEADING American-based fly-tying house. These guys work directly with fly shops and guides to produce the patterns they need to match local fishing conditions. In a world where most shops sell imported flies, often tied in small factories by workers who have never fly fished, the guys at S.S. Flies are bona fide fly fishermen.

According to Peter Smith, when describing the unusual collar on this fly, "Badger fur is wonderful stuff. It has sparse, long black-and-white barred guard hairs and very fine soft underfur. It's a lot like rabbit fur but twice as long. Even better is that the underfur shades from a medium gray at the base to cream at the tips. The Badger Tarpon Fly is tied with the Keys in mind, but this classic profile and the colors have also been consistently effective in the Yucatan."

Several furs are suitable for tying the collar on tarpon flies. Coyote is widely available and inexpensive. Arctic fox tails fur comes in white and almost any dyed color you could wish. All of these materials are easy to use and give a fly wonderful swimming action in the water. Rather than using only hackles for the collars on your tarpon flies, tie a few with hair collars and see which attracts more fish. I think you will be pleased with the results.

Bunny Shrimp

Hook: Regular saltwater hook, size 2.
Thread: Tan 3/0.
Eyes: Black bead chain.
Tail: Tan Faux Fox with a few strands of pink Krinkle Mirror Flash tied along each side of the tail.
Body: Tan or light brown rabbit underfur clipped from the skin.
Legs: Crazy-Legs, barred and speckled bonefish tan.

THIS FLATS PATTERN IS TIED USING A BLEND OF SYNTHETIC and natural materials. Although this is a slightly large shrimp imitation suitable for permit and redfish, you can easily scale it down in size for targeting bonefish; add a few to your fly box tied in sizes 8 to 4.

The tail of the Bunny Shrimp is tied using a synthetic ingredient called Faux Fox. While I often recommend simple craft fur as a substitute for many synthetic hairs, Faux Fox is not the same type of material. Faux Fox is finer and maintains its bulk on the hook and when fishing; craft fur collapses together when wet, creating a thin streak of collar in the water. Add bars to the tail using a brown permanent marker.

The bead chain, tied to the top of the hook, adds a tad of weight and acts as the eyes on the shrimp. When fishing the flats, the pattern swims in the middle section of the water column.

The body is rabbit underfur. Clip the fur from the hide and pull out the guard hairs. Place the underfur in a dubbing loop with the hairs parallel. Spin the loop closed, and wrap the fur up the hook. Brush back the fur between wraps to prevent binding down any of the fibers. The soft body has terrific swimming action when retrieving the fly.

Swimming Crab

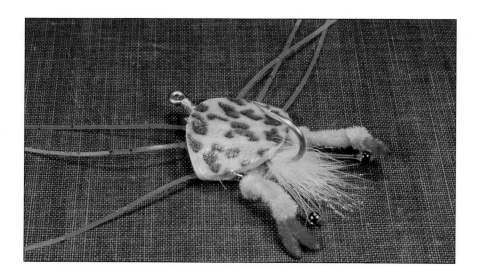

Hook: Long–shank saltwater hook, size 2.
Thread: Tan 3/0.
Weight: A medium lead dumbbell.
Antennae: Tan rabbit fur mixed with Tan UV Krystal Flash.
Eyes: Black plastic beads glued on clear Magic Stretch.
Claws: Puyans Crab Claws.
Shellback: Tan foam topped with Montana Fly Company Crab Skin.
Legs: Tan Sili Legs or rubber legs.
Belly: Tan chamois.

AL RITT'S SWIMMING CRAB IS A NEAT LITTLE PATTERN. A lot of anglers use this type of pattern for catching permit, but it's also a dandy for striped bass. The slap of the fly landing, however, might be a bit much for skittish bonefish cruising skinny-water flats.

The claws are pieces of knotted chenille. They look outstanding!

The eyes are small black plastic beads glued to the ends of pieces of Magic Stretch. The Magic Stretch makes them flexible. You may substitute with monofilament as the eye stalk material, or simply use melted mono-filament eyes. If the melted eyes are not dark enough, paint each eyeball with a drop of black fingernail polish.

The body of this fly is interesting. The top is 1-millimeter-thick foam with a Montana Fly Company Crab Skin glued to the top. You could sub-stitute with Wapsi's Thin Skin, which comes in a wide variety of solid and mottled colors. Be sure to use a flexible, waterproof cement when gluing the top to the foam. Al shapes the body using a cookie-cutter-like tool, but you may use heavy craft scissors. The bottom of the body is a small piece of shaped chamois. Place the rubber legs across the body before gluing together the top and bottom of the fly. The completed body is like a sand-wich with the hook shank running through the middle.

Crab-let

Hook: Regular saltwater hook, size 6.
Thread: Tan 3/0.
Weight: Silver bead chain.
Antennae: Tan rabbit or arctic fox fur mixed with tan UV Krystal Flash.
Body: Tan Cohen's Carp Dub.
Legs: Speckled Sexi Legs.
Belly: Adhesive-backed lead or tungsten tape coated with Clear Cure Goo.

HERE IS ANOTHER AL RITT PATTERN. ALTHOUGH AL LIVES in Colorado, he has a fast-growing reputation for his terrific saltwater patterns. In addition, for the folks who manufacture the Peak Vise, he also leads trips to some of the most desirable fishing destinations in the world.

The Crab-let is a good example of Al's ingenuity at creating flies suitable for catching bonefish, sea trout, and redfish on shallow-water flats. Al weights this fly using only a piece of bead chain. The Crab-let lands gently yet drops through the water column quickly enough to get to the bottom. When the fish approach, tighten your line to raise the fly and make it look like a fleeing crab.

The fur head and rubber legs give the Crab-let a soft, flowing action in the water. You may substitute with narrow-diameter rubber legs for the Sexi Legs.

Cohen's Carp Dub is a new product. Pat Cohen is a leading pattern designer who is setting the fly-tying world on fire. He had an idea for a new type of dubbing. Rather than spending "hours with an old coffee grinder in hand and various bags of materials," Pat teamed up with the folks at Hareline Dubbin to create this new dubbing. Although originally designed for tying carp patterns, Al Ritt quickly adapted this all-synthetic material to his saltwater flies. The completed body looks outstanding. (Of course, you may substitute with your favorite brand of synthetic dubbing.)

For additional weight, Al places a small piece of adhesive-backed lead or tungsten tape under the body. He coats the tape with Clear Cure Goo or another light-cured adhesive, and then trims the body to shape.

Bird Fur Shrimp

Hook: Regular saltwater hook, size 2.
Thread: Pink 3/0.
Weight: Gold bead chain.
Eyes: Black plastic beads on clear stems.
Antennae: Bonefish pink Loco Legs.
Body: Pink midge Diamond Braid.
Hackle: Pink Whiting Farms Bird Fur.

THE BIRD FUR SHRIMP IS AN INTERESTING PATTERN design. Lightweight and wispy, this pattern suggests life when swimming through the water. The Bird Fur Shrimp lands gently so it will not spook fish when wading even heavily pressured flats. This is also another pattern that you can use with lighter weight tackle in the evening when the winds drop or when casting to smaller fish.

Bird Fur is a product of Whiting Farms. Whiting Farms is the leader in producing what is called "genetic" dry fly hackle. In addition to these marvelous hackles, Whiting Farms produces a wide variety of other fly-tying feathers. Bird Fur is one example.

Bird Fur was originally designed as a substitute for heron feathers when tying Atlantic salmon and steelhead Spey flies. These fibers are extremely long and give a fly a lot of life in the water. The problem is that it is illegal to use real heron feathers. Bird Fur is a fine substitute.

According to Whiting Farms, they spent nine years developing this unique product. Although it looks like fur on the skin, these are long, fine-fibered feathers. These feathers come from the saddle areas of roosters. A package of Bird Fur contains one-half of the saddle, enough feathers for tying dozens and dozens of flies.

Although originally designed for making salmon and Spey flies, you can also use Bird Fur when tying original saltwater patterns.

Spawning Ghost

Hook: Regular saltwater hook, size 2.
Thread: Tan 3/0.
Eyes: Gold bead chain.
Tail: Tan UV Krystal Flash.
Antennae: Perfectly barred Sili Legs.
Egg sac: Orange McFly Foam.
Body: Opal Mirage Flash.
Body veil: Amber Antron yarn.
Wing: Perfectly barred Sili Legs.

IT'S SURPRISING HOW MANY IMITATIONS OF SPAWNING shrimp have been created. There are dozens of flies purporting to match shrimp carrying orange egg sacs. A lot of experienced anglers swear that these patterns catch more fish than flies without egg sacs. Why is this?

The fish, of course, are not distinguishing between shrimp—and shrimp imitations—that do have egg sacs and those that do not. One type of shrimp isn't better than the other. Instead, the brightly colored egg sac makes the fly stand out in the water and acts as a target for feeding fish.

In the world of freshwater nymph fishing, flies with "hot spots" and brightly colored beads have become all the rage. Anglers insist that these patterns catch more trout. I have experimented with these patterns, and I also believe they catch more fish. The same is true of a spawning shrimp imitation. The bright orange egg sac acts like a hot spot so the fish can more easily see the fly.

Al Ritt made the egg sac on this Spawning Ghost using orange McFly Foam, but you may substitute with Antron yarn or even chenille. If your local fly shop doesn't stock barred Sili Legs, select another brand of speckled rubber legs.

Note the veil of Antron yarn over the top of the body. This feature gives the fly a slightly transparent appearance similar to a real shrimp. The overall tan color matches a real shrimp; shrimp turn orange, a common fly-tying color, only after cooking.

Foxy Shrimp

Hook: Regular saltwater hook, size 2.
Thread: Orange 3/0.
Eyes: Pink bead chain.
Egg sac: Orange Sparkle Yarn.
Antennae: Black Krystal Flash.
Tail: Tan arctic fox fur.
Eyes: Black glass beads mounted on Stretch Magic.
Head: Shrimp pink UV Ice Dub.
Legs: Perfectly barred Sili Legs.
Body: Shrimp pink UV Ice Dub.
Wing: Tan arctic fox fur.
Topping: Pink Krinkle Mirror Flash.

I HAVE ALWAYS TAUGHT MY FLY-TYING STUDENTS THAT one of the attributes of a good tier is that all of his flies look somewhat alike. Even when the exact patterns change, they look as though they were made by the same tier. The tier has a style. He might make bulky or sparse flies. He might have a preference for using synthetic or natural ingredients. He might emphasize the outline of the bait he is imitating, or he might put more emphasis on movement.

A novice's flies are all over the place, even when tying the exact same pattern: some are sparse, some are bulky, some are small, and some are large. A new tier often pays little attention to detail, and it shows in his collection of flies. Develop a sense for style and proportions, and your flies will immediately become more professional looking.

The Foxy Shrimp is another Al Ritt pattern. And, like all of his other shrimp imitations, it is very sparse and emphasizes movement. The more I look at his flies, the easier it has become to pick them out of a crowded fly box. They have a style all their own, and they do catch fish.

A new tier would do well and catch more fish if they studied Al's tying style and also made sparse patterns that emphasized lifelike action and movement.

Quivering Fringe

Hook: Regular saltwater hook, size 1.
Thread: Yellow 3/0.
Weight: Medium gold dumbbell.
Egg sac: Orange wool.
Claws: Olive hackles.
Feelers: Orange speckled Sili Legs.
Eyes: Melted monofilament.
Head and body: Olive-brown Chick-a-bou.
Back: Olive EP Fibers.

S.S. FLIES CREATED THE QUIVERING FRINGE FOR CAPTAIN Will Benson. In fact, Captain Benson was the first professional guide to work with S.S. Flies—even before it was called S.S. Flies. He wanted custom patterns to match his local fishing conditions in Key West.

The Quivering Fringe was originally conceived as a permit pattern. The heavy dumbbell makes the fly drop quickly through the water column to the proper depth. When resting on the sand bottom, the rubber legs, positioned on the bottom of the fly, keep the claws cocked upright.

Chick-a-bou is another product of Whiting Farms. These feathers come from the belly of a chicken between the legs. Chick-a-bou is used as a substitute for small marabou feathers. The fibers are extremely soft and give a fly a lot of life in the water. You can purchase small patches of Chick-a-bou, or an entire Chick-a-bou skin, at your local fly shop. Chick-a-bou comes in a wide range of natural and dyed colors, so there is something to make almost any fly you wish.

The Quivering Fringe is a stylized crab imitation. Fish it with slow strips to imitate a fleeing crab. Although it was designed to catch permit, it has proven itself on the bonefish flats. It is also a terrific choice when casting to redfish, sea trout, and other species of gamefish that feed on crabs.

Fly Index